# ILLICIT
# MONOGAMY

# ILLICIT MONOGAMY

## INSIDE A FUNDAMENTALIST MORMON COMMUNITY

## WILLIAM R. JANKOWIAK

Columbia University Press    *New York*

Columbia University Press
*Publishers Since 1893*
New York   Chichester, West Sussex
cup.columbia.edu

Library of Congress Cataloging-in-Publication Data
Names: Jankowiak, William R., author.
Title: Illicit monogamy : inside a fundamentalist Mormon community /
William R. Jankowiak.
Description: New York : Columbia University Press, [2023] |
Includes bibliographical references and index.
Identifiers: LCCN 2022026345 (print) | LCCN 2022026346 (ebook) |
ISBN 9780231150200 (hardback) | ISBN 9780231150217 (trade paperback) |
ISBN 9780231520874 (ebook)
Subjects: LCSH: Polygamy—Religious aspects—Church of Jesus Christ
of Latter-day Saints. | Marital quality. | Mormons—Arizona—
Colorado City. | Colorado City (Ariz.)—History.
Classification: LCC HQ994 .J36 2023 (print) | LCC HQ994 (ebook) |
DDC 306.8423—dc23
LC record available at https://lccn.loc.gov/2022026345
LC ebook record available at https://lccn.loc.gov/2022026346

Cover design: Noah Arlow
Cover image: Zuma Press/Alamy

*Our continent went dark,*
*Dark as it was, darker than the sea.*
*It was then the postcard*
*From a scholar in the mountains arrived:*
*"When you don't have any context*
*All you have is theory."*
*Now, coming home, I have half*
*A continent to make sense of . . ."*

—Thomas Paladino, Decanto LXIV, *Presences: A Poem of Decantos*

# CONTENTS

*A Note to Residents of Angel Park    ix*
*Acknowledgments    xiii*

1  Plural Marriage and What It Means to Be Human    1

2  Fundamentalist Polygamy: Contextual Background    19

3  In the Name of the Father: Public Adoration,
Private Qualification    41

4  Different Philosophies for Organizing a Family    67

5  Placement Marriage or Self Choice: Finding Your
Soul Mate    91

6  Managing a Marriage: Expectation, Duty,
and Preference    119

7  Cowife Jealousy, Regret, and Cooperative Exchanges    145

8  Family Politics Revealed Through Naming Practices    185

9  Theology and Mother Care: Full-Sibling and
Half-Sibling Bonding    199

10  Theological Parenthood and the Making of the
Good Polygamous Teenager    213

11  The Lonely World of Polygamous Men   237

Conclusion: Themes and Trends   267

*Notes*   *279*
*References*   *281*
*Index*   *297*

# A NOTE TO RESIDENTS OF ANGEL PARK

ommunities that are conscious of themselves as viable seldom enjoy being the subject of an analytical critique that reveals tacit bias and unvoiced, albeit privately acknowledged, negative behaviors that reflect badly on the community's public face. This presents a dilemma for an outsider who wants to understand the complexity of a community's social life: should only the public face, without qualification, be presented, much like a travelogue designed to highlight the more interesting and wonderfully enjoyable features of the community's life, or should the researcher seek to present the "good" side along with the more objectifiable and less satisfying side of daily life?

Throughout human history, family variation has always been the name of the game. Acknowledging that families often come in different sizes and shapes does not mean that a family system does not have its structural weak point. This is the domain where values often collide and where pragmatic adaptations are required. Because every family system has its tension or contradictory features, it is unfair to criticize a family system through only focusing on its contested domains. There is no culture or family system that lacks some tension arising from the pursuit of personal desires while striving to adhere to social obligations. Every marriage system has its strengths and limitations.

To document that many people find monogamous marriage less than satisfying does not mean monogamous marriage cannot be very satisfying. By the same token, to acknowledge that a polygamous family can be dissatisfying for some does not mean that polygamous marriages cannot work or bring satisfaction to many of its participants.

In discussing those tension points, I do not want to suggest, hide, or advocate that there are only "problems" in the plural family system. This is not so. Many Angel Park residents do find rich satisfaction in their plural marriage, while others do not.

I am aware that many outsiders have visited the community with their minds already made up and, after performing a "gracious open-minded" posture, leave only to criticize the community's family system. I have strived not to do this. I have sought to get it as right as I could without being sensational. In fact, a few community members have, without my asking, provided their life stories, which I found remarkable but, upon reflection, decided not to include in the book. Although their rich stories, however accurate, would have made for sensational copy, I was not able to determine their representativeness, so I decided not to include in the book what I considered to be a hyperdramatic accounts of their lives.

I am immensely grateful to the community and to former community members who have opened their homes and shared their lives with me. I appreciate the time and patience they have extended as they explained their religious beliefs and shared their insights into what has been for me a truly remarkable, albeit at times frustrating, portrait of family life. I recall telling my academic colleagues that some of the most memorable and insightful conversations I have ever had were with community members, whose knowledge and intelligence is second to none. I will be forever in debt to the community for its kindness, tolerance of my presence, and steadfastness in addressing my never-ending queries.

In any culture or small community there are people who "are more successful in upholding or achieving its values" (Lepore 2018:xviii). My primary aim is "to allow readers to form their own opinion about the community I found so compellingly complex" (Bair 1995:xvii). It is the richness of the family system that I wanted outsiders to appreciate more fully. To that end, I strove to provide a rich account of the polygamous family's cosmology and social organization as they shape their members life satisfactions, uncertainties, and dissatisfactions growing up in America's most unique experiment in family living.

Whatever else it is, this book is, like Carol Greenhouse's book, "a testimony to my debt to you" (1986:17). Although over the last twenty years there has been massive national media and scholarly attention (e.g., through CNN, Oprah, the *National Geographic*, the *New York Times*) probing family life in various fundamentalist communities, I have decided, out of respect for the community's privacy, to keep its public name anonymous. I have included the names of some historical or media-centered figures who resided in other fundamentalist communities and have discussed some of those members' published work. I have not done so, however, for anyone who continues to live in Angel Park. Thus I have not included any maps, illustrations, or photos from the community.

My intention is to understand how individuals reconcile often competing ethical obligations with the pragmatic demands of living to provide a clearer appreciation of the plural family's complexity and vibrancy. I have further attempted to "conceptually translate" to outsiders unfamiliar with the plural family's more salient beliefs, norms, and unvoiced nuances. It is also my hope to provide a window for community members to see themselves through fresh eyes. A longtime community member, upon learning what I was trying to understand, said: "Interesting, maybe you tell us what we are doing right and what we are doing wrong and then we can make changes." I have no idea how my effort will be received. I know I learned much from the community and hope in some small way the community can learn something if not from me than from how anthropologists try to make sense of life.

# ACKNOWLEDGMENTS

I was invited in late December 1992 to accompany Emilie Allen on her annual visit to see her grandmother who was being cared for by a member of the Angel Park community. I recall sitting in the car for over an hour thinking of how many studies must have been done on the town. In 1993 I discovered that there were no ethnographic studies of this or any other polygamous community—our knowledge of the community consisted of the occasional, often inaccurate, newspaper accounts. Working with Emilie Allen, at the time an undergraduate at UNLV, I obtained a Nevada Humanities Grant to conduct an exploratory investigation into what it meant to be in love in a polygamous family. We wanted to understand the various meanings spouses and cowives many hold toward living in a plural marriage. The research resulted in a coauthored book chapter: "The Balance of Duty and Desire in a Mormon Polygamous Community" (published in William Jankowiak, ed., *Romantic Passion: The Universal Emotion?* by Columbia University Press in 1995). In conducting that research, we also discovered, almost by accident, that love was also present in a highly idealized form of father reverence. The fruits of our expanded study led to a coauthored professional paper delivered at a conference Walter

Adams organized in 1996 that later resulted in a book chapter: "Adoring the Father: Religion and Charisma in an American Polygamous Community" (in Frank Salamone and Water Adams, eds., *Exploration in Anthropology and Theology*, pp. 235–257 [Lanham, Md.: University Press of America, 1997]).

In 1994, several community members invited me to live with their families. The invitation enabled me to gain further insight into the interrelationship between religious beliefs, kinship, family, and local history. This research resulted in two coauthored articles on sibling relationship and naming practices. I coauthored, with Monique Diderich, the paper: "Sibling Solidarity in a Polygamous Community in the USA: Unpacking Inclusive Fitness," published in *Evolution and Human Behavior*, no. 2 (2000).

In 2018, I was invited to reanalyze my data and explore how different types of polygamous family organizations shape the way parents interact with their offspring. Drawing on data collected from earlier 1990s romantic love and sibling investigations, I reconstructed an analytical framework for understanding how community's youth conceptualized growing up in the community. That paper, "Theological Parenthood, Demographic Restraints, and the Making of the Good Polygamous Teenager" was published in Brien Ashdown and Amanda Faherty, eds., *Parenting as Cultural Practice* (New York: Springer, 2020).

The current volume is the result of research conducted between 1993–1999. In the 2000s, I was invited three different times to visit longtime friends, especially to join them in a son or daughter's postwedding celebration; the ethnographic work that forms the basis of this study, however, is a product of the 1990s. I have kept abreast of community life through reading the numerous media reports and the "escape literature" published by members of the Warren Jeffs FLDS (Fundamentalist Church of

Latter-Day Saints) community, the LeBaron community, and the Allred community.

My research and time used for postanalytical reflection benefited from numerous people who provided assistance, inspiration, insights, and good cheer: Emilie Allen, Brien Ashdown, Thomas Barfield, Jiemin Bao, Jim Bell, Dan Benyshek, Paul Bohannan, Donald Brown, Susan Brownell, Lara Burton, Robert Carson, Napoleon Chagnon, Alyssa Crittenden, Munroe Edmonson, Paul Davies, Amanda Faherty, Victor de Munk, Monique Dietrich, Tish Diskin, Goncalo dos Santos, Amanda Faherty, Helen Fisher, Mindy Gebaide, Peter Gray, Thomas Gregor, Stevan Harrell, Barry Hewlett, Bonnie Hewlett, Sadie Hinson, Libby Hinson, Harmon Holcomb, Sarah Hrdy, Chris Hudges, Cardell Jacobson, Don Jankowiak, Virginia Jankowiak, Philip Kilbride, Pierre Lienard, Charles Lindholm, David Lipset, Gordon Mathews, Francis McAndrew, Alex Nelson, Gary Palmer, Katherine Peek, Len Plotnicov, Barbara Roth, Brigitt Rottger-Rossler, Alice Schlegel, John Schwartz, Ray Scupin, Martin Spencer, Charles Stafford, Yuezhu Sun, Shelly Volsche, Woody Watson, Elizabeth Witt, Claudia Woodman, Xiaowei Zang, Harriet Zurndorfer, and the Fellows at ZIF (Center for Interdisciplinary Studies), Bielefeld, Germany. I also appreciated the feedback I received when I presented my findings at invited talks at UCLA in 2006 and the University of Minneapolis in 2007.

I have benefit from a lively email exchange with Janet Bennion, the grande dame of fundamentalist polygamous studies, who made several thoughtful suggestions. Gordon Mathews gave the manuscript a careful read and made a number of insightful comments.

I remain immensely grateful to Wendy Lochner, editor and publisher at Columbia University Press, for her diligent assistance in shepherding the manuscript through the review process. In addition, I appreciate the keen attention to detail and helpful advice of Lowell Frye, associate editor at Columbia University. I will be forever in debt to Susan Pensak, who gave the manuscript a close read and corrected numerous passages in need of a sharp-edged copyeditor's eye. Finally, a grateful nod also goes to the two anonymous reviewers for their suggestions and encouragement.

To that end, I especially want to thank my longtime friend and editor in chief Thomas Paladino, whose encouragement, suggestions, and support made this book, like so many others, not only readable but hopefully memorable. Finally, my deepest and warmest thanks go to the people of Angel Park, whose patience, openness, and forthrightness made the entire project possible.

# 1

## PLURAL MARRIAGE AND WHAT IT MEANS TO BE HUMAN

*"On my wives' wedding anniversary, birthday, and on Mother's Day, I give everyone a [greeting] card. It can be difficult when you have so many kids and wives. In May there are eight birthdays [including my own]. I would like to do a group celebration, but my wives would not hear of it" (a plural husband).*

### IS THE PAIR BOND A HUMAN UNIVERSAL?

America's fascination with the polygynous (hereafter I will use the community's term, *polygamous*) family arises out of a relentless interest in wanting to achieve a more fulfilling marriage.[1] Mammals are notoriously resistant to forming a pair-bond or a lifelong socially monogamous bond. Of the "roughly 5,000 species of mammals, only 3 to 5 percent are known to form lifelong pair bonds. This select group includes "beavers, otters, wolves, some bats and foxes, a few hoofed animals,"[2] and Homo sapiens. Given the difficulty of establishing an enduring pair-bond, some people ask if humans are really a pair-bond species, or have we been culturally misled into accepting the dyadic bond as our "natural" state of being? (Schacht and Kramer 2019).

David Barash suggests the ethnographic record supports the assertion that thousand years ago the early foragers' marriage system was more polygynous than monogamous (2016). It was only over time and with increasing pressure from society's unmarried male youth that societies gradually shifted to a monogamous marriage system. Even then, wealthy men continued to engage in pseudopolygynous mating arrangements. In partial support of Barash's hypothesis (his position remains a hypothesis, as the ethnographic data on prehistoric foragers is too sparse to reach a firm conclusion) is research conducted on contemporary polyamory (i.e., confluent loves) that argue humans evolved to have multiple concurrent lovers.

Polyamorous or confluent/plural love is intertwined with a new society wide moral revolution that no longer condemns individuals who pursue casual sex and serial love encounters. Confluent love is not organized around a search for a lifelong partner with whom to raise a family, but rather is sustained only by mutual "deep feelings." Once the feelings dissipate, so does the love bond. This "confluent love" stands in symbolic opposition to the historic middle-class configuration of love, sex, and, ideally, a lasting marriage. Because confluent love is based on a moral maxim that holds relationship commitment is a transitory state's best savior when the feelings are "hot," it is assumed that passion will diminish and with it the reason to remain together.

The polyamorous ideal unit is a triad that could be one woman and two men or one man and two women. "Open couples may either engage in hierarchical polyamory, in which they prioritize their primary connection, or they seek to become part of a like-minded pod via an extended family of choice. It is a form of 'entrepreneurial strategy' whereby participants hedge their commitment, while deciding whether they want to remain 'committed'" (Illouz 2012, 2019). Alongside these open couples, solo polyamory has emerged for those who embrace the communication values of polyamory, namely honesty and transparency, but who do not seek to cohabit, share finances, or generate emotional interdependency with a primary partner" (Balzarini et al. 2019; Jankowiak and Wolfe 2021:1).

But "do polyamorous men and women really love everyone they are relationally attached to the same? Polyamorous practitioners insist that they do. It is their official discourse, which they invoke to counter outsiders' claims that they are selfishly sex-driven" (Jankowiak and Wolfe 2021). Most contend that they have formed a heightened spiritual state through the creation of a plural-love bond.

Among practitioners of hierarchical polyamory, Wolfe notes a division of ranked affection whereby one person is the primary or more exclusive love interest, whereas others serve as secondary or even tertiary love interests (2006). Very often, it was the newest lover that generated the most passionate interest and not the in-place primary partner. For some couples, this dynamic might threaten the core of their partnership (Jankowiak and Wolfe 2021).

In a separate study of individuals who did not seek to but nonetheless became emotionally involved with more than one person at the same time, Jankowiak and Gerth (2012) found the two lovers were conceptualized differently: one was an intense passionate romantic love interest, and the other was thought of as a companionate love partner. The existential struggle of such individuals revolved around how best to reconcile loving two persons at the same time (Jankowiak and Wolfe 2021).

Because practitioners of polyamory openly "seek out plural arrangements, they rarely admit they suffer from guilt or emotional angst." Jankowiak suspects, if this is true, "the absence of acute emotional angst arises from all members accepting their relative place within the polyamorous arrangement" (Jankowiak and Wolfe 2021:2). Still, according to Wolfe, embracing poly values is much easier said than done. "Couples new to the lifestyle fear loss of the integrity of their primary bond, while singles engaging hierarchical couples complain that their rightful desires for time and attention may be put aside in favor of the primary couples'" emotional preference (Jankowiak and Wolfe 2021:2).

Although polyamorous practitioners readily assert the superior of plural love over monogamous love, Wolfe found their assertions is "based more in hope than practice" (Jankowiak and Wolfe 2021:2). This effort and subsequent failure to develop and sustain a plural *mutual* love of equal intensity speaks to the human condition, "which has evolved often contradictory inclinations, namely, to be sexually polygamous while also being emotionally monogamous. Individuals in every culture must in their own way reconcile these often dueling and competing emotional orientations" (Jankowiak and Wolfe 2021:2).

If passionate or romantic love is indeed organized around emotional exclusivity, which also includes the reordering of an individual's motivational priorities, what then is the effect of becoming emotionally (as opposed to sexually) involved with more than one person? My research explored how people who claimed to be in love with two people at the same time (a concurrent love) found, as Sternberg predicted, that individuals who were in love with more than one person struggled to balance both lovers in a manageable arrangement. For many, there was, at the beginning of the relationship, little or no tension or conflict. In our sample, these individuals tried to manage the relationships—through establishment of boundaries, either with actual geographical distance or by psychological bracketing, a cognitive technique that helps them to close off or isolate, however short-lived, their involvement with another (Jankowiak and Gerth 2012:95–96).

A number of individuals reported, as polyamorous practitioners claim, experiencing a deeper, richer, and more meaningful satisfaction being involved with multiple lovers. Their satisfaction, however, appears to be relatively brief (Jankowiak and Gerth 2012:98–99). Upon further reflection, all of the respondents told us that it was the worst time of their lives and they would not wish the experience of "loving two at the same time" on anyone.

Clearly, some humans have a capacity for deep-seated concurrent or simultaneous loves, but it seems that these seldom endure for any significant duration. In time, they tend to move toward a more companionship-based love. Whenever that occurs, cognitive dissonance arises, as the two lovers who had been situated in a person's mind at different endpoints on the love spectrum can no longer be easily separated (Jankowiak and Gerth 2012:99).

Concurrent love requires a strong dedication, or even a conscious determination, to maintain simultaneous, albeit separate, life histories or narratives, which for most are simply too trying to sustain. Moreover, the construction of separate personae can lead to various behaviors and attitudes associated with "a dual personality." Regardless of how we might describe the behaviors, separate personae can result in inner turmoil. In effect, such personae can be sustained for a time, but, predictably, at some emotional cost. The very nature of what these individuals hoped to achieve will produce stress on their sense of self, if not substantially fragment it. In the process, the stress on hopes can weaken the very foundation of the bond they seek with another individual. What may have begun as a need to satisfy passion and secure companionship eventually turns into an acute psychological dilemma that is experienced as intensely dissatisfying and personally destructive. The inability to resolve the dilemma of merging both types of love—passionate and companionship—into a sustainable whole underscore the primacy of the dyadic bond, which is based more on emotional exclusivity than on sexual exclusivity (Jankowiak and Gerth 2012:99–100). In the end, love's pull toward dyadic exclusiveness conquers most polygamous and other triadic arrangements such as those found in the polyamorous movement.

"Every culture must come to terms with the relationship between love and sex construct" (Jankowiak and Paladino 2008:1). Because love and sex are independent conceptual and behavioral units that are in a lively relationship with each other, societies seldom give free reign to either impulse, preferring instead to blend them together in support of broader cultural norms related to kinship, inheritance, caste, and class. David Barash and Judith Lipton (2002), focusing on only one half of the sex/love configuration, correctly assert that humans are not a sexually monogamous species. Although many humans do live out their lives in sexually monogamous union, it is not something, the authors argue, that comes easily or naturally. That kind of union requires an ethical commitment and personal dedication to maintain it, which raises the question: if humans need to be vigilant in their moral commitment to remain sexually faithful, does this vigilance extend also to the domain of love? Is it possible to be sexually nonmonogamous while being emotionally monogamous? This is the central question that lies at the core of my investigation of the American polygamous family.

To fully probe the social and emotional nuances fundamentalists associated with what it means to create a loving family, it is essential to first explore the social and psychological complexities often associated with being in love.

## WHAT IS LOVE?
## IS IT REALLY NECESSARY?

Jankowiak and Fischer's (1992) cross-cultural research revealed that passionate love was a universal or near universal, sparked a flood of comparable ethnographic studies on love in a variety of cultures have vastly expanded in breadth and depth. "These accounts illustrate the cultural variability of ideals and practices of love while challenging Euro-American ideals of where and how 'true' love ought to be manifest" (Nelson and Yon 2019). The cross-cultural study sparked cognitive studies (De Munck, Korotayev, and Khaltourina 2009; De Munck et al. 2011), independent ethnographic accounts (Hirsch and Wardlow 2006; Jankowiak 2008; Jankowiak, Sudakov, and Wilreker 2005). and theoretical position papers (Giddens 1992; Fisher 2004; Illouz 2012, 2019; Lindholm 1988, 1998, 2002; Reddy 2001, 2012) sparked a renewed interest into the study of love as a psychological and social phenomenon.

If love is central to what it means to be human, .what is its essence? Helen Fisher (1993, 2004) in a series of publications, argues that love is a drive like sex and hunger rather than an emotion. For her and others, there are thirteen psychophysiological characteristics often associated with being in passionate love (Harris 1995:86). These characteristics are "(1) thinking that the beloved is unique; (2) paying attention to the positive qualities of the beloved"; (3) feelings of "exhilaration," "increased energy," "heart pounding," and intense emotional arousal induced by being in contact with or thinking of the beloved; (4) feeling even more connected to the beloved in times of adversity; (5) "intrusive thinking"; (6) feeling possessive and dependent on the beloved; (7) "desiring 'union' with the beloved; (8) having a strong sense of altruism and concern for the beloved; (9) reordering one's priorities to favor the beloved; (10) feeling sexual attraction for the beloved"; (11) ranking "emotional union" as taking "precedence over sexual desire" (Fisher 2004:6–20; Harris 1995:86–87).

Fisher, speaking collegially, aptly characterizes love as invoking an emotional reorganization of your personal life so that a love object "takes on special meaning." She writes: "Romantic love has a very specific set of characteristics. The first thing that happens when you fall madly in love is the person takes on "special meaning." Everything about that person becomes special, the street they live on, their car, the music they like, the books they read. And you focus on it. So it implies real focused attention, intense energy. You could walk all night and talk till dawn, you feel extreme elation when things are going well, mood swings and terrible despair when they don't show up or call you by the wrong name. You also have all kinds of bodily reactions, such as weak knees, butterflies in the stomach, dry mouth" (2019:1).

Given love's physiological and psychological configuration, it is understandable why there would be a pull toward forming a pair-bond. The strength of the pair-bond preference is readily revealed in polyandrous and polygynous family systems in which there is, in spite of claims to the contrary, a recognized preference for forming an emotional monogamous love bond with one person, who is often referred to as the "favorite wife" or the "favorite husband" (Jankowiak and Paladino 2008; Tiwari 2008).

Forming a pair-bond is never a casual undertaking, nor is it necessarily lifelong in duration. Its persistence arises from its ability to satisfy human sexual desire and need for emotional belonging and fulfillment that is vital to an individual's reproductive interests. Yet societies that do not approve of marital choice construct elaborate mores and norms to ensure that their offspring's behavior is based on something more than physical attraction (Jankowiak and Nelson 2022).

To guard against the formation of unexpected and unplanned love bonds, cultures have developed a multitude of forms of social regulation (Collins and Gregor 1995) that can include "harem polygamy . . . seclusion of women and chaperonage, obsession with virginity, descent systems that create primary allegiances to parents rather than spouses, clitoridectomy, the men's house complex, association of women with impurity and contamination . . . and patterns of sexual promiscuity that undermine enduring relationships" (Collins and Gregor 1995:338). Cultures that adopt these strategies of direction strive to uncouple passionate love bonds from feelings of sexual satisfaction. The senior generation in most cultures, Alice Schlegel reminds us, seeks to "control the young through control over their future sexual [love] lives" (Schlegel and Barry 1991:186). In these societies, the passionate love bond is held to be a potential rival to other, more important, nondyadic loyalties (Schlegel and Barry 1991). It is further understood that feelings of sexual attraction can lead to deeper relationships of human feeling that can, in turn, develop into full-scale resistance to parental authority. In the case of passionate love, parental guidance is often one of definition: Is it supposed to exist? If so, when and how should it be expressed (Jankowiak and Paladino 2008:23).

American history is filled with novel attempts to embrace, ignore, deny and reimagine the proper relationship between sex and love. Historically these have ranged from the nineteenth-century Oneida Community, stressing that romantic love was a psychological dead end while frequent sex with numerous partners would be led to a more fulfilling life. The nineteenth-century

Shakers came to the opposite conclusion, that the source of human suffering is too much passionate sex; in its place they practiced sexual abstinence. In the late twentieth century, American youth would once again experiment with communal living that denied love in favor of unrestricted sexual partners or withdrawal into themselves to avoid human intimacy and thus the potential for acute disappointment.

I suspect that, while there may be occasional and thus highly idiosyncratic concurrent love relationships that are successful, ethnographic and historical studies have consistently documented that these relationships are not feasible on a larger community scale. For example, Benjamin Zablocki's (1980) comprehensive sociological research into plural or group love arrangements among, for example, the Oneida, Kerista, and New Buffalo communes found that group love arrangements presented insurmountable difficulties for its members. In fact, the arrangements are often abandoned in a relatively short time for some type of pair-bond relationship (Jankowiak and Paladino 2008:22).

The problematic nature of concurrent or plural love, I argue, stems from the dyadic nature of love. It is telling that research into plural love communes found few reported experiencing happiness or emotional satisfaction or nourishment in their concurrent love relationships. This conclusion strongly underscores the burdens of departing from a pair-bond relationship that is organized around emotional exclusivity. It raises the question: would the experience of the individuals in our small sample have been any different if they lived in a community that supported plural or concurrent loves? What impact does a society's cosmology that regards plural love as superior to monogamous love have on dampening the desire and willingness to form a dyadic love bond? Can religious belief, commitment, and moral dedication overcome the tug toward forming an emotionally exclusive pair-bond within the larger social unit?

## MY QUESTION: CAN A COSMOLOGY BASED IN PLURAL LOVE ABOLISH ROMANTIC LOVE?

The Mormon fundamentalist community I studied is organized around a notion of harmonious or familial love that encourages the development of a spiritual love bond between all family members. The bond includes cowives and their children, who collectively learn to love and care for each other. In effect, it is an idealized state that is neither individualized nor dyadic in orientation. Harmonious love, unlike a dyadic love bond, is akin to communitas in being unbounded in its potential for forging, strengthening, and sustaining affectionate bonds. It is somewhat equivalent to Reddy's (2001) idea of "longing for association." Because it encourages respect, empathy, helpfulness, and lasting affection, harmonious love often serves as the principal means to bind and unite the polygamous family. Its nondyadic focus stands, however, in sharp contrast to romantic love, a tolerated but kept secret or seldom openly affirmed emotional experience. Although harmonious love is fervently stressed as the ideal, it is vulnerable to personal sexual desires and romantic preferences.

Because social relations in the polygamous Mormon family, like many other polygamous societies (Jankowiak, Sudakov, and Wilreker 2005), revolve around personal sentiment as much as duty, there is a twin pull of almost equal force—that of the personal pushing against the societal and doctrinal. Whenever a conflict arises, an individual's response is unpredictable, threatening the social order. The tension hovers: Which partner will uphold family harmony, which will seek to satisfy personal gratification? The threat is dominant in the case of romantic love, which, more than any other emotional experience, not only can overwhelm a person's judgment but also reorder his or her priorities. The duration of the priorities is unpredictable.

For Mormon women, romantic love's presence or absence—much more than role equity—constitutes the primary measure of the quality of their relationship. In many ways, the present-day fundamentalist community is similar to nineteenth-century Mormon polygamists whose love letters were filled with expressions of romantic yearnings, descriptions of emotional turmoil, and heart-rending disclosures (Young 1954). At a biopsychological level, these expressions of passionate love resemble those found not only in mainstream America but also those reported in other cultures around the world.

My working hunch was that humans as a species are not so much sexually monogamous as they are emotionally monogamous. It is very difficult to love two people at the same time. To determine if the hunch was correct, I embarked on a six-year investigation into a Mormon polygamous family that believes plural, not romantic love, is the highest form of love. In plural love, wives, children, and husbands hold a high mutual regard for each other and actively work, and often struggle, to build a harmonious love bond that will unite them in this world and in the next. The plural family is held together as much by a collective will or communal effort to maintain a strong image of a harmonious family as it is through individual actions and decisions. The community's own belief that this harmonious love bond can be accomplished has received support from few anthropologists. For Bohannan (1985) and Harrell (1997), the pair-bond is a culturally constructed ideal, more a by-product of a specific type of social organization and thus not a cultural universal. In this way, it is not inconceivable that communal efforts at complex family living can be successful. Others disagree, arguing that an impulse to form a pair-bond is present in every known society, even in those that strive to deny its existence (Hatfield and Rapson 1996).

So who is more correct? Can the "impulse" to form an exclusive pair-bond be easily reconceptualized and relegated to a secondary or minor consideration? In the following chapters, I will explore how members in Mormon fundamentalist communities strive to form and uphold a cosmology that deeply values the creation of a harmonious plural loving family, recognizing yet devaluing dyadic love. To acknowledge the personal and ethical dilemmas that may arise from individuals embracing the often-dueling values of dyadic love and plural love provides a framework for understanding how these values have and continue to shape family life in the fundamentalist community.

## METHODOLOGY

Through observation and interaction, anthropologists strive to understand the people they live with before they evaluate them. This approach requires, as Tanya Luhrmann (2012) reminds us, a "delay in judgment" in order to maintain an openness to the phenomenon that is under study. As is typical for most long-term field research projects, the subject of the study often changes. I initially set out with a simple focus: to find out whether the polygamous family is a viable family system in which wives and offspring lived more or less satisfying lives. Specifically, I wanted to determine if a man could be romantically in love with two or more women at the same time.

This aim raises questions that are fundamental to anthropology. How does one understand another way of life? What does it mean to live inside a polygamous family? Sometimes people's lives are more dense and multivaried than they can recall. How can we make sense of what is believed to be remembered and what is believed to be forgotten? I tried to address these questions by focusing on what individuals told me about their lives, paying special attention to the uncertainties and qualifications in their descriptions and comments about the quality of family interaction, especially as they pertain to marital satisfaction.

Angel Park is one of those towns where "although everyone doesn't know everyone, many know a lot about many" (Barker 2018). Between 1993–1999, I visited the community. My visits included overnight stays with different families and attendance at church service. I never hid my identity, and everyone in the community knew I was an anthropologist interested in understanding their lives. Many members were highly respectful in answering my questions and helping me understand what it was like to live in a complex marriage system. In the process, I obtained insight into the voiced and unvoiced values that structure individual lives.

I found that almost everyone in Angel Park had a keen ethnographic eye about polygamous family life. I further found that females had better knowledge than men of the community's social contradictions. This might be because women socialize with other families more often than men and that the interaction provided them with a wider range of experiences and a greater opportunity to hear personal stories, especially from their sisters who had married into other families.

My sample included anyone who was living at the time in Angel Park as well as those who once lived there. Because there is frequent mobility of individuals between the various polygamous communities, my sample expanded, enabling me to come to a better understanding of variations between communities. In addition, I relied on the ethnographic accounts and descriptions found in some "escapist literature." I functioned in one important sense as a divorce lawyer, but not one who represented any party. This stance allowed me to maintain skepticism about their autobiographical accounts of marital pain. Because the concerns and problems they acknowledged and discussed are like those voiced in other studies, I became less skeptical of what I read or was told and decided to include, with proper citation, some of their voices.

One role of an ethnographer is to provide others outside the discipline insight into and understanding of a lifestyle that most people are unfamiliar with. Whenever this occurs, Michael Agar stresses, "it is imperative to be extra cautious in interpreting their way of life" (1996:4). This is especially the case when that life has received many false, erroneous, and, at times, malicious descriptions, and opinions, and still did when I was actively in the field there. Every social system has its unique tension points and conflicted perspectives concerning its own identity. This fact should not diminish or negate the values that define for itself the essence of the good life.

In focusing on some of the contradictions within the Mormon fundamentalist polygamous family system, I do not mean to offer an adverse or negative evaluation. Every society has its own contradictions, personal disappointments, and existential doubts. Identifying and describing them does not delegitimize the society's goals or ideals. Rather they can highlight or underscore the underlying structures and possible difficulties that confront individuals living in either a monogamous or polygamous family. We can learn much about how society seeks to manage its structural tensions and difficulties when we look at how individuals seek to manage, overcome, adapt to, and cope, sometimes reconcile with those same societal tensions and difficulties.

Because I wanted to understand how the community's beliefs were internalized by individuals and shaped the way they expressed their personal desires, especially within the intimate domain, it was essential to probe the family system as a holistic institution that is organized around interdependency of family members and their membership within a religiously ordained community. I have focused on men and women as unique, independent individuals who accept or deny the roles of husband, wife, parent, or sister-wife. I found the key for understanding Angel Park's implicit ethos was to focus on the way affection is expressed and denied.

It is imperative to understand how women, especially in their role of sister wives, negotiate, manipulate, and support or even undermine other sister wives as well as their husbands in pursuit of their own self-centered interests. I wanted to understand the everyday pressures and struggles between husbands and wives, between cowives, and their teenage children. I do not look to criticize the complex family system, but rather to understand the values, both voiced and unvoiced, that shaped and impacted how they sought to resolve specific difficulties, especially within the domain of love.

To maintain the anonymity of my subjects, I have given aliases to nonpublic figures and altered any identifiable characteristics of those who shared their own or others' life histories. I have used the real names of public individuals if they had been used in earlier historical or sociological studies and in newspaper and television accounts. To protect privacy and confidentiality, I have modified or reshaped details that could help to identify someone. The modifications do not diminish or distort the representativeness of the social values of behavior within specific contexts.

Instead they modulate and dampen the harsher tone of reactions that people who live outside the community might have toward accounts of ordinary life in a fundamentalist polygamous community.

Dan Bradburd reminds us that "we have an obligation to reality such that the anthropologist and the historian are charged with representing the lives of people who are living or who once lived" (1998:165). To get it right, long-term ethnography is necessary to probe "what is going on, who is doing what, and to the degree possible, why they are doing it" (Bradburd 1998:151). It is, thus, a biographical and ethnographic imperative that "any given life [or society] must serve to present evidence for further scholarly inquiry" (Bair 1995:xviii). To do otherwise and get it wrong is to become either a one-sided advocate for the community or a narrow-minded critic of it, thereby blocking the road to inquiry (Peirce and Buchler 2012). This is what I have tried to achieve.

Cardell Jacobson and Lara Burton's important edited book *Modern Polygamy in the United States* (2011) makes a related call to ethnographers to stop dividing "polygamous communities" into either good ones or bad ones that are harmful so that there can be a more fruitful discussion of "the way in which different types of polygamous communities, its members, and social institutions create, support, or suppress the human drive to find meanings and life satisfaction" (2011:7).

We need more informed studies highlighting the plural family by using psychological and sociological methods that show the liminal zone in between cosmological convictions and the pragmatic realities that arise out of self-interest. In the following chapters, I will probe the complex plural family as it has been shaped and reshaped in response to local politics and wider social historical events. The social hierarchy and ideas of kinship of communities are probed to better understand the critical role that fathers play in structuring the family as a symbolically male-centered religious system. I intend to probe the power of romantic love as a dyadic force within marriage because it can act in opposition to the plural ideal of harmonious love. I will further argue that men, especially in the role of husband, and in spite of occupying a higher, albeit symbolic, privileged position, are often emotionally vulnerable and feel guilty whenever they cannot financially provide for their family. This internalized guilt accounts for some of the negative and positive behaviors that husbands often display toward their wives and children. Focusing exclusively on women's plight in a plural marriage, especially as escapist literature and popular media have, compromises the possibility of, and narrows the focus needed for, a full presentation of men and women who are often in negotiation with each other and others in the family as they strive to live a more satisfying life within a complex or polygamous family system.

# 2

# FUNDAMENTALIST POLYGAMY

## Contextual Background

There have always been numerous ways to construct a family, with each society believing its own family model is the best, while ignoring all the possible variations and exceptions found within their ideal model (Stacey 2011). This bias is especially the case in contemporary American society where the nuclear family, and its corollary, monogamous marriage, remains the commonly affirmed ideal, despite the increasing number of people who either reject the ideal or are unable to achieve it. Anthropological research finds that "the family is the most adaptable of all human institutions, changing with every social demand" (Bohannan 1985:1). Judith Stacey concurs, reminding us that there is a: "stubborn lag when it comes to legally recognizing different family forms" (2011:111). The reluctance to acknowledge and accept different family forms may stem from the understanding that *family* is a code word for societal gender ideals about "the place of women and children in the social world" (Bohannan 1985:7).

There are numerous journalistic accounts that focus on women's attitudes toward living within a plural family system, but there are few long-term ethnographic studies of the polygamous community as a social system that includes both men and women's perspectives. Most people draw their views and opinions about polygamous life from such cable TV shows such as *Big Love* and *Sister Wives,* which provide a public face to a potentially viable alternative to the nuclear family—the polygamous family.

The absence of a more balanced approach to understanding the polygamous social system as a lived experience and symbolic reality has left the discussion of the relative benefits and disadvantages of a polygamous lifestyle to two opposing groups: advocates for the plural family and critics of it. Consequently, we continue to have exaggerated or distorted, often erroneous, images of what is America's most complex family system. Further, we lack an accurate assessment of the emotional benefits and costs living in a theologically governed plural family entails.

## THE POLYGYNOUS FAMILY: AN ANTHROPOLOGICAL EXPLANATION

Although most humans across the planet live in monogamous marriages, there are people who choose not to. Historically polygamous marriages are more common when a specific material factor is present: need for female farm laborers (Boserup 1970), a high morality due to war (Ember 1985; Ember, Ember, and Low 2007), or a high pathogen stress that favors nonsororal polygyny as a means to maximize genetic variation and disease resistance in a progeny (Ember, Ember, and Low 2007:2).

Moving beyond structural factors that influence whether a culture is organized around a polygamous as opposed to monogamous family system is the issue of "female choice." Do women really have a choice in deciding to accept or reject a plural marriage? The cross-cultural investigation of James Chisholm and Victoria Burbank (1991) found social coerciveness was a stronger factor than female free choice. They report that, even when it appears that free choice is present, there are always, though often unstated, material and social restraints. For example, among contemporary Palestinians, polygyny remains a viable family system. This is due, in large measure, to local norms that marginalize unmarried middle-aged women. Many unmarried Palestinian women delayed marriage in favor of pursuing a professional career. In delaying marriage, these women could no longer attract a suitable mate because the men of their society prefer a younger wife. This practice has resulted in a middle-aged woman agreeing to become a second wife (Sa'ar 2004). Her decision to become a second wife is based less on a desire to enter a polygynous family than it is upon local norms that make it essential to marry and not live alone. In the Palestinian social hierarchy, a second wife has a lower status than a first wife; a woman who has had a college education and a professional career is no exception.

Satoshi Kanazawa and Mary Still (1999) developed an expanded version of Burbank and Chisholm's social coerciveness model. For them, a female's choice to enter or reject polygyny is determined, in large part, by resource allocation. In contrast to Kanazawa and Still's model, Stephen Sanderson found that poor, uneducated rural women are more inclined to enter a polygynous marriage, while wealthier women overwhelmingly shun polygyny (2001:330). The social coerciveness thesis applies to some Western agricultural societies. But does it hold for understanding women's motivations and their position in fundamentalist Mormon communities?

The polygamous family of contemporary Mormon fundamentalist communities is unique because its formation stems from the intentionality of a populace of like-minded individuals who have made an earnest commitment to living according to specific values, principles, and ideals. Individuals who live in intentional communities place a high value on fostering a sense of community or a feeling of belonging and endorse an ethos of mutual support that "is increasingly hard to find in mainstream Western society" (Kozeny 1995:18). Nonintentional societies are the by-product of economic and ecological circumstances that establish the norms by which people live their lives. Intentional societies emphasize personal choice; a person can choose to join the community or not and, if they so choose, can leave it. Intentional communities are, therefore, very different from tribal social organizations.

Material considerations are seldom the primary reason for joining an intentional community. The more powerful motivation is an individual's quest for a meaningful, spiritual experience that, many believe, can best be realized through participation in a community designed to create "a better world." This millenarian vision lies at the heart of early Mormon identity (Bennion 2012, 2020). It is a vision that continues to preoccupy fundamentalist polygamous communities today.

## THE PUBLIC'S PERCEPTION OF THE POLYGAMOUS FAMILY

Americans have a long-standing ambivalence toward polygyny. It acts, on one hand, as a kind of affair of the imagination that produces an allure, and the allure leads to speculation about its possibilities and, at times, a wonder that polygyny may have positive benefits. On the other hand, there is a strong antipathy, based on the belief that polygyny must be a hellish existence for those inside it (Jennings 2016). Despite television programs such as *Sister Wives*, which portray polygyny as a positive and healthy lifestyle, many Americans, remain convinced that no one, without some cultural repression or indoctrination, would willingly live in a polygamous family.

Contemporary American fascination with polygyny is not unique. Europeans have been captivated by the image of a polygamous harem. As early as the sixteenth century, travelers to the capital of Ottoman Turkey speculated on the experience of living in a harem filled with beautiful women (Pierce 1993). It was a common view that the sultan's wives were abject slaves who existed only to serve him in unimaginable, albeit sexually arousing, ways. Three hundred years later, a similar view, but with more clearly stated objections, extends to nineteenth-century Mormon settlements.

Objections to present-day Mormon fundamentalists center around two key points: the tenet that women necessarily occupy a low position in the family and that male sexual appetite is out of control (Bohannan 1985:79). This is not new. As far back as the nineteenth century, anti-Mormon novels blamed "mystical magical influence on the Prophet who learned the art of mesmerism (a form of hypnotism) from a German peddler" (Ulrich 2017:337). Tales of cruel "sister-wives," along with accounts of their suicide, desperate escapes, and torture were frequent subjects in antipolygamous literature. It was further believed that "women were slaves to a system worse than death" (Ulrich 2017:1). These views outraged nineteenth-century Mormon women who adamantly insisted they were not "pawns of the patriarchy" (Ulrich 2017:385). To reassure a skeptical America that the polygamous family is a valid alternative to monogamy, nineteenth-century Utah legislators overwhelmingly voted to give women the right to vote, with the understanding that Mormon women would readily support the polygamous family system.

The European and American phobia toward the polygamous family was not shared in Imperial China. Keith McMahon's study of Qing dynasty literature (1644–1912) found that the polygamous family was positively portrayed as a utopian ideal in which successful men had numerous "erotic romances with co-wives who were beautiful, sexy, and not jealous" (1995:7). Instead of something to be avoided, a polygamous arrangement was, at least in some males' fantasy, something to strive for. This is a common issue in many Islamic societies where the religion allows a man to have four wives. A Somali man shared a local folklore expression that noted: "Best to have three wives, with two they know who you are with, with four you are exhausted."[1]

Twenty-first-century Chinese males, "like their great ancestors continue to view marriage as the realm of responsibility and respectability, and extramarital relationships with lovers and mistresses as the true domain of romance and passion" (Zurndorfer 2014:16; Osburg 2013). Not everyone wants a mistress, however. Among China's single-child generation, many professional men actively seek to establish a rich, emotionally satisfying relationship with their spouses (Jankowiak and Li 2017).

Contemporary Americans, like the Chinese, retain a mixed view of polygamy. Today there are numerous websites for and against polygamous living. It is a busy time for these websites. One of the more popular antipolygamous sites is Tapestry Against Polygamy.com. It presents alleged cases of incest, underage marriage, and various problems of living in a plural household. In contrast, positive online websites (e.g., exmormon.com, Truthbearer .com, lovenotforce.com, and pro-polygamy.com) uphold polygamy based on religious conviction, the right of Americans to live the way they want, and as an effective answer to poverty, where single women with children can find a home that supports them. Clearly, Americans' conflicted fascination with the polygamous family as a real and an imagined community continues.

Some of the misunderstanding, to say nothing of the distorted views of outsiders, often stem, in large part, from an unfamiliarity with individuals who live in a plural family. This is due, in some substantial measure, to the fundamentalist's pragmatic retreat from mainstream society. But this was not always the case. Despite mainstream society's persistent hostility to the polygamous family, nineteenth century Mormons, even when they were a besieged community, were open and friendly to visitors (Brodie 1984). This hostility, which at times was outright persecution, compelled fundamentalist communities to seek safety and security in self-imposed isolation. Polygamous communities, like their nineteenth-century counterparts, retreated to more geographically isolated areas or desert environments (Bennion 2004; Bradley 1993). However, the self-imposed geographical isolation did not lessen outsiders' speculation, often erroneous, about what went on inside a polygamous community. Mainstream America's misconception and its distortion of polygamous family life has been compounded by the negative but accurate presentations in the news media of the bizarre and nonrepresentative behavior of the Fundamentalist Church of Latter-Day Saints (FLDS). This church is a large polygamous community whose mentally disturbed leader (Warren Jeffs) turned long-standing community marital norms upside down to disturbing ends with disorienting results. Both past Mormon fundamentalists as well as contemporary ones (the latter strongly opposed to FLDS) celebrated their isolation and marginal status as a positive value—an affirmation readily invoked in the common saying: "The Gentiles do not need to know about those doing God's work."

The socially imposed isolation has often had negative consequences. Jonathan Turley, a law professor, states that most of the abuses associated with polygamy flourish amid the isolation, stigma, and secrecy spawned by mainstream society's criminalization of the lifestyle (2004). In effect, Turley suggests that, if polygamy had not been deemed a crime, it would be just another type of nontraditional family. Legitimizing the polygamous family would enable women to seek legal protection whenever they or their children are mistreated. Stacey agrees, emphasizing that criminalization ends up "driving polygyny underground enabled patriarchal sexual abuses to proliferate unregulated" (2011:117). Turley writes that "societal law would discipline and alter behavior inside the polygamous family," dislodging the harmful effects and making for a supportive environment.

The American family is increasingly composed of one-parent households, blended families, singles, unmarried partnerships, and same-sex unions (Legros 2014:4). Polygamous community members are aware of these changes in family composition and wonder why their choice of living in a plural family is often viewed as unethical and un-American. They insist there is no such thing as a "natural" or common marriage type. Monogamy, they maintain, is not the only way to form a satisfactory marriage; there have always been notable variations in form and substance.

What most polygamous people want is social acceptance. They do not perceive themselves as abnormal; they see themselves as people who have a different way of living than others. They share a deeply felt concern for family, home, and neighborhood. They have their own view of society—their own sociology, as it were—and this view is more often likely to include thorough criticisms of secular institutions, apprehensions about the downward trajectory of morality, and a firm belief in their vision of what needs to be done. Their opposition to mainstream society enhances their social identity, in some ways strengthens it, and it contributes to the motivation to cooperate with community members (Hardacre 1991:47).

## RESEARCH ON FUNDAMENTALIST POLYGAMOUS SETTLEMENTS

There are not many empirical studies, as opposed to journalist accounts, that focus on how fundamentalists live their lives. Irwin Altman and Joseph Ginat (1996) were the first to provide a groundbreaking investigation through use of a social-psychological survey to provide an overview on local beliefs, attitudes, and practices found in their sample of twenty-four polygamous couples (twenty-three I suspect are from Salt Lake City region and one elite family situated in Colorado City). Janet Bennion's study (1998), set in a different location, produced a pioneering ethnographic account that explored how women, and, to a lesser extent, men, adjusted to living in the polygamous community of Pinesdale (alias the Harker community), Montana. In a later study, Bennion (2004) provided a macro or ecological account of why various polygamous communities tend to cluster in ecologically restricted environments. This study also allowed insight into the smaller LeBaron polygamous community, which migrated in the 1950s from Salt Lake Valley to northern Mexico. Her study was not intended to be a long-term investigation; thus there remains much to learn about life in that settlement.

My ethnographic investigation of Angel Park constitutes the second long-term ethnographic investigation into an American polygamous community. It probes how individuals and their families strive to create meaningful lives within a religiously sanctioned community. It is the first to explore how men and women perceive, understand, and endeavor to live according to fundamentalist religious principles and to sustain a structured effort to achieve dignity and life satisfaction in the roles of spouse, parent, and community member. Moreover, it is the first study to explore the role that romantic passion exerts in undermining and reshaping the plural family.

The community of the Fundamentalist Church of Latter-Day Saints is the most written about polygamous community in U.S. history. Most of the writings are journalistic in approach and are provocative, interminable, and ethnographically thin. Never before have so many people living in a similar community had their life histories—often referred to as "escape literature"—published. The result is that FLDS is well documented. Yet, despite numerous accounts, analysis of the community—how it is composed in terms of relationships, its organization, and how it functions—remains remarkably unsubstantial and far from thorough. This is due, in part, to the fact that "the story," as told by journalists and most researchers, has centered on women's regrets and disappointments in joining or remaining an active participant in a polygamous lifestyle. The media accounts and the published life histories downplay the plural family as a viable multidimensional social system that has benefited most members living in the community. In other words, the dissatisfactions and failures have taken center stage when they belong to the sidelines. Nowhere in the journalistic writings is any discussion of how marriages and the meaning that individuals attach to them change over time. Nor do they explore the impact of theological precedents on the formation and transformation of a person's ideals and, thus, do not report on conduct. The overall portrayal is one of stasis, a community lacking in any dynamic, without development and response to changes inside and outside it. The biggest journalistic oversight is a lack of recognition of the wide variation in family norms and organization in a single community. The emphasis falls almost exclusively on documenting behavioral abuse—which rightly can be termed sensationalism. What is needed is a massive correction, a refocusing that presents a comprehensive perspective on the essential components of polygamous communities.

## FUNDAMENTALIST LIFE ORIENTATION: A BLEND OF AMERICAN VALUES

Given the uniqueness of the polygamous family system, it is easy to overlook the commonalities that fundamentalist Mormons share with mainstream American culture. Forged out of the eighteenth-century American frontier experience (Ulrich 1982), fundamentalist Mormonism embraces many American middle-class values: basic frugality of means, emphasis on controlling one's destiny, a striving for upward mobility, and a belief in individual responsibility. Fundamentalist Mormons never rejected mainstream culture as much as it feared provoking its wrath. Nonetheless, for most of its seventy-year existence, the Mormon community has repeatedly encountered political persecution and social harassment. From the 1930s and into the 1950s, numerous polygamous communities were subjected to governmental raids, with the last and largest taking place in Short Creek in 1953. That one resulted in the arrest of 39 men and 86 women and the placement of 263 children into foster care for up to two years (Bradley 1993:110; Van Wagoner 1986. An unintended consequence of the raids was to "strengthen everyone's conviction and dedication to maintain their lifestyle. Outside pressure had in effect turned everyone who embraced the lifestyle into a community of firmly committed believers (Bradley 1993:110). In this way, the external pressure ensured that U.S. polygamous communities would remain "enclave cultures."

Given the present-day tolerance of mainstream culture toward cohabitation, alternative child-rearing practices, and other related social experiments in family living, the polygamist community has become a "public secret." Since the late 1960s, there has emerged a greater tolerance, though often reluctant, within different states and various polygamous communities (Cragun and Nielsen 2011).). Although the Western states remain adamant in their view that the polygamous lifestyle is illegal, they have tacitly adopted a "live and let live" policy toward the more than thirty thousand polygamous people living in western North America (Quinn 1991).

Because "Mormons, as free agents, were left to find out for themselves how to conduct their affairs" (Bradley 1993:3), it is not surprising that there is a range in types of community, stretching from reactionary-conservative to orthodox-liberal. Fundamentalist Mormons live in a variety of communities, many of them alongside formerly polygamous households. Independents (or individuals who believe in Mormon scriptures, but do not belong to an organized community) total around fifteen thousand people (Heaton and Jacobson 2011). The largest community is the Fundamentalist Church of Jesus Christ of Latter-Day Saints, which includes Hildale, Utah (2,726 people), and Colorado City (4,821 people), whereas the smallest is Pringle, South Dakota (112 people) (Bennion 2004, 2012). In between are communities located in Pinesdale, Montana (917 people), in Centennial Park, Arizona (1,264), in Kingstons, Salt Lake City (1,500 people), in Bountiful, British Columbia (800 people), and in Angel Park (2,700 people). The communities are in solid agreement as to the four foundational theological books: the

Bible (the Old Testament), the Book of Mormon, the Doctrine and Covenants, and the Pearl of Great Price.

However, they profoundly disagree with the Church of Latter-Day Saints (LDS) in its rejection of the centrality of a polygamous family in this life. Like the nineteenth-century Mormons, fundamentalists perceive plural marriage as an essential means to salvation. Their defiant affirmation of plural marriage resulted in ongoing strife between Mormon fundamentalist communities and the LDS, which after 1890 officially prohibited polygamy. The theological, often antagonistic, disagreement between them is ongoing and constitutes a conspicuous eyesore for the mainstream LDS. Regardless of the strong "similarities between Mormon fundamentalist and mainstream Mormon theology . . . the fundamentalists insist their organization is not an 'off shoot'" (Bennion 1997:20), but rather a more authentic representation of Joseph Smith's religious teachings; LDS, however, vehemently disputes their interpretation of Mormon history and scripture.

Over time many fundamentalists reinterpreted LDS church doctrine and began to accept the consumption of two forbidden drinks, coffee and alcohol. The change signaled that some of their differences are not merely theological. This point was made clear to me when I asked a friend: "If you are a true Mormon, how can you drink coffee?" Without saying a word, he opened the Doctrine of Covenants and turned to section 1-9, which reads, the *"use of wine, strong drinks, tobacco, and hot drinks is proscribed."* After reading the section, he said: "where does it say you cannot drink coffee?"

The consumption of alcohol came to Short Creek with an increase from the 1950s migrations from the Salt Lake City region. It is estimated that 50 percent of the FLDS community drinks alcoholic drinks, with some, mostly men, becoming heavy drinkers. In the 1990s, a four-member Alcoholic Anonymous

Group was formed, which met every week in Colorado City (Bennion 2012). I was not able to determine if Angel Park had a similar problem.

Unlike evangelicals, fundamentalist Mormons do not view the standard Bible as an accurate literary translation; they are aware of different translations and their interpretative discrepancies. They are divided on the view that God is a wrathful God who sits in judgment of their behavior. Although many in the senior generation believe in the wrathful God of the Old Testament, I found the junior generation to be open to a God who is kind, understanding, and loving. Still, the essential teaching remains clear, as it did for the early Christians: one must be ever "vigilant and godly, lest you too slide into the abyss" (Luhrmann 2012:102).

The conventional feminist critique of the polygamous or plural marriage states that the dissatisfactions of women are the by-product of their dependency on their husbands, who monopolize both their earning power and sexuality. However, recent research of the polygamous family has not found this dynamic to be typically the case. Most Angel Park women have their own earning power and are more than ready to engage their husband in the give-and-take negotiations that potentially benefit themselves (Bennion 1998, 2004; Altman and Ginat 1996). Moreover, fundamentalist religious doctrine and its ethical guidelines also restrict men's sexual behavior. For both sexes, premarital sex is condemned. Also condemned are affairs that married and non-married men might have outside a church-sanctioned marriage. Contrary to the feminist critique of the polygamous family, it is not women but young men who are more likely to lose out in the evolutionary struggle to obtain a wife (Bennion 1998, 2020; Jankowiak 2019).

Although the polygamous communities share certain core theological beliefs, they vary enormously in social organization, residential preference, and the value of individual agency, marital practices, and flexibility in family organization and in the sexual division of labor. It is inaccurate and misleading, therefore, to think of the fundamentalists as a composite monolithic cultural entity. There is far too much variation to generalize across communities or even within them. It is critical to recognize and acknowledge that descriptions and commentary apply to a particular community or to even a smaller subset within it.

Fundamentalist polygamous Mormons are in solid agreement concerning: 1. the doctrine of eternal progression that holds God was once human and progressed through many transformations to become a god, and therefore ordinary men can follow in his footsteps and become a god in the next life (Bohannan 1985:66); and 2. if a man is successful, the more children he has, the greater his kingdom, with wives sharing their husband's position in the next life. Because a woman's celestial ranking is linked to her husband's, it is to her benefit to advance his reproductive interest (Bohannan 1985:84). The religious leadership customarily lecture their congregations about the importance of living up to the plural ideal. A keynote of the lecture is the principle that "if you have two wives, and you are a monogamist at heart, I am afraid the One Mighty and Strong will not be able to use you." From this perspective, the plural family is at the heart of the communitarian impulse to establish and nurture a spiritually unified and socially harmonious system of order. The maintenance of harmony, unity, and regularity depends on the strength and vitality not only of the relationships of father to son and mother to children but also the relationships between cowives. The plural family is held together as much by a collective will and communal effort as it is by any other action or pattern of behavior. In this and every other way, fundamentalist communities have remained throughout their history, both demographically and culturally, a male-centered, family-oriented, theologically governed religious community.

Nineteenth-century Mormons, unlike other Protestant sects, embraced a premillennial theology that the fullness of the Gospel experience could be achieved in this lifetime before the Second Coming of Christ and the end of the world (Chmielewski, Kern, and Klee-Hartzell 1993:39). The ideal of identifying America as the new Zion and the consequent search for a New Jerusalem is not uniquely Mormon (Wieseltier 1993:26). It is an orientation that appeals to every millennial-reaching orator from Oral Roberts, Pat Robertson, and Jimmy Swaggart to Warren Jeffs, the current, albeit imprisoned, leader of FLDS.

Most Mormon fundamentalist communities continue to believe, at least as an abstract ideal, in the millennial narrative with the possibility of constructing a new Eden that will see "the end of suffering, the righting of wrongs, and the coming of New Jerusalem." New Jerusalem is the meeting place of the twelve tribes of Israel or God's chosen people (Jennings 2016:350). Given the community's strong religiosity, it is not surprising that most Mormon fundamentalists desire to create the material and spiritual conditions for bringing about the Rapture, whereby the faithful are immediately uplifted into heaven.

In Warren Jeffs's sect, the premillennial ideal gave way to a more immediate millennial worldview in which members of the community gather to enter "the Rapture" and be taken immediately into heaven. Their failure to achieve this cherished goal is, according to their view, the outcome of the sins of the world, especially those found among kinfolk living in Angel Park.

## ANGEL PARK: A RELIGIOUS COMMUNITY AND MAINSTREAM CULTURE

Angel Park is a sectarian religious community situated in western North America and northern Mexico. Like other fundamentalist communities, it is separately governed and sustains nominal, if any, contact with other fundamentalist groups. The population of Angel Park is around twenty-seven hundred, with over half of it under the age of twelve years old. It is an intentional community in which members live, or expect to live, in a plural family. Unlike nineteenth-century Mormonism, where an estimated 10 to 20 percent of the families were polygamous (Embry 1987, 2011; Foster 1991), more than 45 percent of the Angel Park families in the 1990s formed polygamous households.

Like many small American rural communities, all of Angel Park's main roads are paved; its side streets not. Its houses, however, are anything but typical of rural communities. "The Big House" (or their ideal house) is for the entire polygamous family to live together. The houses range in size from three-bedroom mobile trailers to huge 35,000-square-feet mansions. Many are forever undergoing renovation.

The realities of insufficient materials often undercut deeply felt theological axioms. For example, many polygamous communities need outside funding to build, expand, or renovate, and this compels women to seek work outside the community. Jobs for these women range from simple service work to school administrators and teachers, nurses, lawyers, and local police. Others pursue college education, obtaining professional degrees to earn higher salaries. Angel Park places more value on education, encouraging its children to graduate from high school and, if the interest is there, to attend college. In this goal, they have been successful: a local community college is composed of 70 percent females and 30 percent males, all from polygamous families.

Although the residents of Angel Park feel that certain aspects of the larger culture are immoral (e.g., premarital sex, abortion, X-rated movies), there are other cultural activities in which they do participate, and, at times, the participation includes discussion and criticism of national and international events. Several polygamous families have even appeared on various talk shows to defend their religion and lifestyle. Others have discussed their lifestyle with magazine and television reporters. Contemporary fundamentalists in general are not like the Hutterites; they disapprove of mainstream American culture and seek to minimize their interaction with it. For most Angel Park's residents, life is to be enjoyed, and they do not hesitate to partake of some of its many delights (e.g., drink coffee and alcohol, visit the national parks, shop at a nearby mall, and feast at all-you-can-eat $13.99 buffets). Significantly, whenever Angel Park's more liberal family members "go to town," they seek to avoid being singled out but instead try to blend in by changing their clothes from the everyday, more conservative community dress to mainstream culture's dress. More conservative members avoid the issue of "proper" wear by simply not leaving their community. For families that allow or encourage dinner conversations regularly, they discuss topics that range from religious issues, current events, the entertainment value of *Saving Private Ryan*, the representativeness of *Little Women*, to the 2020 national election, its reflection of American culture, and the benefits of flaxseed oil for preventing illness. The community celebrates the Fourth of July and Pioneer Day (July 24), the latter holiday when Mormon pioneers settled in 1847 in the Salt Lake Valley.

Politically, Angel Park, like other small rural Mormon communities, is a closed community organized in a male-governed theocratic political system (Bennion 1998). Few town officials are selected without proper religious credentials (Parker, Smith, and Ginat 1973:693). Angel Park leadership espoused an orthodox-liberal stance, which maintains adherence to a strict interpretation of the fundamentalist doctrine of governance by a collective priesthood and a more open attitude toward interactions with mainstream society. The leadership affirms personal agency and responsibility, which is contrary to other fundamentalist communities who insist on a firm to absolute obedience to religious authority. The orthodox-liberal faction is not only more educated but smaller, with a sizable number of businessmen interacting regularly with outsiders. Moreover, the leadership, when establishing community rules or changing them, favors consensus to unqualified obedience. For example, the fundamentalist reactionary-conservative leadership prefers to end a sermon with "Obey," whereas the Angel Park leadership typically ends its sermons with "Think about it." The FLDS community believes that their leader is a god who requires them to stand up whenever he walks into a building. Angel Park does not believe that leaders are gods, but are instead called by God. When the leadership walks into church, members do not stand. Regardless of different beliefs and attitudes toward mainstream society, every fundamentalist community remains a theologically governed society.

Because of its location, Angel Park's economy cannot support all its residents. Most are required to work outside the community in a variety of professions. Most men are employed in currently booming regional construction and interstate trucking industries. Women and other men work in various jobs such as accountants, architects, janitors, masseuses, caretakers, principals, teachers, nurses, and mechanics. The town boasts a remarkable zero unemployment rate. But, overall, Angel Park is not a wealthy town. Although its average median income is higher than Appalachia's $8,595, it still has one of the lowest median incomes in the western United States.

The need to improve their economic conditions often compels fundamentalist communities "to go public" more than many members may want (Wuthnow and Lawson 1991:38). Although more conservative fundamentalist communities have become less closed to interaction with mainstream culture, Angel Park is more open to talking with reporters. As a result, members face new experiences, encounter new opinions, and witness typically mainstream behaviors at odds with the community's cherished values and seldom-questioned beliefs. For example, a forty-something-year-old woman noted with pride that the "time Angel Park got wealthy is when we shook hands with the world." She later added: "I now have doubts. Why should we treat people living in other cities as evil? Why hate outsiders and see them as being from the Devil? I wonder about this religion. As I go out into the outside world and work and visit, I discover what I've been told is wrong. Not everyone outside the community is bad." Her existential dilemma is not new.

In most cultures, people typically take the ways of their lives, the habits, and routines, for granted, seldom reflecting on the natural order of things. This is not the case for fundamentalist Mormons, whose marginalization contributes to an ongoing reflection on their lifestyle—introspection really. Theirs is a life that most are ready to defend and discuss. If a community is defined by "what the group aspires to be and not only what it actually is" (Peterson 2005:102), then Angel Park is a community that is in constant dialogue with itself. Its commitment to religious doctrine keeps the community bonded together. The introspection stimulates an equally intense interest in its history and mainstream criticism of the plural family. Because the community believes its family system is legitimate and sound, it often reacts defensively to any criticism or condemnation from outside it.

Although it is easy to assume that communal living began in the sixties when the "hippies" sought alternative ways of living, the truth is that this kind of living has been around for thousands of years. There are six hundred known communes in America, beginning in colonial times up until the 1960s, the last surviving less than five years. But those that held out more than five years were religious communities (Pitzer 1997:11). Richard Sosis and Eric Bressler (2003) found that one of the primary factors that made for the longer duration of religious communities is the higher degree of cooperation that seems to come from an individual's willingness to give up their belongings and invest in the community (Johnson 2017:185). Norenzayan and Shariff contend that the "survival advantage of religious communes was due to the greater [often exorbitant] commitment of the members, rather than other aspects of religious ideology" (2008:61). In effect, "the number of costly requirements demanded by the religious organization" was less powerful (Norenzayan and Shariff 2008: 61). Yet, it seems clear that, without a fully developed religious cosmology, communes would not be able to justify the cost of their self-sacrifice. The research by Sosis and Bressler of nineteenth-century religious and secular communes found that "religious communes last four times longer than secular communes" (2003:270).

Martin Marty and Scott Appleby's comprehensive study of fundamentalist communities around the globe found fundamentalists do not want to impose archaic practices and lifestyles on its membership, nor "return to the golden era or sacred past, although nostalgia or retrospective fondness for such an era is a hallmark of fundamentalist rhetoric. Instead they want to recreate a political and social order that is oriented to the future rather than the past" (Marty et al. 1991:3). In seeking to do this, fundamentalists must straddle the gap between what they believe "the divine" requires and what is required to live in the reality of the mundane life that exists outside their community.

The gap, this challenge, of needing to bridge two different worlds was a recurrent problem in the Middle Ages too. In those times Christians argued about what was reserved for the City of Man (or public citizenship) and what was meant for the City of God (or private piety) (Lilla 2008). It is a gap that few fundamentalist communities have satisfactorily bridged. I found that most community members adopt a pragmatic, often ad hoc, response to the problems of living a religiously inspired life within a secular, highly commercialized society.

Individuals' pragmatic responses are not only triggered over how to accommodate religious convictions and the very real need to interact materially with the "outside world" but also involve how best to manage private emotions that are neither valued, glorified, nor honored. Specifically, this often involves men and women forming, almost against their better judgment, an exclusive love bond, the behavioral preference for dyadic exclusivity in a moral universe. In the following chapters, I will probe how the community and its members promote, rationalize, justify, and encourage one type of love while, at the same time, initially resisting and subsequently tolerating another form of love, albeit one more dangerous.

# 3

## IN THE NAME OF THE FATHER
### Public Adoration, Private Qualification

*A mature woman with excitement informed me: "I want to create a public celebration that will tell the story of my father's life." I asked: "Did you love him?" She replied: "Not really.*

I f religious meanings, like cultural meanings, invariably reflect the interplay between official creed and other structural and psychocultural factors, then there are few modern cultures where meaning is derived entirely from theological tenets and religious doctrines. Because every culture must adjust to individual and collective needs, religious tenets are seldom upheld as consistently or as uniformly as religious leaders want or practitioners profess. It is my contention that the interplay between theological axioms and social realities accounts, in large measure, for the institutionalization of what I call father glorification or adoration in the fundamentalist Mormon cosmology.

Father adoration is a complex psychocultural configuration that arises from four separate yet intertwined factors: 1. a theology that confers on men a supernatural essence that is more father-centered than husband-centered; 2. a closed-corporate theological community that confers its greatest esteem on men in leadership positions; 3. a polygamous family system organized around a father-husband combination, which is, at a symbolic level, the primary focal point and that unites, real or imagined, the often competing female-centered units into an integrated cultural system; and 4. a post-1970s American ethos that encourages increased involvement of a father, replacing a detached parenting role (Jankowiak and Allen 2006:382).

## MORMON THEOLOGY, CHRISTIANITY, AND HONORING THY FATHER

Fundamentalist Mormon theology is grounded in the teachings of four books: the Bible (especially the Old Testament), The Pearl of Great Price, The Book of Mormon, and The Doctrine and Covenants. The latter two books are prescribed to its members as holy scripture and in turn contain the words of God as they were revealed directly to Joseph Smith (Musser 1944).

There are several non-negotiable tenets at the core of Mormon theology. One is that God is a polygamous man who loves all his children but who confers on men, in particular, an elevated spiritual essence, asserting that men who live "righteously" will obtain a higher spiritual standing. The second is that men will occupy leadership positions in the family, sit on the church council, and have the possibility to become godheads in the next life with dominion over all their descendants. The community considers those who are called to serve on its Priesthood Council to be more spiritually enlightened, and thus their kingdom, like that of the Priesthood Council brethren in other polygamous communities, "is ranked higher than other men's kingdoms" (Bennion 1998:44). Within this cosmological creed of status, the father is charged with the duty to expand, and continue to expand, his kingdom by entering into the institution of plural marriage (Musser 1944).

Women's official standing, on the other hand, is determined by their performance in the highly valued complementary roles of mother and wife. Like Southern Baptists, Mormon fundamentalists interpret the scripture literally. In short, "a woman should submit herself graciously" to her husband's leadership and a husband should "provide for, protect and lead his family" (Niebuhr 1998). It is considered essential for fundamentalist women who want to achieve salvation to be obedient, first to their fathers and, then, to their husbands, by becoming sister-wives (i.e., cowives) in a "celestial" or plural family. There are two types of marital contracts: one "seals" a man and woman together "for time and eternity" in the Heavenly Kingdom. The other seals the couple only for time in this life but not in the next (Musser 1944). Because this bond extends beyond the grave into an eternal world, it is in a woman's "best interest to advance her husband's interests" (i.e., she should bear a large number of children) (Bohannan 1985:81), at the same time striving to uphold her husband's public status and authority in front of his children.

A second tenet holds that the father-son relationship is the core axis for the transmission of cultural and spiritual essence. First articulated by Joseph Smith in 1832, this tenet is the "theme that predominates throughout the Book of Mormon" (Clark and Clark 1991:286). It is based on the belief in a Melchizedek priesthood, the lineage of which extends back to Adam, who is not the first man on earth but rather a god who married several wives, including Eve from the garden of Eden and Mary, the mother of Jesus. Jesus, the first son of Adam, his first son, later became the supreme god over Earth. This belief constitutes the cornerstone legitimization that the only acceptable form of religious expression is based in the Melchizedek priesthood.

The polygamous family's behavioral expectations are derived from these two religious tenets that elevate men as the religious center and authority in the family. Men as fathers occupy the dominant role. From an organizational perspective, its function is to ensure that consistent familial attention is given to the father because of his dual role: the ultimate adjudicator of family affairs and the representative of spiritual authority. In effect, the family is a patriarchally governed system. The father is not only the religious specialist in their family, that is, the final arbiter of all spiritual and ethical conflicts. He is also eligible by virtue of his gender to become one of the high priests of the entire community. Dorothy Solomon, reflecting on growing up in a Salt Lake Valley polygamous family recalled, "Daddy was the patriarch governing the household and all within it. Only God was greater" (2004:21).

A father's centrality is routinely reinforced as he leads the family in Sunday school service (conducted at home) and daily family prayers (especially before meals). He also provides guidance in his offspring's choice of mate, disburses the family income, and, on occasion, reveals his religiously inspired dreams to his wives and children. As the family specialist, the father is the final judge of spiritual and ethical conflicts. This role is most clearly demonstrated when he calls "a home meeting," usually held on Sunday, where the family comes together and everyone has the opportunity to voice his or her concerns and discuss solutions.

It is revealing that it is the father, and not the leader of the church, who hands out, as part of the sacrament of communion, the holy wafer to family members who want to participate. In leading the family in prayer, the father further signifies his importance as spiritual head of the family. In his interviews in the 1880s with Mormons raised in a polygamous family, James Hulett found that fathers were similarly perceived as the "bread-winner, head of the family, and spiritual leader" (1939:285).

In coming together as a family, there is a tacit, albeit salient, honoring of the father. In the community where I lived, I never witnessed fetishization of the father who places himself as equal to God like Solomon's father. I was told, however, about a man living in a different community who had his children write the word *Father* over the name of God in the family songbook. When family hymns were sung, the children were in effect singing to their Father and not to God. I did not find this to be typical among the families that I knew or was told about. I learned about the dynamic of the hymn singing from an individual who lived in a different community but grew up in that household. Given the religion's underlying axioms that elevate a husband/father as the supreme family authority, it is not entirely unthinkable for a few misguided men to conceive of themselves as godlike in this world as opposed to the next.

## HONORING OF FATHERS/IDEALIZING THE FATHER

The history of any group is often shaped by the stories it tells itself and reinforced by their telling. The community I lived in often holds a gathering that is open to everyone where a deceased founder's deeds, or those of the head of a large family, are remembered and reflected upon. These gatherings, which take place at the Church Meeting Hall, serve as public remembrances of the father's laudable deeds and accomplishments that, in the view of the members, advanced or improved the community. Given by the father's offspring or closely related kin, they are testimonials, devotional in tone and presentation, that honor the deceased father's memory through the selection of hagiographic accounts that ritualistically praise the fathers' actions while overlooking his shortcomings. The participants listen closely and nod, reaffirming their sympathy for loss and respect for the deceased.

Every culture has its own narratives. Angel Park's hagiographies provide possible solutions or answers to the problems of daily living. In addition, they serve as exemplary models of behavior. In this way, the fundamentalist hagiographies are remarkably similar in their content. They typically tell a story of a just and honorable man whose steadfastness in his religious convictions demonstrates, often in the face of personal hardship and financial loss, his commitment to cherished community ideals and participation in important community activities. These activities can include the building of some structure (often a drainage ditch), the operation of a much-needed sawmill, the creation of a company that will employ numerous residents, donations of a large contribution to the congregation's legal defense, and a public commitment to live within a United Order.

Because people use stories to organize and store cultural traditions (Bohannan 1985:45), the public testimonials serve as powerful expressions of loving devotion that are supplemented by important reminders of how to live the proper life. By providing an opportunity for the community to idealize or praise an individual's life, the core values its members endorse and promote are remembered and reaffirmed. The devotional tone of the testimonials can be heard in a mid-twenties woman's fond remembrance of the role her deceased father played in her life. Delivered during a church service, she stated how "my father always explained the importance and meaning of the Gospel to his family." "Although," she added, "he was strict and diligent in his work, he was also a concerned and loving parent who always worked with his children so they never got in trouble." She concluded her testimonial by saying how she loved to "see him in the morning, pouring milk into his coffee and that even today, every time I make coffee, the smell reminds me of his wonderful presence." The palpable presence of a deceased father is not uncommon in the memories of adult children everywhere, but in Angel Park it has a ritualistic component.

The love of the father is found, too, in the public remarks of a woman in her mid-thirties who affectionately recalled that, as a young girl, she would go on walks with her father, who never failed to explain the importance of the living God's law (i.e., polygamy). She declared, with an emotional timbre in her voice, that through "his kindness and love, I am a better person." An unmarried teenage girl, whose father had passed away when she was eight years old, remembered her father as a sensitive man who "I appreciated for his kindness and commitment to the family." She added, "He will always be an inspiration to me." The respect that people have toward their father can be seen in a young male's acknowledgment that "I could not bear to disappoint my father—I was afraid I could not live up to his ideals." I also heard it voiced by a female in her twenties who told me that "she never knew her father" because he died when she was an infant, but nonetheless she adored his memory and would never let anyone say anything bad about him.

If rituals are essential to promote group loyalty, then they should be readily expressed in a variety of group gatherings. For example, at a wedding reception I attended when everyone was congratulating the bride, someone called out, "Let's remember Papa Bill (now deceased) for his role in raising a good person." Everyone sighed in agreement.

Father adoration is often expressed during the family's Sunday dinner, a time when the entire family tries to eat together.

At one such dinner a man in his forties told his wives and children that his father had always stressed the importance of eating at least one meal a week together as a family. "Dad always said," he added (with tears in his eyes), "the family that eats together stays together." He continued at length about his father's enlightenment and how he, too, as a father, wanted to continue what was, for him, a memorable family tradition.

The honoring of the father as either an important founder of the community or the founder of a family line is reinforced by Angel Park's private school requirement that every graduating senior must write a report about his or her family's history or the history of a significant community founder. In this context, the community founder is defined as anyone who made a significant contribution to Angel Park's growth and development. Such a man is regarded as a kind of father to the whole community and, in a way, everyone's father. Significantly, women, as mothers or wives, while revered in conversation and the routines of daily living, are seldom the subjects of these student essays. Nor are they ever commemorated during church services. Hagiographies, in Angel Park, are reserved only for fathers.

Father adoration can extend beyond the glorification of an individual's biological father to include community leaders who, some believe, can, after death, offer some form of community guidance and protection. Like Chinese ancestor reverence, Mormon fundamentalists believe death does not immediately break the bonds of social kinship. Another example of the community celebration of fathers is found in the commemoration held for one of the original pioneers of the community. Several months after his passing, his family organized a celebration of his long and productive life. At the end of the ceremony, his 315 grandchildren and 144 great-grandchildren stood (infants were held by a standing family member) so that everyone present could bear witness to his large prosperous family. I heard that his father once told his family that "the sun never sets on our family." It is a remark voiced with pride and received by the community in admiration for a life well lived.

These examples do not mean that mothers are less loved, or regarded as unimportant, in Angel Park. Adults are quick to acknowledge their mother's contribution. Appreciation of the mother is more private, though not necessarily less emotionally given or acknowledged. In the public arena, however, fundamentalists prefer to speak entirely in the idiom of father adoration and seldom in terms of mother love. And this is a difference in attitude and significance—adoration for the father, love for the mother. Typically, after the father has "passed to the other side," he is commemorated by the placement of his photo in a prominent place in the family living room. A deceased mother's photo, however, is usually smaller or, if it is the same size, is placed under his or inconspicuously on an adjacent wall. The placement of the photos of the deceased constitutes the highest form of remembrance and the most potent declaration of filial affection. In this sense, there is a restricted or exclusive form of ancestor reverence in Angel Park. The focus, the emphasis, is on the father.

## FAMILISM: COMPETING WITH A FATHER'S REPUTATION

Group loyalty is not based on a relationship as much as "membership in a group competing with other groups" (Flechter 1993:34). Although fundamentalist Mormon theology and church leadership discourage familial ranking (i.e., the ranking of families into a hierarchy of relative social worth), the practice nevertheless flourishes, unofficially, in Angel Park. The social repercussions encourage a kind of clannishness whereby individuals seek to advance their family status and, indirectly, their own reputations through economic achievement and superior moral performance. Although an individual's actions are felt to be either an aspect of family inheritance or something unique to one's own personality, status competition often involves the advancing or denigrating of a father's reputation. It is not surprising that children in particular often believe their relative social standing depends upon advancing or criticizing one another's accomplishments. In other words, there is evident competition, and there is nothing novel in this panhuman propensity. What is significant is the fact that gentle and not so gentle "digs," directed in a back-and-forth at each other by the children, are typically couched in a father-centered discourse, which is often nothing more than an exercise in status-leveling or status assertion. Such interfamily competition takes place in a variety of settings: "song duels" between children of rival families, general peer-group teasing, and public criticism and ridicule of another's behavior.

One popular form, in the song duel, takes place only between children and never, as in the case of the Eskimo song duel, between adults. As an example, an eight-year-old girl encounters two seven-year-old half-sisters from the rival religious faction and immediately sings: "Your family is too simple, just too simple . . ." The seven year olds, just as quickly, repeat the song fragment but substitute the eight year old's family name in place of their own. Claims and counterclaims are flung back and forth between the peer groups. In a way, a truly interesting one from anthropological perspective, the back-and-forth of individuals using song rhythms resembles American rapping where individuals usually but not always rail against each other. There are rap showdowns where groups are pitted against each other. The chief difference is that the content of rap is not predominantly about one's family status, but one possible ingredient in the repertoire. Song duels or contests are not uncommon in some tribal cultures; often the song protests are directed between members of opposing tribes.

Teasing always involves mockery in the name of one's father; unlike American rap that much more often involves mockery of another rapper or a girlfriend. Another child's supposedly family-centered personality traits (wherein the family, and its figurehead, the father, are implicated by the defect) can be seen in the interaction of children at play. When one boy repeatedly kicked the ball, some children ridiculed his physical clumsiness as "typical of all the Jacksons." In a reversal of father adoration, the Jackson father is belittled, for he's the real source of the clumsiness. Father mockery is inevitable in a community where his adoration is crucial. The exact reverse is true in American rap. Mothers are loved, and in many cases, greatly revered, and thus the mockery is similarly directed at the family member with the elevated status. In Mormon fundamentalist society, if the father is mocked, he can also be praised. Positive attributes are seen as a trait typical of a certain family. For example, when a particularly gifted musician performed at her school reception, she was warmly applauded, with many in attendance noting in appreciation that "all the Boyd's are gifted musicians, just like their father." When one wants to push back in awe or ridicule, or deliver a counterattack, the image of the father is invoked as the indicator of strong feelings either way.

Unlike children's status competitions, which take place in a semipublic arena and are directed at a specific person, adults prefer to voice their negative evaluations in private settings among family members and close friends. These evaluations invariably take the form of teasing put-downs such as the so-and-so family "puts on airs" or "they think they are so special," in order to uphold, on one hand, a community ethos of fellowship while also defending, if not advancing, one's own family reputation. There is, thus, in Angel Park a kind of balance of power involving mockery of fathers and adoration of them as a way of preserving the historical continuity of status. Mockery is one way of keeping certain fathers in their place within the local social hierarchy.

Adult family rivalry often involves the embellishment of one's father's accomplishments through the manipulation of historical facts. Before the religious split in the community, a man from a prominent family instructed his children who were preparing to perform in a school play to glorify his communal contributions (many of which never happened) while neglecting to mention other men who played more pivotal historical roles. Immediately after the performance, other members of the community returned home and retold to their children the special exploits of their own fathers in building up Angel Park. Of course, there is status competition or the manipulation of local history in communities and cultures all across America, but in Angel Park these are invariably expressed in the name of honoring or dishonoring someone's father.

Not every embellished historical account is made to advance a father's accomplishments. Some accounts are invoked to defend what the family considers to be slanderous charges made against him and, indirectly, themselves. A family's low status can be altered with determined, concerted historical revisionism. In the 1930s, for example, police charged one man for sexual indecency. Fifty years later, his middle-aged daughter habitually explains to anyone who will listen how her father was framed and thus never sexually immoral. This consistent defense is one example of historical revisionism among many others. In this way, adults try to maximize their father's memory in order to advance or maintain their own position in a social hierarchy that is only partially shaped by principles derived from its fundamentalist theology. It is also partially the strength and consistency of elevation of the father. Fathers can be instrumental in providing sons and daughters with opportunities for employment or, in the case of a son, withhold his blessings, which will delay his appearance before the priesthood council to request a wife. Significantly, a father's status within the community is linked to a perception of him as being active within the religion. For example, I heard of a man who asked a favor from the church leadership. They politely turned his request down since he did not regularly attend Saturday evening priesthood meetings or Sunday service. Another example of the importance of a father's social status in providing potential opportunities for a son is found in a conversation I overheard between a teenager and his mother about whether his father had a "high standing in the community." The teenager felt that he suffered because his father was "not being highly respected in the community." A daughter's concerns and complaints about her father are typically discussed privately with her mother. Issues of respect for her father diminish marriage prospects less for a daughter than those prospects for sons.

## THE CHARISMATIC FATHER: IMAGINING THE POLYGAMOUS FAMILY

The polygamous family's social organization is derived, in part, from theological axioms that hold up men as the religious specialist and authority in the family and, in part, from the social dynamics of polygamous family life that make men, both as fathers and husbands, the pivotal axis by which wives and children organize their attention and internalize family identity.

From an organizational perspective, intense and persistent familial attention is given to the father as the ultimate adjudicator of family affairs as well as the representative of spiritual authority. The father's idealization (in some instances, *glorification* would be a more precise term) carries within it a psychological component that acts as the foundation in constructing children's identity. So, strong is the children's identification with the father, both as a concrete reality and an abstract ideal, that children are reluctant to withdraw from it, its power, and the allegiance that flows from it. If they do withdraw from it, they only do so with grave and unsettling misgivings. For individuals to leave the community, they must, in psychological terms, "kill the father" by rejecting his religion and way of life. In some individuals, there can nevertheless be a lingering fondness for the community's more socially supportive programs, such as helping others to rebuild a house. The connections to the community, and certain people in it, sometimes remain, but without fondness for the father.

For children of a plural marriage, the notion of familism and thus a sense or feeling of belonging stems from an image of the all-powerful father who is the social and religious authority. In a very practical way, the plural family is held together as much by the effort to maintain a strong image of family as it is by actual memories of interaction with one's father. It is an image that needs the active involvement, participation, and affirmation of fathers and cowives.

American psychologists have long noted that, for American children of both sexes, the "mother is the most important figure" (Sered 1994:57). Because families tend to be organized around the mother, there is a general tendency, especially among white American middle-class families, toward the development of greater emotional ties between mothers and children than of those between fathers and children. Sered (1994) points out that matrifocal units often arise within patrilineal social organizations. In Angel Park, as in the Salt Lake Valley region, the tendency toward matrifocality is weakened but not entirely eliminated by the cultural emphasis on the spiritual and administrative authority of the father (Parker, Smith, and Ginat 1973).

Unlike in other polygamous societies, Mormon polygamous women expect to develop strong, intensely emotional relationships with their husband. Such relationships run counter to church teachings about the nature of a man's role, that of an emotionally neutral and preferably egalitarian attitude toward his wives. It is the desire for romantic intimacy (discussed at greater length in chapter 5) that intensifies a woman's identification with the role of wife/lover in addition to that of mother. This identification stands in sharp contrast to the official ideal of marriage as a primarily procreative institution.

Because cowives are often in competition for their husband's attention, they tend to emphasize, even perhaps overstate, their idealizations of him in order to overwhelm the other's claim on his attention. In the struggle children are often used as a means, a tool or prize, to that end: to become the desired object of their husband's attention. The use of children for this purpose can be deliberate as well as unconscious. Because wives focus their attention on their husbands, the children, who want to please both their mother and their father, will follow suit. The children participate because they have their own aims. By cultivating father adoration, mothers hope to demonstrate their commitment to religious ideals and tacitly express their superior worth among cowives. Consequently, mothers play a crucial role in "transmitting the pervasive symbolic presence of their husbands" (Parker, Smith, and Ginat 1973:697). They will instruct their children to love and cherish their father while striving to fulfill his expectations. Parker, Smith, and Ginat (1973:696) found, for example, that, whenever a father was away on business, his wives would teach the children special songs or have them learn short stories to be recited or sung upon his return. If the wives want to uphold their husband's public image after his death, they will actively and habitually defend his reputation over the course of their marriage and afterward. I learned of a family whose older sons disliked their father, but his wives were united in promoting their husband as a unifying presence and symbol and therefore did not listen to, or agree with, the sons' negative opinions. These efforts, along with the child's own desire to bond with the father, enhance the father's stature as the spiritual leader of the plural family. The father is the key presence and symbol that links the church, the family, and the self-together into a unified cultural system.

In spite of the devotion to upholding the father as an idealized and, almost sacred, symbol, everyone is aware that a plural family can fragment relatively easily into separate matrifocal units. In the effort to achieve a tighter family cohesion, church leadership emphasizes the value and importance of rededicating the self to higher ideals, encouraging obedience to the husband, and demonstrating respect for his fatherly duty to care for everyone.


## SPIRITUAL AFFIRMATION:
## VISIONS AND DREAMS

The experience of visions and dreams are the most vivid evidence of a person's ability to interact with the spirit world. By describing them and their meaning to his children and wives, a father's authority is unmistakably reinforced. It is his accounts and the meaning he gives them that demand the attention of wives and children not just because of his recognized authority but because they are understood by the community to have profound religious significance.

Polygamists seek to find and understand God's will through the aid of visions and dreams. Prayer, visionary dreams, and one's own inner promptings are evaluated by their effectiveness in advancing that understanding. The process is not unlike the approach taken by American Puritans to spiritual conflicts, similar with regard to the belief in the applicable power of these experiences. Belief in the validity of visions and dreams as a vehicle of truth is so strong in fundamentalist religion that these often serve as the critical or central guide for important decisions. A middle-aged man, for example, told his family about an angel who instructed him that his oldest son would live the fullness of the Gospel (i.e., would stay in the community and form a plural family). Another father had a dream that affirmed his son's ability to support the family and sustain its unity. Still another father recalled for his wives a vision he had as a young man that told of a short yet very fulfilling life. The dream underscored his religious righteousness, pointing to the family's need to follow his instructions and cherish their time with him. Dreams like these not only circulate within the family but at times move out into the community. They are manifestations of the father's authority. They establish his influence as a moral force and attest to his charismatic presence within the family.

In every moral community, there is identification of the self with the leader. If "identification is the process of developing bonds to an object and altering one's actions because of these attachments" (Ross 2007:58), then the interdynamics particular to the American Mormon polygamous family likewise contribute to transforming the father from an important, albeit respected, parent into an all-powerful charismatic figure; therefore the family privately cherishes his memory and, in most cases, the community at large elevates that memory to the highest level of admiration. Since the father is given God's will, he is the voice of spiritual idealism. Consequently, he imposes the conditions for transcendence, which derive, in part, from social organization and, in part, from emotional identification with the father, the man himself. As this voice, he must be heeded. The voice and image may or may not be at odds with the actual experience of a son or daughter and the remembrance of their father. Even when there is a discrepancy between the experience and the remembrance, the power of father adoration is so strong that it can erase the discrepancies.

## LOVE, AMBIVALENCE, AND HOSTILITY: RESOLVING THE FATHER

The religious ideals as well as the internal dynamics of polygamous family life contribute to the production of a charismatic awe felt toward the father. It often translates into an adoration that will continue through the lives of most family members. The adoration is not automatic, however. Men still need the support of their wives, and this means they need to be clearly proactive in the life of their family. There is an exchange here that, when functioning in the customary way, reinforces each other's roles. Men require that their wives sustain their reputation in front of the children, they cannot completely withdraw or be seen as abandoning their children.

The essential religious goal in this dynamic is that wives express their support by endorsing their husband "in righteousness." In the event that a husband abandons his family through complete indifference to its needs, particularly to those of the children, there is a crisis. Such a disregard to their well-being will lead the abandoned wife to turn against her husband and seek to undermine his authority and representational importance. When that occurs, the children, typically acting in solidarity with their mothers, will reject the father. If the father has a bad or rocky marriage yet maintains actual involvement with his family, his teenaged children often disagree with their mother and will not leave their father. The power of the father's elevation is shown in the widespread feeling that there is no other side to take. Even when the children clearly see that their parents have a less than satisfactory marriage, the close bond (one that is not intellectually presumed but a simple fact of the dynamic of father adoration) with their father restrains or blocks them from leaving. For example, a wife wanted to divorce her husband and leave, but her teenage children refused to go with her. This resulted in the wife moving out of state without her children. Another instance occurred in which a teenager defended his father before his mother after she vehemently criticized his father. He yelled, "Stop speaking bad about my father," and then walked out of the room." The quality of the husband-wife relationship is secondary to the quality of the father-offspring relationship, and it shows in every aspect of life. The adoration of the father is strong, and the bond and identification with him is nearly impervious.

Among infants whose fathers died, there is an unqualified or total adoration of the father. Before exploring the complicated world of father-child interaction, I want to look at the children's perspective, especially those whose father died when they were too young to have had many meaningful or memorable interactions.

A prevalent theme and a common complaint in Angel Park is the yearning of children for a closer relationship with their deceased father. This results from the age difference between older fathers having children with younger wives, with those fathers often dying before the child is grown. When asked about the importance of a father, a fourteen-year-old boy, whose father had passed away six years earlier, said: "A father is so important for a boy. He will give you guidance, leadership, and direction. I regret I didn't have a closer relationship with my Dad before he passed to the other side." The intensity of such a feeling of loss growing over time into an idealization is revealed in the following event. An eleven-year-old girl was walking up a mountain path when she spontaneously exclaimed, "I remember going up here with Dad. It was so wonderful." She turns to her mother and asks. "Mom, did I go up here with Dad?" The mother nods, and the girl said: "Yes! I remember it was so wonderful." The absence of the father can produce a memory of an experience that may not have occurred, or whose outlines are unclear if not entirely uncertain, because the power of father idealization permeates the community. Out of the idealization, the father's vital presence continues beyond his life, which demonstrates the strength of its power.

Individual identity is based, in part, on the recognition of one's biological roots and, in part, on rendering homage, regardless of biology, to whoever is the patriarchal family head. An example of an offspring's need to idealize the father is found in a married woman's unrelenting efforts to come to terms with the relationship to her father, or the lack of one—a father who abandoned her when she was a toddler and never returned to the community. For most of her youth, she refused to accept her stepfather as her real father, yet maintained a somewhat respectful attitude toward him. She believed her father would return to the community and then be worthy of her love. She also embraced the idealization of the father. It was her struggle to reconcile the loss of her father, that is, absence, within the community's cosmological framework that exacerbated her experience of loss and undercut her identity. But the force of her continued respect for her father served as an anchor throughout the struggle. Now in her forties, and with several children, she regularly calls her biological father "just to talk about things with the man I adore."

Although this example seems typical by mainstream standards, it goes against the community's theological tenet, which holds that the only candidates for honor are those who remain in good standing in the church. For this woman, the emotional bond with her birth father took precedence over the standards required to honor the current male head of the family. She honors him. There are many similar cases where a daughter or son is caught between a commitment to the ideal of father adoration and her or his negative view of the father. In most cases, the decision affirms the ideal of father adoration despite the negative view.

The grounding of these idealizations is dual, combining imaginative projections with actual interactions. The proportions vary by individual, but I found that a large number of the idealizations are dual. As positive psychological projections, children's imaginative projects (many can more accurately be termed fantasies) about a deceased or "lost" father are a familiar theme. What is unusual about them in Angel Park is the tendency to exaggerate and embellish the experiences of their fathers that are most enjoyable or blissful.

Although fundamentalist Mormons want nothing more than to honor and admire their fathers, more often than not, despite their best efforts, the honor is qualified, not absolute. Nonetheless, the depth and persistence of the desire to honor underscore the hold of father adoration as an institution, which is foundational for the entire family dynamic. Outright rejection is the rare case. Because the father's actual involvement with his family ranges from intimate involvement to outright indifference, it is not surprising that there exists a deep underlying ambivalence toward one's father, who, as a sacred symbol, is nonetheless the focal point of family organization and identity.

There are two often-competing images of the father in Angel Park. The cherished and revered public image that forms the community's hagiographic accounts are often modified, if not overturned, in private conversation, by more guarded and ambivalent attitudes. The range goes from clear affection to smoldering resentment and outright rejection, with variations and degrees in between. Given the community's social dynamics and its religious core tenets, most people are uneasy in acknowledging or revealing their ambivalence and instead praise their deceased father's memory. However, the actual reality of the father-child interaction often gets in the way. The reality of the interactions is not unlike the interactions between fathers and children across American culture. The distinguishing feature is the consistent and widespread expression of father adoration in the polygamous Mormon community.

The quality of feelings toward one's father depends on the degree of the father's involvement in his child's life. If the father passed away when his children were young, the children's tendency is to view him as a valued and revered symbol. The idealization here is personal in tone and substance. It is based mostly in a fantasy of reconstruction, but it is still a salient value.

When the father is present and had either developed a warm or somewhat aloof relationship with his children, there appears to be no contradiction between the father's public image and the child's actual remembrance (as an adult) of their interaction. However, if the father-child relationship was grounded in what a child believed was an abusive relationship, then that child's attitude often veers from absolute adoration and denial to resentment. For those who felt anger toward their father and remained in Angel Park, there were customarily attempts to reconcile the anger with one of the most fundamental axioms of the community: the father as an ideal vital to the community's identity.

The reconciliation often takes place in three ways: absolute devotion, guarded adoration, or rejection. Guarded adoration, by far the most common attitude toward the father, maintains a clear distinction between the symbolic accomplishments of the father and his fatherly qualities as a man. For example, sons of a prominent family repeatedly praised their father's accomplishments and what he meant to them. In private, however, some acknowledged a lack of emotional closeness that left a gap in their lives. Significantly, brothers more than sisters admitted to a fear of their father—even, at times, a deep resentment. One brother recalled how much he admired his father, but often wondered if his father loved him. The fact that the brother couldn't tell is an indicator of how fathers can be detached from or aloof to their children, or generally uncommunicative. This brother noted that he had no difficulty, unlike the case with some men in the community, in distinguishing his father as a viable cultural symbol from his actions as a man. Such a capacity to compartmentalize was not shared by most of his brothers, who were too reluctant not to completely honor their father's memory. He further observed, "My brothers are afraid that, if they acknowledge that our father has some shortcomings, it might undermine their view of him. They do not want to acknowledge that he was also a man. They can only remember him as our honored father. They think they have to completely adore him in every way, or not at all."

Another example of guarded adoration can be heard in one middle-aged woman's reminiscence that she "wasn't that close to my dad. The only reason I want to write about my father's life history is to do it before someone else does. Then I can read it at our church service." For her, it is celebrating the father's public image and her role in doing a public performance that holds the appeal. The motivation is not drawn from unqualified adoration but rather from the importance of the church service to the community and her own personal wishes.

Another attitude is total rejection. When a son or daughter rejects his or her father, especially in conversation, it is usually because they no longer participate in the community's social life. By rejecting the father as a symbol to be venerated, the individual effectively severs his or her ties to the wider cultural and religious order. Rejection of the father entails a kind of self-exile from Angel Park. So deep is the necessity of father adoration that when rejection occurs, the child will often bitterly curse his or her father. For example, in one family where the father had abandoned his children, less than half the family attended his funeral. Although some return after being away for a long time, they will never idealize their father, preferring to hold onto a deep hostility and to keep the suppressed anger to themselves.

The various attitudes toward the father hide a deep-seated ambivalence and emotional volatility, which nonetheless lead to the idealization of him as bearer of family pride and identity. The ambivalent anger toward the father actually contributes to the institutionalization of father adoration in Angel Park, primarily because the guilt that accompanies the rejection gets rechanneled into support of the father and that institutionalization. The characteristic ambivalence does not satisfactorily reconcile the father-son relationship or solve it and, as such, constitutes an emotional reservoir for the unresolved emotions that shape the style in which father adoration is manifested in ceremonial and ordinary life in Angel Park. The bifurcation of the father into the symbol and the man is one means that men and women in

Angel Park use to manage what is, for many, a ghost they can never shake.

In sum, the emergence of father adoration arises from the peculiar social dynamics of the polygamous family household as much as it does from the theological centrality of the father in the fundamentalist Mormon religious system. From this perspective, father adoration is a by-product of specific social factors and theological axioms that, coming together, result in its institutionalization. The public adoration of fathers is a distinct type of noble love that is bottomless in its essence and available to everyone. It is never seen as a zero-sum commodity—not the more I have, the less you can get. In this way, the periodic gathering of families in the name of the father not only sustains the intertwining of one family with other families to solidify a strong cultural heritage but also celebrates that bond while, at the same time, renewing the dedication to striving for the creation of the Heavenly Father's ideal family unit—the polygamous family (Jankowiak and Allen 2006:382–391).

# 4

# DIFFERENT PHILOSOPHIES FOR ORGANIZING A FAMILY

HUSBAND: *You lost your identity rights as soon as you said I do.*

WIFE: *I did not.*

HUSBAND: *You are supposed to obey me and my first wife.*

WIFE: *I will not do this; it is inhuman.*

HUSBAND: *You are supposed to come to the first wife's home and cook every other week.*

WIFE: *This is not fair.*

HUSBAND: *When I am with my first wife you cannot call and ask for me.*

WIFE: *No other home is this strict.*

*"The brethren often tell us during Sunday meetings that "women are not a husband's slave! They have rights too" (a plural wife).*

*"We are going to do it, but we didn't—we are working on it, but forgot" (a plural wife).*

Despite the glorification of the father, the ultimate embodiment of male patriarchy, there is a wide range in the way men organize and manage their respective families. In Angel Park, there are three predominant management orientations: stern authoritarian, diffuse or consensus, and indifference.

The authoritarian orientation follows a classic patriarchal ideal of top-down male leadership. This orientation resembles eighteenth-century Austrian government, which valued centralization, discipline, and military discipline (Judson 2016:53). It is centered upon a ranking official—in this case, the husband—who provides instructions and support to those under his command. The military metaphor is frequently invoked during church sermons and is commonly voiced in many family homes. Although the metaphor is invoked throughout the community, the more elite or prominent families seem most able to organize their families around a viable hierarchical system. As one man told me, "I tell my family we are like the military and everyone needs to follow orders." Another man who was immensely more flexible tried various ways to organize his large family and concluded that everything had to be run through him. As he noted, "It just becomes too confusing to let each wife organize the family the way she sees fit—you no longer have a united family but several monogamous families under one roof." Another husband stressed, "My house is a hierarchy. I pay the bills—everyone needs to step in line or ship out." A youth recalls, "My father did not allow conversation or debates at the dinner table. He wanted absolute silence and obedience." An adult offspring recalls his father's favorite mantra: "You will do it and you will love it."

Another illustration of the authoritarian approach is found in the way some fathers take control of the dinner menu. A youth recalled a time his father took the entire family to a restaurant, and when the waitress handed everyone menus his offspring (who range in age between one to sixteen years old) never opened them. They knew from experience their father would order for everyone, whether they wanted a particular food item or not. In retrospect, they perceived their father's behavior as another opportunity to assert his authority over his family. Other men reinforced their patriarchal position by engaging in family rituals designed for no other reason than to reinforce his dominance over the family. In one case, a father commanded his family to "fall into line" (his favorite metaphor) and parade around the house. A less dominant, albeit patriarchal, orientation is revealed in a young woman's remembrance of her natal family, where family members often query their father about the possibility of going to college or visiting a friend in another town or, in the case of a wife, visiting her parents. The youth recalled that his father often agreed to their request, but a few times he said no, and his offspring and wives followed his directive. Women often testify during a church meeting that they "will do whatever my man tells me." It is more a statement of embracing and accepting cherished community values than an actual account of their daily interaction. In effect, the patriarchal or authoritarian orientation asserts that women obtain salvation through obedience to their husband, a point echoed in a mature wife who recalled that "I obeyed my husband, until he had dementia."

Women's perception of themselves within the plural family can be strikingly at odds with the more formal religious image. Most married women are more than capable of pushing back and redefining their familial role as well as influencing and changing their husband's marital behavior. Women on several occasions asserted that "men have the priesthood [or religiously ordained authority], and we have agency [or freedom to decide]." Thus, a commitment to a patriarchal ethos does not mean an absolute blind obedience. Although authoritarian-oriented men and women would rather give preference to the teachings of religious leaders and believe obedience is more important than self-reliance, women are not above engaging in their own form of quiet resistance. In this way, women are active players shaping the emotional tone of their marriage. It is not unusual for a wife to resist or counter what she feels is her husband's unreasonable command by invoking the following phrase: "We are going to do it." But then note she "did not do it but she is working on it but forgot." Angel Park's women's response is similar to what researchers have found working in monogamous patriarchal families around the world. In this way, patriarchy carried within it its own internal logic. What is striking in Angel Park is the presence of polygamous families that follow a more pragmatic approach to family organization.

An insightful husband who practiced a modified version of the patriarchal family ethos appreciated Angel Park's wives' pragmatic response. He observed that "wives are obedient to her man in principle, but only when it serves their interests. Otherwise, they just ignore the man." The discrepancy between the religious ideal and the more common pragmatic response accounts for family misunderstanding, resentment, and confusion, as one youthful wife readily admitted: "I should be more obedient, but I am a disobedient girl." Her assertion is not atypical.

In contrast to the authoritarian approach, the consensus family management orientation encourages open discussion and freer expression of personal doubt. Such families tend to be headed by educated or immensely introspective men who are not insecure discussing what "makes life worth living." Husbands/fathers who prefer a consensus approach enjoy instructing, guiding, and nurturing their wives and offspring in their life journey toward becoming a better person. Men who favor a consensus management household are acutely aware of their responsibility to provide a supportive home environment. A mature man reflecting on his marriage noted, "A leader cannot sit back and give orders. He has to become a manager and try to satisfy all the various interests of a society without being dictatorial." Another man conveyed his family management philosophy; " A man must lead, but not absolutely. I practice a more open approach to management of my family. My brothers ask: 'Are you crazy to let women do this? Why are you so open?' I realize I have confronted my father's ghost. I realize my father is a man with fragility. This realization allowed me to go my own way and be more open and pragmatic with how I organized my family."

One man tried various ways to organize his large family, ranging from cowife independence, then group negotiation, and finally male leadership. He realized that the pragmatics of organizing a large family required that the husband actively manage his family. In his family, he requests that each wife ask what needs to be done today. A well-organized family requires group coordination to complete the daily tasks that sustain it and thus keep the family in order. To that end, they insist on upholding family rules they think will contribute to a more harmonious home. They repeatedly stress that when everyone behaved in a morally appropriate manner harmony should prevail. Consensus families can be large or small and prefer to emphasize the value of cooperation and reporting (or telling others where you are) as their family's foundational principles.

I estimated that in Angel Park, unlike FLDS or Short Creek polygamous communities, around 40 percent of the families for which I had data preferred to organize their families around a consensus, albeit still father-centered, orientation; while another 40 percent are organized around an authoritarian or patriarchal orientation, with the remaining 20 percent lapsed into essentially separate family units with no thought of living in a unified plural family.

The indifferent approach or posture, which is neither respected nor admired, is more the by-product of a male's rejection of the responsibility of family leadership. A middle-aged wife reflecting upon her marriage and the absence of male leadership captures some of the frustration wives often experience. She observed, "I wanted him to head the family, but he refused and then he wanted to but then he walked away." The husband's indifference invariably results in family members becoming disinterested in and refusing to work together to promote any semblance of plural family unity. Rather quickly, this leadership style results in a monogamous living arrangement with a wife living upstairs and another downstairs. There is no sharing or family unity; thus no communal meals or joint child-rearing. In every way, this absence of leadership undercuts core theological principles and practices, which results in a less than satisfying material and spiritual life for family members.

Whatever a man's family management philosophy, he will require his wives to support his vision of how a proper family should be organized and managed. Many wives try to protect their husband from some of the harsh realities of family life. Other wives, however, do not. For example, a mature woman recalled that her husband had lapsed in having regular home Sunday service. She informed me that Sunday service was more than just about reaffirming commitment to the religion. It was also an opportunity for the family to voice their complaints or reservations about an individual's actions. For example, one senior wife thought her husband drank too much (which is a common pattern in the community). Her husband was irritated and told her to "solve her problems and he would deal with his." In another family, a sister-wife thought everyone was taking advantage of her by asking her to do their laundry. She felt used. In still another family, the husband admitted that "he did not like to be a father"—a second wife asked him, however, "to at least hold a Sunday service for the large family." He agreed. So, after the Sunday family meal, the family would read and discuss scripture. "These meetings," the woman noted, "seem to have a calming effect on my sons. I was grateful for this." The woman continued, "A week or so later my husband thanked me for supporting him in front of the children. He even admitted with some discomfort that he needed "my support in upholding his vision of how we can become a better family. Now every time we hold a Sunday meeting we chant: 'I am so grateful for the religion, for knowing God, and for the priesthood.'"

There is a generational difference in family organization style. The authoritarian or patriarchal orientation is more common among the community's elite families where the husband was born in the 1930s to early 1950s. This generation is more conservative than later generations. It is within this generation that the husband remains the central organizing focus of family life. The husband/father manages his family firmly while trying to be fair. In these families, meals are taken together, and children are bathed and put to bed at similar times. Significantly, family prayers are also recited at a regular time each evening.

The regularity or consistency is less apparent in families with indifferent leadership. These families' variability is associated with nonelite status; there is a greater variation in the way a family is organized, with meals taken at different times and individual sleep schedules varying with a mother's inclination.

In every consensus-organized family, women embraced the religious principle that their husband is the head of the family while also offering an important qualification. Ideally, women should be "submissive" and follow her husband, as long as he follows the principle of Jesus Christ. But when he becomes too selfish and dishonorable and is not fair one may resist. In the various family approaches, there is a continuous appeal to religious texts as justification for allowing or forbidding certain behaviors, which is a constant reminder that the family is at heart a religiously based system. That devotional commitment is often expressed in family settings: "I am so grateful for my religion, for God, and the priesthood." It is a refrain voiced with reverence and deep appreciation.

It is an Angel Park core belief that if harmonious bonds of friendship and love can be achieved within the larger community, they can be achieved within the plural family, thereby enabling individuals to transcend self-centered impulses in favor of a fuller, richer, more collective-oriented state of being. To that end, many families believe the plural family requires some form of a hierarchical arrangement directed toward promotion of the common good. Given this life orientation, high-functioning polygamous families tend to organize themselves around a division of labor whereby individuals are assigned different tasks.

In the community's high-functioning families there is often a complementary division of labor that is put to use for good effect. For example, a family is organized around each wife working and thus controlling her own money. The sister-wives contribute to a common pot that, if low, the husband enhances with his funds. He hires a child caretaker the wives all continue to pay for; he does this as he believes wives could worry that a cowife is treating her own children better than the others. To eliminate this potential anxiety, it is best to bring in a more neutral person. His wives are fine with this practice.

## DIVISION OF HOUSEHOLD LABOR

Angel Park families believe that the division of household labor makes for a more unified and supportive family environment. Plural households are organized around work zones: yard and garden, washing, house cleaning, kitchen duties, and childcare.

It is rather mundane and yet how it is organized can make a family highly functional or immensely dysfunctional.

It is difficult for anyone who grew up in a small family to imagine the difficulties of managing a large family. There is a pragmatic reality in managing a large family—some families use a cafeteria-style line to feed their small children, others use separate tables with each mother sitting with their children. Some families allow table talk; others prefer to eat in silence. A wife recalls: "we had thirty kids with fifteen babies in diapers. We went through six diapers a day for each child. You finished changing one and had to start all over again." She admits that "I was overwhelmed at times but" (noting, with pride) "I did it." She also recognized that "our polygamy and our poverty made us different, but it also bonded us to each other, especially our sense of persecution heightened" (Spencer 2007:17).

In spite of the official ideology that holds motherhood as one of its highest ideals, there are women who prefer not to spend every day caring for children. It is not unusual for a woman to admit—sometimes and, for a few, most of the time—she can feel lonely and believe those who work outside the family have a more fulfilling life. I knew two homes where the family discussed this and tried to provide an opportunity for the housemother to visit friends and, in one instance, rotate childcare between cowives so no one felt too confined. In high-functioning families, a common feature is its members wanting to care and being actively responsive to each other. Moreover, it is assumed that the best family organization is a hierarchical arrangement oriented toward the promotion of the common good. Given this life orientation, high-functioning families tend to organize themselves around a familial division of labor with members being assigned different tasks.

The patriarchal and consensus approach are both common in many nonelite families. That of consensus, albeit still hierarchal in design, is more common in families whose members work as educators or are actively engaged in business interactions outside the community. In consensus families, members have come to appreciate the opportunity to have a voice in family affairs. For example, a thirty-something woman recalled her father stressing "the importance that we all agree and support the larger goal of living united. If anyone pointed out a contradiction, Dad would say, 'OK, let's sit down and talk about it. Let's see how we are working for unity and achieve the larger goal.' Everyone in the family was impressed, and we would say to each other, 'See, he does believe in the big plan and we should help him.'" In another family, the father encouraged free discussion and debate. For him, a table full of conversational vibrancy was the essence of life. Other men, however, prefer more control, tempered with little to no conversation. In short, there is wide variation in Angel Park family organization.

Altman and Ginat (1996) found that Salt Lake's Allred families are organized more around a consensus approach that is most readily manifested in kitchen authority. Some families alternate the weeks in which a different wife is in charge of family cooking and laundry; other families assign on a more permanent basis specific tasks "with one wife managing child care, another wife doing the family sewing, laundry and ironing and another preparing meals" (1996:369). I discovered that it is not in the family backyard or in the living room, but rather in the kitchen or cooking arena where sister-wives often come to voice their displeasure, asserting their relative family position or cooperative unity. For example, a family disagreement erupted over the amount of apple sauce that should be placed on a child's plate. The sister-wife who oversaw the kitchen thought each child should be given "just a little," while the child's mother thought it was OK to give "a bit more." The disagreement resulted in a quarrel, which for those present was less about the food item and more about the opportunity for each woman to voice her relative positionality, authority, and irritation. In another family the sister-wife who oversaw the kitchen often informed her sister-wives it was "too late to use the kitchen" only then to heat up a frozen pizza for her own kids. In another example, a mother, in a highly dysfunctional family, often hid treats (e.g., cookies or cake) in her bedroom closet so that she could later give them to her children. If her sister-wives discovered she was hording treats, they would have demanded a share, which would have resulted in a public quarrel. If the kitchen is a center where sister-wives exert public displays of authority and control, it can also be quickly transformed into a memorial of cowives' cooperation. In many families there is pride in collectively organizing a large family meal. In this setting, sister-wives praise each other's contribution to the special meal. They will say in front of the visiting guest: "Sun is the best at preparing this dish" or "No one can cook as good as Mei." Bennion (1998) noticed a similar pattern among the Pinesdale polygamous community, where "the proximity of wives can result in increased conflict, increased cooperation or both" (1998:135).

Another more conservative family delegates tasks within the family through the assignment of skill sets. An especially talented young woman was sent to college to get a professional degree, which enables her to earn a higher income and thus bring much needed funds into the larger family. Another woman who has less education was assigned to be the family's car driver who takes her sister-wives to shop for groceries and related household items. She also will drive other sister-wives to and from work. Because most families stress modesty, women who want to remain in physical shape run in the evening wearing men's clothes so no one will mistake her for a female.

A man's political philosophy of family organization impacts the way he resolves family conflict. In more consensus households the preferred means is to let women "work things out" among themselves; whereas in more authoritarian families the ethos is to obey a husband's directions and commands. Justification is always to religious scripture, which is repeatedly asserted. It is the rare family that discusses how to solve a common problem. The preferred response is to assert and reassert theological axioms, as if repeating them often enough will successfully transform the questionable behavior(s).

In the indifferent and highly dysfunctional families there are few guiding principles with which to organize the family. An indifferent husband contributes to promoting a female hierarchy if he withdraws from daily activities. Whenever a husband no longer wants to "work with" or strive to create some semblance of family unity, his aloof behavior results in family anarchy. The withdrawal of the husband from a leadership role invariability results in the more assertive, or in local parlance, the "queen bee," wife seeking to take charge of the family. If the assertive wife is decent and respectful to her sister-wives, the family without male leadership can still function as a cooperative unit, but if the assertive sister-wife is spiteful and dictatorial it will undermine family unity and result in each cowife going her own way with complete contempt toward her husband and other sister-wives.

A longtime community member acknowledged that he knew "very few [dysfunctional] families that lived in harmony. In those families the wives and their children constantly fight amongst themselves. They needed a man with leadership skills who actually leads. In those families, the teenagers can't wait to leave the big family. They find it too oppressive." When a husband retreats from family obligations, his wives will counter his occasional commands by instructing their children to ignore their father. Over time, this practice will undermine his family standing and authority. In some instances, it has the reverse effect, where his children decide they will not be like their mother and will assume a different marital persona. For example, a middle-aged woman remembered with disgust how her mothers and not her father ran the family. She recalls, "It was horrible. They were constantly disagreeing amongst themselves. Nothing got done. I decided when I married I would not treat my husband the way my mothers treated my dad. I would do whatever I could to make my husband the center of our family. Our children know their fathers always comes first because he is a special man."

In high- and mid-functioning families, home Sunday religious meetings are a critical time to bring members together as a formal unity. In consensus homes it is a time to express themselves over what may trouble them. This style is, however, only common in those families that approve of consensus and are thus open to discussion. In some families the Sunday meeting can last an hour or so, while in others it can last over seven hours. In the more authoritarian families, the goal of Sunday school seems to be for the man to assert his authority and remind his wives and children of their obligations to each other as well as to their father/husband.

## CONTROL OVER A WIFE'S WAGE

The cultural ideal is for wives to give their salary to their husband, who will redistribute what each wife needs. It is thought that this system encourages personal responsibility and is easier to manage. The redistributive practice can promote a stronger sense of sharing and unity in a large family that also upholds the husband as the family's benevolent banker. Other husbands, in managing their large family, prefer to adopt a more pragmatic stance and tolerate wives keeping some of their wage money if they also contribute to household expenses.

Angel Park families, like the Allred communities, adopt "some combination of the communal and the dyadic [or individualistic] systems" (Altman and Ginat 1996:310). In Angel Park, I estimated that in around 25 percent of the families the husband and wives kept their wages and contributed a percentage to a collective fund, with around 30 percent symbolically honoring their husband as head of the family by giving 50 to 60 percent of their wages, retaining the remainder for themselves. This pattern is especially evident when the husband is away for a long time and the wives must manage the household among themselves. In 20 percent of the dysfunctional families, women give nothing to their husband, with the remaining 25 percent giving all their wages to their husband, who redistributes it according to need. Similar patterns are found in the Salt Lake City Allred community (Altman and Ginat 1996) and in the Montana Pinesdale community, where Bennion observed that women who earned a salary had enhanced status and more authority in their respective families. In Angel Park, women who bring in a steady income are more respected. Housemothers' service is recognized and appreciated, though, as in mainstream society, less respected. As an astute working wife noted, "Mothering issues and household management are seldom discussed. Bringing home a paycheck is [positively recognized]." She continued: "Things are so expensive, and with so many kids you need extra income. You have to work. I need to do so much to manage my home" (i.e., her offspring). No matter what financial system a family adopts, there is always the threat, especially among the community's poorer families, that funding will be insufficient.

## SEXUALITY ACKNOWLEDGED AND DENIED

Because reproduction was thought not to be "about personal pleasure or even about creating a bond between husband and wives" (Ulrich 2017:231), nineteenth-century Latter-day Saints embraced contradictory ideas whereby they glorified reproduction while "urging sexual restraint" (Ulrich 2017:232). Angel Park is no different. A man justified his desire to have multiple wives as the only way he could produce numerous offspring. He pointed out that "Jesus Christ had eight wives—why? How could one woman have four billion children? She needed to go out and find help."

In Angel Park, nineteenth-century Mormon prudishness is giving way to a more responsive and at times playful sexuality expressed between a husband and his wives. This is not recent. Musser wrote that "sex in the name of love is okay but enjoyment in and of itself is bad." (1944:103). In Angel Park, especially among its more junior generations, sexual satisfaction, within a marriage, is acceptable, decent, and proper. For example, a youth told me his father instructed him that "sex is for reproduction and for bonding—both reasons are important." Another man, who had instructed his family that the "true polygamous only has sex to have children," later revealed to an old friend that he experienced an intense physical attraction to one particular wife: "Every time I see that girl I would run after her—we did it in the kitchen, on chairs, and everywhere." In his eyes, because he wanted to have children with her, his sexual desire was legitimate.

In the nineteenth century, husbands who continued to sleep with postmenopausal wives were classified as adulterers (Hardy 1992:91). It is an idea that continues to be voiced in the LeBaron Mexico community (Spencer 2007:39) as well as among some in Angel Park. There are exceptions, however: I was told of some men who had close feelings for a particular postmenopausal wife and continued to sleep with her. Moreover, it is thought that once a woman is pregnant the sexual relationship should cease (Miles 2011:203). In Angel Park, I found that not every couple followed that folk admonishment. The refusal to cease sexual intercourse can be also found in the FLDS community. Carolyn Jessop, for example, reflecting on her own father's sexual behavior, wrote that he continued to be sexually active with all his pregnant wives (2007:178). The point is that within families there can be a greater tolerance for expressing sexual desire. It is a desire that is seldom voiced in a public setting due to the fear that mainstream culture continues to hold the erroneous stereotype that polygamy is an institution designed to satisfy a male's gluttonous sexual appetite. In this regard, I repeatedly discovered that the mainstream cultural perspective was completely fallacious.

If sexual desire is a legitimate emotional state, then sexual restraint is also considered proper. Although the community deems using birth control unacceptable, I was aware of one (highly unrepresentative) woman who did not want to have any more children and did use birth control. Her husband supported her, saying he would wait for her to change her mind. Another husband responded to a wife, who already had several children, when it was her turn to sleep with him, and requested that they not have sex as she feared becoming pregnant, by hugging her, saying he understood. If intimacy is based on the degree of emotional affiliation present, then many Angel Park marriages are far from aloof and indifferent. In this way, there is wide variation between families and much more pragmatic adjustment to an individual's fears, needs, expectations, and hopes than can be tightly summarized in the community's theology.

## MANAGING INTIMACY

In the Allred and Angel Park communities there are two predominant rotation systems: the laissez-faire (or irregular visitation) (Altman and Ginat 1996:287) and a fixed system (seeing wives in a regular schedule). The fundamentalist fixed schedule is similar to sub-Saharan African cultures who also use a standardized schedule designed to ensure that every wife is treated the same. In contrast, in the laissez-fare system the husband does not organize his visitation around a standardized schedule but instead sees whomever he wants whenever he wants for however long he wants. This can result in spending weeks, if not months, on end with one wife who feels wanted and thus more special than her sister-wives. For example, Floria Jessop (2009), who lived in the FLDS community, writes that her father would have sex with her mother then "he would climb out of bed and go back down to Elizabeth's (his favorite wife) room." She adds, "I lay in bed in my room, just across the hall, and listened to Mom cry herself to sleep every night" (2009:24). A mature male noted, "A man cannot be fifty-fifty with each wife. Only one-third or one-fifth [involved with each wife]." The fundamentalist rotation pattern is similar to the Imperial China wife/concubine and the Ottoman harem pattern where the emperor or sultan had the choice of a different concubine or, in the case of the Ottomans, a continued preference for his first wife over his other "wives" (Peirce 1993).

Another pattern that is closer to fixed than the laissez-fare preference is to stagger visits over the weekend or rotate one week at a time—it is thought the longer time allows for special feelings to develop. Still others just use a system in which they sleep with a different wife every night. Unsurprisingly, the preferred "rotational system" reflects a man's idea of how a good marriage should be organized. But the rotational system is not without its difficulties: for example, the husband's emotional adjustment in switching between households. A wife notes, "we [she and her husband] get along fine, and then he leaves and two days later he returns and he is angry about something—it takes us the entire day to get used to each other—and then he leaves, and the cycle is repeated all over again."

If a husband no longer is interested in a particular wife, he will invoke a religious justification for not sleeping with her. It is not unknown for some Angel Park men, like LeBaron men, to stress that while they still love their wife they no longer think it is essential to sleep with them as "we have to learn to control our passion and use them only for procreation (Spencer 2007:120). The wife's reassignment to an asexual relationship is willingly or grudgingly accepted, while she often wonders why her husband continues to be sexually active with his other wives (Spencer 2007). Many, but not all, wives adjust and accept this state of affairs. As one low-profile wife acknowledged: "Sex is not everything." Other women use their sexuality to manipulate their husband to provide them with a necessary or valued luxury item. Other women suggest that a woman should refuse sex if her husband does not provide them with sufficient funds to support her children. In contrast, some married women complain that they do not have enough time to sleep if they are required to have frequent sex with their husband; they are grateful not to be the primary object of their husband's attention. Although a preference for sexual restraint is not representative, it is occasionally voiced among sister-wives. For them, the sexual domain is not an essential arena.

## MATERIAL AND PRAGMATIC REALITIES

There are ongoing tensions between community theological principles and the need to make pragmatic adjustments in managing a large family. To fully grasp the polygamous family, it is essential to understand the "role of women in the construction and maintenance of the household system" (Leslie 1993:149). After marriage, women often visit married sisters who are ready to engage in details of their married life. Given the depth of a woman's kinship network, I found that, compared to men, they had a richer, more nuanced understanding of the plural family. Because they frequently visit each other, they form an alternative support system ready to help with childcare, illness, and travel to the hospital, and they performed a supportive role sharing happiness and sadness. Although visiting sisters are tolerated, mothers are less so. Mothers are regarded as intrusive outsiders who may attempt to undermine a man's family authority. But, like most Angel Park's folk norms, there is variation. If a mother does not comment on a man's family organization and offers valued assistance to her daughter, his wife, men often tolerate a mother's visit. A woman reminded me that among fundamentalists there is a dominant norm holding that no one has the right to interfere with another man's family, even when there is abuse in that family. Carolyn Jessop, commenting on life inside the FLDS community, noted the presence and strength of a similar norm (2007:37). Given this pronounced, albeit unvoiced, norm, mothers can, in the words of a recently married woman, "visit you, provided she is helpful and never emotionally intervenes in family affairs." In spite of these injunctions, I found female-centered visiting networks that resulted in the intertwining of different kin/family groups to be a rich source of meaning. For most, it is what makes life worth living, with its constant celebrations of birthdays, dinners, and personal outings (e.g., going to the movies or bowling).

While some wives are obsessed with assessing the quality of their husband's emotional interest in them, other wives more acutely focused on whether their husband can provide the necessary material resources to support his growing family. Because the polygamous family is organized around rapid reproduction, it can outgrow "the boundaries of the household [finances], taking women's interests with it" (Robertson 1991:41). Whenever this occurs, it is not uncommon for a wife to comment, "I do not worry about a fall from grace, I worry about being put out in the cold." Concurring, Irene Spencer's commentary on the LeBaron community's family finances is representative of most fundamentalist polygamous households: "the family grows in size much faster than the husband's paycheck" (2007:10). Children are expensive; there are diapers, food, health needs, which means there is seldom enough money to go around (Schmidt 2007:30). An Angel Park woman, with numerous children and insufficient funds to support them, seconded that observation, crying out, "I have all these kids, and no one will help me."

Adequate financial support is a problem. I estimated that around 20 percent of Angel Park families had insufficient funds, with a much higher percentage of FLDS households, lacking adequate resources to support their plural family. In homes that are financially solvent, women are less defensive when their sister-wife uses communal property or serves food treats to her children. In financially stable homes, there is no psychology of "limited good," whereby if someone uses or receives something of value others believe there is less available for them. In well-functioning families, material considerations are seldom an issue; whereas in low-functioning families it remains a theme that augmented personal anxiety and resentment and serves as a source of frequent family quarrels. To that end, men need their wives' income to support a growing plural family.

Unlike tribal and agricultural societies where a small percentage of men is polygamous with women making the best of tough economic circumstances, Mormon fundamentalist communities are unique in that they are intentional polygamous communities who need women's reproductive labor more than their economic labor. In spite of economic costs, the religiously inspired community strives to create a family system that is not conducive to economic growth. In fact, except for the wealthiest, most polygamous families could not survive without support from external sources. In the U.S., that is the federal government. The community fears government intrusion and yet needs it to survive. It is almost impossible to form a polygamous family without most wives working or, if not, depending exclusively on government welfare. In this way, most U.S. polygamous communities have been able "to transfer the costs of reproduction to other social institutions rather than" bear the full cost themselves (Robertson 1991:39).

A. F. Robertson suggests that without wider social institutions to support a large family "the compact pattern of domestic developments offers little insulation from the pressure of the reproductive process. On the other hand, if people know that

they can count on external assistance in dealing with reproductive instability, it's easier to manage and sustain a large household" (1991:39).

Robinson echoes the economic conventional wisdom in pointing out that in the "face of the family's shrinking ability to provide for all the needs of its members, the state [or in this case
the U.S. federal government] may assume many of the family's
former functions" (1991:137). The 1940s Short Creek polygamous
community, aware that many families could not support their
families, urged its members to seek federal assistance in order to
supplement their irregular income (Bistline 1998). Wallace Stegner reports that in the 1940s Short Creek residents regularly
received relief checks (1942:217). Most fundamentalist communities continue to resemble 1940s southern economies, about
which William Faulkner once observed, "our economy is no longer agricultural but is the Federal Government" (cited in Lepore
2018: 540). This has not changed. Today, most fundamentalist
polygamous communities continue to receive some sort of government support (Bennion 1998).

Among FLDS, there is fear about a potential raid—whether
the government will show up because of their fraudulent use of
food stamps (Bennion 2012)—which contributes to an "under
seige" mentality. Still, many FLDS members justify their "right"
to federal support, as they feel they should use every means possible to fulfill God's design for creating and upholding his preferred family system. The government is aware of the potential
for fraud, but is handicapped in enforcing the law since fundamentalist women are not legally married and as single mothers
are thus eligible to receive federal support.

By the 1900s, Short Creek, which was now referred to as
FLDS, was ranked among the top ten townships in the West for
the WIC (i.e., Women, Infants, and Children) support program

that supplies food to low-income mothers and pays for Medicaid participation (Zoellner 1998:A1–A6). The community's reliance on WIC and Medicaid rivals only Western Indian reservations. Moreover, 33 percent of residents were on public assistance, with Medicaid paying for one-third of all babies born in town (Jeffs and Szalavitz 2009:202; Zoeller 1998:A6). Because the town has a self-funded birthing clinic, the percentage of townships that use Medicaid is lower. In 2002, 66 percent of FLDS residents received federal assistance, with 78 percent receiving food stamps (Bennion 2012:294). The fundamentalists justified their dependence on government welfare as God's creation, to be used by his chosen people to help them survive and continue to create his ideal plural family (Western 2005:11). The FLDS leadership had for decades encouraged its members to obtain every government benefit they could apply for. Over time, this pattern developed into a fraudulent practice in which members were instructed "to buy food items with their food stamp cards and give them to the church warehouse where the leaders would decide how best to redistribute them. The food stamps could also be used as a form of payment at the sect-owned stores without the users receiving any cash in return" (McCombs 2016: A1). State prosecutors further revealed that "the money was then diverted to front companies and used to pay thousands of dollars for a tractor, truck and other items (McCombs 2016:A1).

In contrast to the FLDS community, Angel Park, with its emphasis on self-sufficiency over reliance on government welfare, does not promote, encourage, or idealize its members turning to the federal welfare system for support. I learned of only two families whose primary financial support had lost his job, which meant the family was eligible for federal assistance, but, in each case, as soon as the man found employment his family no longer accepted federal assistance. The community has a long history of resourcefulness in legitimately pursuing available federal and state grants. They have obtained funding for town infrastructure improvement as well as individual help with a particular medical problem. The grants are obtained legally and demonstrate a keen talent and willingness to adapt to certain features of modern life.

In sum, family management is a process that is ongoing. It depends on the philosophical convictions of a family as to whether it will rely upon government support or will try to manage the larger family using its own resources. Angel Park, unlike FLDS, has decided to strive to be more self-sufficient and not depend upon government largess. Although the community embraces a unified theologically grounded cosmology, individual families repeatedly discover that it is essential to adopt a more pragmatic response to life crises and daily family management. In the end, there is tremendous variation within the community, with individual men embracing the theologically orthodox authoritarian approach, while others make pragmatic decisions in expanding and adjusting to the various personalities present within a big family.

# 5

## PLACEMENT MARRIAGE OR SELF CHOICE

### Finding Your Soul Mate

*Ella Hunt, a nineteenth-century wife, in a letter to a future sister-wife wrote, "The subject in question [plural marriage] has caused me a great amount of pain and sorrow, more perhaps than you could imagine, yet I feel as I have from the beginning that if it is the Lord's will I am perfectly willing to try to endure it and trust it will be overruled for the best of all" (Ellsworth 1992:45).*

In the Mormon fundamentalist community, there are two competing ideas about what love is and what it should not be. Both ideas are salient and often contentious, as the logic of one can undermine the logic of the other. The official ideal is noble or harmonious love and thought to have a higher calling than what many believe is the more self-centered sentiment of romantic love. Noble love is a "hierarchical love that reflects a sense of duty, while also justifying an ethic of protection, care, and reciprocity" (Parish 1994:176). In this scheme, "a sense of self is founded in relatedness within the family and this is what is most valued" (Parish 1994:176). Angel Park families believe that patriarchy or a male-dominated hierarchy is necessary to maintain family's coordination and an individual's overall well-being (Parish 1994:168). In Angel Park, like other fundamentalist communities, a wife is instructed to follow her husband's directives, respect him, and show him acquiescence and loving affection, while he, in turn, is obligated to love all his wives.

Angel Park's members justify the superiority of their faith and lifestyle with the valuation they give to harmonious or noble love, which some anthropologists would characterize as the essence of *communitas*. It is a feeling of being unbounded in its potential for forging, strengthening, and sustaining affectionate bonds between family members. It is somewhat analogous to William Reddy's idea of "longing for association" (2001:4–10). Because communitas encourages respect, empathy, helpfulness, and lasting affection, harmonious love often serves as the principal means to bind and unite the polygamous family. It is seldom dyadic, and it is not in opposition to differential status, familial rank, or a sexual division of labor. It is distinctly more hierarchical than it is egalitarian in its daily manifestation. Unlike passionate love, which tends to be egalitarian, emotionally intense, and dyadic in its orientation, harmonious love celebrates involvement with every family member. In fact, it thrives on it.

Edmund Morgan, in a series of publications explored the relationship between Puritan belief and the efforts to form God's ideal family, that is, a father-centered or patriarchal hierarchy in which everyone accepts their place, content to live in a community of like-minded believers (1944:48). This view is similar to the Puritans belief that "love is rational and controlled, not voiced with passion" (Morgan 1944:48). At an abstract level, most community members are in good agreement with the Puritan outlook on love and marriage. At the personal level, there is wide variation.

The early American view of love and marriage is affirmed in church sermons, where it is a virtue to embrace responsibility and share kindness with everyone in the larger family. In stressing noble love's superiority to romantic love, the community finds solace in personal sacrifice. It is considered an excellent preparation for living in the next life, where polygamous wives will achieve a higher glory and celestial rank than their monogamous counterparts.

The community is aware of this pull and works in good faith at trying to overcome "our natural" yearnings in order to embrace a higher calling: to form and sustain a loving plural family in which the husband and his cowives honor and respect each other. Although harmonious love is fervently stressed as the preferred family ideal, it is vulnerable to sexual and romantic desires. Its nondyadic focus stands in sharp contrast to romantic love, a tolerated but seldom publicly glorified emotional experience. This is one of the reasons for the community's celebration of the virtues of sacrifice, loyalty, and commitment to the plural family. Everyone is aware of the personal commitment that an individual makes in deciding to participate in a plural marriage and live according to the way their God wants them to live. The experience of a first wife who had a deep love for her husband is instructive. After several years of marriage, she accepted a second wife with the acknowledgment that "she and I will adjust, we will learn and both of us will become a better person."

## THE DOCTRINE OF PLACING MEN AND WOMEN IN A MARRIAGE

In the 1940s Short Creek community, the priesthood leadership, or the brethren, had collapsed into rival cliques which assigned a community member's daughter(s) to bind men together into a more personalized alliance (Bistline 1998:69). This practice was similar to that found in late–nineteenth-century Utah polygamous family life. Hulett considered this a natural outcome whenever "it is permissible for every man to look upon every unmarried girl as a prospective wife, and where there is [potential] to form a personal rivalry between men from different ecclesiastical strata" (1939:186): competitive contests within and between generations is inevitable. Irene Spencer, who grew up in the LeBaron polygamous community in Mexico, observed that when "I turned seventeen I was approached by at least ten men many claiming they had divine revelation that I should marry one of them" (2007:302). Decades later, Angel Park leadership, alarmed at the way swarms of Short Creek men would "hustle" young women when they reached marriageable age, tried to regulate courtship practices through institutionalizing the doctrine of "placement marriage." Angel Park's religious leadership saw this as a first step toward avoiding what it considered to be Short Creek's and nineteenth-century Mormon's harmful "mating frenzy." The leadership, or the brethren, thought it best to restrict, and if possible eliminate, any such frenzy around courtship by having membership defer to its authority. It alone would make the marital determination as to who was the true celestial mate. In agreeing to abide by the leadership's judgment, community members institutionalized a more orderly marital process and thus created a more orderly community (Jessop 2007:23).

There is a compelling cosmological logic behind the Angel Park membership agreement to be "placed" in a marriage. Mormon fundamentalists believe there are different spheres in which a person's soul has dwelled and will dwell. According to doctrine, they are the preexistent state of being, when the souls live together before receiving their earthly bodies; the earthly existence, or here and now state; and a future state of being, or time in the next life, where a male, provided he has lived a righteous life, will become a god and live with his wives who will act as his spiritual advisers to oversee his own planet. Given the different spheres of existence, it is imperative for men -and women to enter the spiritual union of earthly marriage whereby each person makes a life commitment to his or her "true love" or soul mate. Angel Park believes the leadership of its priesthood is endowed with spiritual or celestial insight to guide the selection of the correct spouse so that they can live together for all eternity. Many individuals believe there is a danger in following one's own personal inclinations or feelings. Doing so could result in selecting the wrong spouse or someone who belonged to someone else. If this were to occur, the couples would have to separate upon death so that each could be rejoined with their preexisting celestial spouse. Therefore, the community agrees it is best to ask the brethren (e.g., a member of the priesthood council or one's own father) to pray for guidance or insight as to who one may "belong to."

Not every fundamentalist community believes it is vital to have a religiously inspired placement marriage. The LeBaron community in Mexico, founded by fundamentalists who originally lived in Salt Lake City, with the FLDS, and in Short Creek, does not practice placement marriage because it restricts female choice. The community founder, Alma Dyer LeBaron, believed that women would be happier if they could choose their own spouse. An astute woman who lived in Angel Park and in the LeBaron communities observed that "those who date as opposed to being placed seem to be able to discuss things and come to some understanding about what marriage should be and what individual roles should be easier and smoother. I suspect they may have better marriages." I contend that she is only partially correct.

## FATHER'S AUTHORITY, DAUGHTER'S FILIALITY, AND ARRANGED MARRIAGES

Besides the search for a former or "true love," there are other pragmatic realities that can impact marital decisions. Perhaps the most important is a belief in the "will of the father." Because the father holds religious authority over his family, he can influence who his children, especially his younger (under seventeen years old) daughters, will marry. If a man believes he was promised to a particular girl, it is expected that he will first seek permission from the girl's father. If the father approves and the daughter agrees, then the couple will go to the brethren and ask for its approval and blessing. If there are no complications, such as someone else who also desires the young woman's hand, the request is readily granted.

In the early 1950s and 1960s, the community operated as a closed corporate society (i.e., inwardly oriented and economically self-sufficient). In this setting, a few fathers exchanged daughters with each other. There were tacit rules that structured these exchanges: 1. A man can give his daughter to anyone he wants but cannot tell another man that his daughter belongs to him or his son(s), and 2. high-status men can ask for and receive two daughters in exchange for one daughter. These daughters then enter the man's home as plural wives. Since these exchanges were seldom immediate, individuals had to wait until the girl passed puberty and became a teenager. There was always some anxiety that a promised daughter might be given to someone else or, worse, that she might refuse the arrangement and elope. These agreements were fragile and, consequently, they remained privately negotiated "agreements" as opposed to official ones. However, once the exchange was completed they became official.

Men therefore wanted to marry their daughters off earlier, before they had the opportunity to find, within their age cohort, a potential mate. By the 1990s, if not earlier, some Angel Park fathers were less interested in organizing an exchange agreement for themselves than they were in arranging a marriage for a son or, in some instances, a grandson. In contrast, the FLDS community lessened the sway of agency or free will, preferring to make it absolutely subordinate to hierarchical religious authority. Having a pronounced emphasis on obedience as its core value enabled several fathers to continue to construct daughter exchanges among themselves.

Ascertaining, with any degree of accuracy, marriage patterns among the FLDS has been almost impossible. Based on newspaper reports and conversations with friends associated with the FLDS, the practice of young (under eighteen) marriages did occur. However, it is not at all clear whether these were "spiritual" marriages, legal marriages, or simply marriages between underage teenagers. I did find evidence that many early-age marriages were artifacts of efforts to build a political alliance between ordinary families and the religious leader or prophet. This practice was common in the FLDS and in Bountiful, the Canadian fundamentalist community. Parents are aware of the material (e.g., not paying rent, taxes, water and power bills, and other types of assistance) and spiritual benefits (a higher place in the afterlife) in arranging a spiritual marriage with the community's prophet. In the 1990s, the FLDS leader was well into his seventies yet still was accepting young wives. It was known that he would never consummate these marriages, informing his younger wives that he preferred to wait until the next life when his body was replenished and he could once again produce children. The prophet's age, however, did not restrict families from eagerly offering their daughters to him. When the FLDS prophet died in 2000, he was reported to have had nearly one hundred wives, with the youngest being fifteen years old.

## SEEKING THE IDEAL SPOUSE: A CORE EXPECTATION

Fundamentalist men and women believe a successful marriage should have certain essential qualities or traits. Perhaps the most critical is that the person must have a firm commitment to the fundamentalist cosmology and thus to forming a plural family. The devotion of contemporary fundamentalists to their religion and the practice of plural marriage are similar to their nineteenth-century counterparts. Ida Udall, for example, explained how she broke off from her engagement. She reported that "the man she plans to marry did not want to practice polygamy, something she wanted to learn to do: sharing her husband with other wives to become a better person" (Ellsworth 1992:41). Most Angel Park women and their Montana Pinesdale counterparts assert that, from the ideal perspective, "romance is secondary to the primary criterion of finding a man who is strong in his priesthood" (Bennion 2012:98). In concurrence, fundamentalist men often query friends and associates about a woman's freedom to marry and the degree of her commitment to upholding the religion. Men will typically inquire in this way: "Does she have suitors, and does she believe in the Principle (i.e., polygamy)?"

Besides commitment to forming a plural marriage, fundamentalists also believe a successful marriage requires that a spouse has a number of traits. The ideal wife should be willing to make a full commitment to her husband, never ask to be adored, be quiet, patient, and obedient, and not trouble her husband with the little details of child-rearing. Further, she accepts having "to go without" and bears her poverty cheerfully and with dignity, while taking care of the house, the children, and, most of all, her husband. In addition, she actively seeks to recruit other women to marry her husband and join her in forming a loving plural marriage. In contrast, the ideal husband is a man who surrenders himself to the priesthood (or the community's religious leadership), is kind, generous, compassionate, fair, faithful, favors his family over his friends, and respects each wife's unique personality, while striving "to work with all his wives" to build a loving, harmonious plural family.

The desirable traits of the ideal wife are not always present. Fundamentalist men often talk about the need to have a submissive and obedient wife, and many men find obedient low-profile wives uninteresting spouses. In actual everyday living, men will not infrequently become uninterested, indifferent, and annoyed, even if they have obtained an "ideal" mate. This contradiction is illustrated by some candid comments made by a low-profile wife looking back on her first marriage: "I was a yes-yes person. Then I learned I did not have to be. My father taught us to bow and scrap, and to do whatever your husband tells you. But I noticed my husband was indifferent to my agreeableness. So, I changed. I started to disagree. My husband, used to my timid obedience, was surprised and began to treat me better, but still remained disinterested, as he already had a favorite wife who was seldom obedient. Realizing the truth, I soon left him and the religion."

Ulrich's historical research found that nineteenth-century Mormon men, "despite their patriarchal posturing's, [still] wanted to attract, not command, female loyalty" (2017:107). Although late-nineteenth-century Mormon women continued to be legally subordinate to men, many men favored a "good deal of the rough and ready comradeship and partnership" (Hulett 1939:250). In the marriage domain, Angel Park men are no different from their historical cousins.


## FINDING A SPOUSE: THE NEED FOR GUIDANCE AND SUPPORT

Angel Park members agree that the wise individual will seek out the counsel of one's father or the priesthood leadership and be guided in the choice of mate by them. Because the father has religious authority over his family and is, in most families, also admired if not adored, his opinion can be a pivotal factor in influencing a woman's marital decision. For example, if a man believes he was promised to a particular girl, he often first seeks permission of the girl's father rather than going to the priesthood. If the father approves and the daughter agrees, then the couple will go together to the brethren and ask for its approval and blessings. If there are no complications, such as someone else also desiring the young woman's hand, the priesthood believing they belong to someone else, or the woman outright rejecting the man's proposal, the request is readily granted.

Some men prefer seeking out a potential spouse through first asking a girl's father for his permission. For example, a mature man visited the father of a nineteen-year-old girl because he believed his daughter was placed with him in "the preexistent state" and requested her hand in marriage. The girl's father, an ambitious man, though from a low-ranking family, intently listened and replied: "She is special to us." "Well," said the suitor, "she is special to me too." The father replied, "I will think about it." Several weeks later, the man learned that the daughter had been placed by the priesthood with another man who came from a higher socially ranked family. Another example of a father's active involvement in helping his offspring marry revealed a different kind of story. A young man had been courting his daughter and made a good initial impression on the father. When the father discovered that the young man wanted to take his daughter out to the movies but did not have the money for it, he gave him the money. Sometime later the young man told the father that he "cherished" his daughter and "wanted to make her his wife and a mother." The father, who was pleased by what he said, tried to persuade his daughter to say yes if he proposed to her. Another father, when asked by his daughter where she may have belonged, never uttered the man's name, even though his daughter gave his name a few times. In stating what he thought would be her future spouse's name, he restored her confidence and security that she would be well placed.

## PLACEMENT MARRIAGE: SEEKING THE PRIESTHOOD OR BRETHREN'S GUIDANCE

Besides seeking a girl's father's permission, there are other methods that individuals use to obtain a spouse. The properly sanctioned church method, at the appropriate age, begins with the imperative to "give yourself to the priesthood." Then the brethren pray with the supplicant and through reflection discover one's celestial mate. The second method is for the individual to search on her or his own, then request the blessing of the priesthood if it concurs that one has found one's celestial mate. Another method, though not religiously sanctioned, is to develop a deep attraction or love for another person and then arrange for a civil marriage with the priesthood's approval.

I found an example of the first method in the story of a nineteen-year-old woman. Her father told her not to become involved with any young man in high school. When it came time to marry, having followed her father's advice, she went to the brethren. They prayed on her request, and she was placed with her current husband in what is a successful marriage. An eighteen-year-old man followed the second method; he prayed, seeking spiritual guidance for his celestial mate. He told me this account of his progress: "I recently did this, and a feeling came over me and I know I am in love. She is older than I am. She is nineteen years old. But we must wait, as I am too young. I will go to the head of the priesthood and see if he thinks my feeling is correct. If it is, he will be able to tell her to wait for me. If not, then she is not the one for me." During the waiting period, he was informed that she "belonged" to someone else. He accepted the priesthood's judgment and, with some disappointment, searched elsewhere for his celestial partner. A few years later, he did find another woman who, with the priesthood's blessing, agreed to marry him.

I found another example of the second method. A twenty-two-year-old woman who initially had left the community later returned to request the priesthood's help for placement in a plural family. She recalled her experience this way: "At first I thought I was going to be placed with an elderly man. If that happened, I would have 'rejected the placement' . . . I did not want to be married to an old man. I was set to refuse. However, when it turned out to be a different man [who had one wife], I agreed to the marriage. In fact, I felt relieved and sank back into the couch in a state of calmness. I knew it would be OK."

While some placement marriage deliberations can be a straightforward process in which the individuals readily accept the brethren's recommendation, there are others where personal convictions result in avoiding, ignoring, or rejecting the recommendation. The community itself continuously thinks about who may be promised to whom, believes it important to listen to a father's suggestion or follow the priesthood council's guidance, while at the same time does not discount inner promptings or agency (i.e., the local expression taken from nineteenth-century transcendentalist philosophy for free choice). This can sometimes result in acute internal conflict. Youth are taught, on one hand, to seek moral guidance from the priesthood, while, on the other, instructed to understand that they are independent agents responsible for their own lives. The tension between authority and independence is often most vividly played out and answered when individuals seek their "true love" without asking for the brethren's guidance.

Men and women are active agents in seeking out a "true love" that they believe they were bound to in their celestial preexistent state. To help discover their "true love," men and women rely on prayer and introspection for a sign of who they were promised to and thus should marry. For example, a young woman intensely devoted to her religion prayed for several weeks. Then she experienced a vision of who she should marry. Her "true love" was a married man whom she had never spoken to. Immediately she sought out the priesthood for an assessment and, she hoped, a confirmation of the authenticity of her vision. It was confirmed to be authentic. A few days later, she approached the man and suggested that her vision was a sign from God that he should take her as his wife. Although he did not know the woman very well, he agreed. The woman was filled with anticipation and excitement over being united with what she believed was her "true love." The man, however, adopted a reserved, almost emotionally guarded, posture toward his new bride. For him, marriage was more of a duty, and, in this case, a moral duty to accept a woman's visionary dream that he felt he could not ignore or reject.

The account that a young woman gave of how she came to decide who she should marry typifies the internal dialogue many youths go through as part of their search for the ideal mate. She said that "I thought about this, prayed on it, and realized that nothing was coming from my prayers. So, I just picked a young man who seemed interested in me." She went on to explain, "I did not want to be placed with an old man, I know so many girls who cry for years after the wedding, 'cause they were placed with an old man and could not have the young man they preferred (i.e., had an earlier " love crush" on). I got a young man who is nice, and I am happy."

Another illustration of a young woman's active search for "true love" is Sherry's story. Sherry came from a prominent family and ignored her father's request to marry someone he believed she belonged to. She disagreed. She believed that she belonged to a man who had three wives and whose home she often visited. After a time, she went to talk to the wives' husband and told him that she was certain she belonged to him. He asked her to continue to visit his family and get to know his wives. He reasoned that, since she would be with them more than him, it was essential she got along with everyone in his family. She agreed and, over a period of time, she was pleased with the way the plural family interacted. She told the man about her feelings, and soon thereafter they married.

I found a number of other examples of young people listening to their own feelings. At the age of nineteen, a young woman rejected her parents' mate selection. The brethren recommended that she marry a man who had two wives. She summed up the experience this way: "He was so sure that I would agree that he immediately began to build a new house for me, while keeping his first wife in his larger house. After several years of waiting and pleading, he finally got the hint and accepted the fact that I would never marry him. I wanted to marry someone whom I love, and eventually I did" (Jankowiak and Allen 1995:288).

If a couple does not obtain the approval of their family or the brethren, elopement is another way youth can influence marital decision. Elopement is a form of youthful defiance that is not unusual in societies organized around some form of arranged marriage system (Nelson and Jankowiak 2021). Elopement is a primary means youth use to direct who they want and do not want to marry. In Angel Park, parents, especially fathers, are usually the most upset whenever there is, in local parlance, "a Romeo-Juliet marriage." This occurs where a couple runs away, with the girl becoming pregnant, only to then return knowing that her family will take her back and accept her new marital status. For example, a twenty-seven-year-old man told me the story about how his future wife's parents liked him "until they found out that I wanted to marry their daughter. Her father wanted her to marry someone else. But we loved each other and knew we were meant to be together. My wife was eight years younger than me when we left the community to marry. A few months later we returned and were accepted back into the family." In this instance, the disagreement was between the girl's parents and the man, not the brethren, which had taken no strong position in the matter. Another example of agency in selecting a spouse is a young woman's decision to reject the proposal of a man who insisted they had been a spiritual couple in their previous life in favor of marrying her high school sweetheart. The brethren respectfully requested she reconsider his proposal. The girl's parents believed their daughter had chosen correctly and supported her decision. Given the firmness of her conviction, the man withdrew his request, and the girl married her high school sweetheart.

Another young woman's decision to elope with a much older man was based solely on her own experience, which she had confidence in; she told me, "I just knew he was the man for me, and nothing was going to stop me from marrying him." Her marriage ended twenty years later, only with his passing. By everyone's account, she had a solid, satisfying marriage. Still another case of youthful freedom to choose is the case of a young woman who worked in a nearby city when a local teenage boy began to flirt with her. She explained that "I knew he liked me, so I gave him my T-shirt and he gave me his picture. I told no one about him and nothing ever developed but sweet memories [long pause]. . . . I think it was the discovery of earlier freedom to flirt with a boy that gave me the strength to more actively seek out the man who would later become my husband. I knew after the first month of meeting him [her future husband] he was my soul mate, and we were meant to be." The simple fact that a young person knows she or he has the freedom to choose can provide a boost of self-confidence and the satisfaction of showing good judgment. Another example of Angel Park women's freedom to reject a dissatisfying placement marriage in favor of a marriage to their "true love" is that of a twenty-four-year-old woman. She was placed with a forty-four-year-old man whom she thought was the "most hideous creature I ever saw." After a few months together, she left him for her high school boyfriend who lived in another state.

The authority of Angel Park's fathers and of the brethren is seldom absolute. The brief examples or cases I describe highlight how the community's implicit values extend, though not unchallenged, to an individual's right to choose her or his own mate. In this way, the notion of personal "agency" serves as an effective counterpoint to the community's more formal religious organization, one that encourages deference to the brethren's judgment or recommendation. Although an individual's belief that his or her choice of a mate is divinely inspired is seldom directly challenged, the community's most common reaction is to wonder whether God or the Devil is the real source of the inspiration. Some community members will ask the individual: "How can you be sure he or she is the one who you made the heavenly convenant with?" (i.e., the one you were married to in the preexistence or spiritual state of being). The customary response of couples either together or separately can be paraphrased, emphasizing certain words over others, this way: "I do not know. But I picked [him or her], and it was a good choice. We know God has blessed us."

The freedom of youth to choose to resist their elders' mate selection or recommendation underscores the value and strength that the romantic love bond can exert whenever an individual becomes involved with someone. These examples and accounts run counter to mainstream opinion that fundamentalist youth, especially its young women, lack autonomy or the right to reject an unwanted marriage proposal approved by parents or religious authorities. In Angel Park, women always have the right of first refusal.

## "LOVE CRUSHES": MEN'S ANXIETIES

Without the brethren's guidance, it is more difficult, but not impossible, for a man to find a wife. It is imperative for men to prove that they can be financially capable and spiritually worthy. Although men maintain a detached, if not cynical, posture toward romantic love, they do have fears of emotional vulnerability. Many dismiss or downplay the value of emotional love, stating that it is, at bottom, an illusion and not the best basis for a marriage. The strength and consistency with which this sentiment was expressed originally convinced me that fundamentalist men seldom felt romantic passion for a spouse. However, more in-depth probing found that two-thirds of the men had a "love crush," though often one sided, in high school. For many, the experience was so distressing, so disappointing, that they determined to never become so emotionally involved again. I asked one man if, on his wedding day, he was in love with any of his four wives. He said that he was not, but told me that, when in high school, he had fallen in love with two women who rejected his overtures. He added, "It hurt so much I decided never again to let myself experience that feeling." Twenty years later, he found a deep, and, at times, passionate love for one of his four wives. Still, in Angel Park, his anxiety, prolonged in many cases, is common.

Polygamist men and women, when discussing the benefits of placement marriages, often mention as one of the primary benefits the avoidance of emotional entanglements. What is significant is the difficulty that individuals have in avoiding emotional entanglements. Because social relations in the Mormon polygamous family, like many other polygamous societies (Jankowiak, Sudakov, and Wilreker 2005), revolve around personal sentiment as well as duty, there is often a twin pull of almost equal force between two often-competing preferences. As noted, one preference is to follow the brethren's instruction, whereas the other is to follow one's own personal romantic impulse. Whenever a conflict between the two preferences arises, a person's response can be unpredictable and, as such, can become a potential disruption to the community's moral order. The basic question that is thought and considered is the following: will he or she uphold community harmony and follow the priesthood leadership's direction, or will he or she ignore the priesthood and follow their own intuition?

## UNMARRIED AND MARRIED MEN'S: COURTSHIP STYLES

A man's courtship style depends upon whether or not he is married. Unmarried men, primarily young men with limited material resources, must wait to either be "placed" or to develop an active and private emotional bond, under the guise of friendship, with a woman. For example, one successful marriage began as nothing more than a bicycle encounter. A married woman told me that her first meeting with her future husband began as a request to go on a bike ride. The memory and its impact on their future is clearly recalled: "The first time we rode together I kind of liked him, and the second time I felt even closer to him, but it was the third bike ride when I realized I was being drawn to him and I felt strong emotions toward him. He asked me a few days later to marry him, and I agreed, and the priesthood agreed too, and we were married within a month." Some men attract a potential mate by demonstrating their commitment to the girl's family. For several weeks, one man volunteered to work on the house of the parents of his future wife. During this time, he interacted with her, their daughter. Her parents were appreciative of his generosity and did not oppose his interest in their daughter. She, in turn, appreciated his hard work and willingness to help her family. When he proposed, she immediately accepted.

Married men court differently. For them, new courtships include his other wives, though not directly. No matter the strength of attraction, a married man must take into consideration how the addition of a new wife may affect his family. Some men are reluctant to take a new wife out of concern that she may disrupt the established harmony of the family; other men assume that, whatever the disruption, it will be short-lived and family life will be able to become reintegrated with everyone getting along. There is, for men, a benefit to adding wives. The community admires men who seek additional wives to enhance his reproductive capabilities, a critical feature of polygamy.

The majority of married men in Angel Park prefer to adopt a practical as opposed to a romantic approach to courtship. The man will prepare a list, functioning something like bullet points, of all the things he expects from a wife so that she will not be surprised or thrown off guard after they are married. The goal is to ensure a mutual understanding. After listing his requirements, the man will ask the woman if she is still interested in marrying him.

Whatever a man's courtship style, it is usually brief, or, in the case of the Allred community, it "does not [at all] take place" (Altman and Ginat 1996:109). In Angel Park, the courtship lasts anywhere from one day to a month. There are a few exceptions to the brief courtship. Some men prefer to "court" their new bride for one or two years, after which she will be reintegrated into his plural family and visited on a rotational base. Wives find this kind of courtship and the necessary integration difficult to adjust to because they may have been accustomed to being treated as his 'only' wife or are expecting to be treated as such. It is critical that prospective wives understand beforehand that sharing her husband with his other wives is a key responsibility for the plural family to succeed.

In every fundamentalist community, courtship, sexuality, and marriage are conducted within a clear and firm moral framework that most members strive to uphold. Unlike American mainstream culture where courtship is time for experimentation with physical intimacy (Karandashev 2019), the fundamentalists are adamant in insisting it essential that the courtship period is chaste and that a sexual relationship is not initiated until after the priesthood administers the wedding. I did learn of a case where a low-ranking man in the community was courting a potential wife and, knowing that he was going to marry her, saw no reason not to sleep with her. When his other wife found out, however, she wanted to leave him. From her perspective, he had committed adultery, which is defined as having sex before being spiritually blessed and married. After much soul searching, she decided to remain with him since she considered him to be a loving husband and wonderful father.

No matter how firm a community's moral framework, there are always ambiguous or action settings that require new interpretation. For example, a married man was courting a married woman who had been abandoned by her husband. When he suddenly kissed her in front of his first wife, she screamed: "You have no right to kiss a married woman." He replied: "I have a right to get another wife." To which his first wife declared: "Not if she is still married." They took their disagreement to the brethren and learned that it was acceptable for married men to approach a married woman whose husband had abandoned her and discuss possible marriage. The brethren did not comment on whether or not he should have kissed his possible spouse.

There is also a silent type of courtship—a stepfather-stepdaughter arrangement that is conducted, often in abject denial, over many years. This form of marital courtship involves a middle-aged woman with a teenage daughter(s) whom the man briefly courts and marries. Unstated is the possibility that the man will be able, at a later date, to marry the woman's daughter. For example, a recently remarried woman admitted to her best friend that "I worry about how my new husband is focusing on my teenage daughter. He shows her lots of kindness, gifts, and attention. She does not know what is going on—when she does she will hate him." She added a qualification: "Unless, he is very clever . . . I heard of a teacher from another polygamous community who started courting a girl in his class, and he bought her things and took her places. Then, when she turned eighteen, he married her." Irene Spencer noticed that in the LeBaron community a delayed stepfather-stepdaughter courtship is not unusual. It is neither common nor unknown in Angel Park. For example, I was told of a case in which a divorced woman who had remarried was worried that her husband was too attracted to her teenage daughter. The young woman's stepfather was often angered whenever he found a poster of a male movie star in her bedroom. One day, in a fit of jealous rage, he tore down the poster. His courtship, which included acts of generosity, proved fruitless, since the young girl requested that the brethren place her in another man's plural family.

## MARRIAGE SATISFACTION: PLACEMENT OR ROMANTIC LOVE?

It should not be assumed that placement marriage results in greater unhappiness and marital dissatisfaction than a marriage based on romantic love. Some placement marriages do, but some do not. In most placement marriages, individuals, particularly teenage women, who follow the matrimonial recommendations of their parents or of the priesthood council, are often not emotionally involved with their new spouse. Individuals who enter such a marriage expect, as do members of many other cultures, that in time "love will come." In effect, couples fall in love after agreeing to marry and not before. A twenty-seven-year-old woman, on the eve of her tenth wedding anniversary, revealed, "During the first three years of my marriage I did not even like my husband, but now I can say I truly love him." Hers is not an atypical case. A few women disclosed to me that, once placed, or told who they belonged to, and thus would marry, they imagine, or fantasize about, their future husband and their forthcoming marriage. As a result, they fell completely in love with their husband to be, based, to some unknown extent, on an abstract ideal.

The importance and value placed on passionate love can be seen, albeit by a negative inference, in the habitual cynicism that many mature women have toward plural marriage. I found that middle-aged women often privately counsel younger women not to fall in love with their husband. For example, one older woman told a prospective bride that, "if you do fall in love, he will hurt you." In this instance, the young bride confessed that it was too late since she had "already fallen in love" (Jankowiak and Allen 1995:285).

Several women that I came to know fairly well acknowledged that they fell in love after they were placed. One woman was surprised: "It was wonderful. Without placement we never would have found one another." Other couples remain optimistic, noting that "God would have directed them to each other anyway." An especially vivid example of this unfolding process is found in a fourth wife's memory of her marriage. When she married, she found him tentative, unsure of himself, and almost completely indifferent toward her. His aloof posture was so severe that she thought the priesthood had made a mistake in her placement. She had willingly given herself over to the priesthood's judgment with no idea to whom she belonged, but believed in her heart that the priesthood would choose wisely. Early on, she felt that she may have belonged to a different man. But she decided that the priesthood could not have been mistaken and must have selected wisely. She then became determined to be patient and work hard at "upholding up" (a local expression for a commitment to the patriarchal hierarchy). She wanted her marriage to be a loving one and worked at making it so. It took a few years, but her painfully bashful husband came out of himself and grew to love and cherish her. For her part, she helped him to renew his bond with the other wives, who, in turn, were grateful that she brought their husband back into the family. I found her story highly representative. In the marriages that began with indifference, I found that more than half developed into a warm, deeply authentic love that the community recognized and admired.

Romantic love marriages also have their ups and downs. What begins as a passionate crush can give way to detachment and, at times, resentment. Most of the women who rejected the religion and left the community began their marriage in a love crush. I did find that, if a marriage began as a romantic love-based marriage and later developed into a plural marriage, the originally loved wife invariably became the "favorite wife." No matter how many additional wives a man may add, the first-loved wife seldom lost her status within the family. In the end, it remains unclear to me which is the better basis for a marriage: one that begins with love or one in which love emerges after the spouses marry. In Angel Park, both avenues are a source of marital satisfaction and disappointment.

# PLURAL MARRIAGE AND THE PULL
# TOWARD DYADIC INTIMACY

It is the desire for romantic intimacy that intensifies a woman's yearning for emotional exclusivity. It also leads to advancing her own interests and asserting a claim on her husband to be. In Angel Park, it is customary, on a wife's wedding anniversary and birthday, to be taken on a trip or outing to see a theater show such as *Les Misérables*, attend a local rodeo, go on a river trip, or dine at an upscale diner. Whatever is selected, everyone knows that this is a dyadic event that reaffirms the presence of a special relationship. A wife's birthday is celebrated more than her children's birthdays, and this is based on a dyadic impulse. Money is often tight, but husbands know they must find time to celebrate the bond with their wives, but do not feel the same pressure to do so for a child's birthday. The children do not place as much importance on their birthdays as their mothers place on creating a temporary zone for the enhancement of couple intimacy.

The priesthood council has suggested that this practice be modified. Instead of bringing only one wife, a husband should bring all his wives to group celebrations. The council stresses that the arrival of a new wife is just as much about her marrying into the entire family as it is about her taking a husband. The council reminds everyone that the wedding ceremony (a highly secretive and exclusive ritual) is organized around the idea that marriage is less a dyadic relationship than a pluralistic institution. A fundamentalist Mormon wedding ceremony requires all the husband's wives to be present and, at the appropriate time, to place their hands over the incoming bride's hands as she publicly agrees to marry her husband (and, of course, join with all his other wives). In this way, the recommendation of the priesthood council is not a foreign notion. After church service, a twenty-seven-year-old man, with only one wife, seconded the council's recommendation. He stressed that their religion "teaches us to put our natural desires at bay and live a spirit life." To that a middle-aged man who had two wives responded: "OK, a good goal. But let's be realistic here. A woman needs to have time alone with her man. It is difficult or impossible to prevent this from happening. A woman wants to develop a special relationship with her husband." The younger man responded: "I agree, but I think we should strive for perfection." Significantly, the community continues to ignore the firm suggestion of the priesthood council. The vast majority of fundamentalist men find it easier to honor each wife's request to be treated as special or unique, even if only for one day. Clearly this attitude stands in contrast to the religious ideal that marriage is primarily a procreative institution organized around an ethos of harmonious love for the entire plural family. For most Angel Park women, it is also, albeit for a short period of time, a coupledom institution.

Over the years, Angel Park's attitude toward marital placement has evolved. Throughout the period from the 1930s to the 1950s, either individual choice or a father-arranged marriage was the preferred way to find a marital partner. By the 1960s, for the priesthood leadership, placement marriage became the preferred norm, whereas in the 1990s, and beyond, there has been among some families, but not all, an increased tolerance for the personal-choice or romantic-love marriage. The value extended to personal choice often serves as an unvoiced but effective counterpoint to the community's formal organization stressing compliance to the wishes of one's father and the priesthood council's recommendation.

Mature women, especially if in a bad marriage, tend to be more skeptical, at times cynical, about men's motives for joining the community and going to the Saturday male-only priesthood meetings. One woman thought that "a major reason to go to the priesthood meeting is to get a wife. . . . If you want a wife, go to the meetings and give money." Her more cynical remarks cannot be taken at face value, as I discovered. The majority of the men who regularly attend have no interest in marrying another woman, but feel it their duty to be present at what is for most the gathering of the faithful. The woman's cynicism is further tempered by the additional fact that a few men who were not raised in the community but converted at a later date, and who regularly contribute to the church's tithing funds, have never been given a wife. The decision to place someone in a marriage is based on a variety of factors outside of a straightforward monetary exchange.

Although the desire to form an exclusive husband-wife bond runs counter to the community's theology, one that advocates a detached, less exclusive spousal relationship, it is a woman's expectation and desire to have a more exclusive husband-wife bond that accounts for much of the plural family's internal turmoil. The preference of Angel Park women for becoming their husband's favorite wife, along with their insistence on celebrating their birthday and wedding anniversary alone with their husband and not with their sister-wives, stands in sharp contrast to the fundamentalist assertion that the family is primarily a procreative institution. For many Angel Park women, the family is also the site or place in which to celebrate their "coupleness." The reflection of a wife on the material benefits of a plural marriage reveals the strength of the pull toward creating a dyadic love bond. She explained: "It is cheaper to run a plural family household and not have separate households where everything is bought twice. You use the same dishes, drive one car, and share clothes among different wives and their children." But she added as a qualification that, for her, "the positive benefits of a shared economy are not worth the emotional cost of sharing a husband. The only reason I do is because I deeply believe in our religion."

# 6

## MANAGING A MARRIAGE

### Expectation, Duty, and Preference

*A husband who had been married to two wives for over six years compared his placement marriage with mainstream monogamous marriages: "I am so lucky—I have two wives who love me. In the outside world [i.e., mainstream society] you must work to find a woman, then do everything for them, and after all that they often just leave you."*

*The worst mistake of my life was getting married during March Madness (college basketball playoffs). Every year we go to a motel and just sit there and watch the games (a plural wife).*

Every American marriage is complex; plural marriages are even more complex. The complexity arises, in large part, from women embracing three potentially incompatible values or schemas: equity or fairness, an obligation to fulfill the expected gender role of putting one's husband's career ahead of one's own, and a commitment to the development of one's own personal potential (Quinn 1991; Lindholm 2000:259). Because these schemas are often incompatible, they can engender a moral conflict over which schema should be given priority (Lindholm 2000:259).

In contrast to mainstream American women, Mormon polygamous women are not as conflicted. They embrace the community's gender role expectations and have no trouble supporting
their husband's work. The major conflict arises out of a perceived
difference in the distribution of emotional equity within the family, which is entirely dependent on the husband's capacity to be
a financial and emotional provider to *all* his wives.

In this chapter, I will explore the folk meanings that Angel
Park attaches to the notion of the good husband and the good
wife. What are the unwritten "rules" or tacit norms that men and
women hold in defending and asserting their interest, while
remaining committed to a religious orthodoxy that insists that
noble or harmonious plural love is one of God's most sacred
ideals?

## THE GOOD MARRIAGE DEPENDS
## UPON A GOOD HUSBAND

It is a core community assumption that the success or failure of
a plural marriage depends on the husband/father's ability to
effectively manage his family—an essential attribute for having
a successful marriage. The way a man organizes his family, as
noted in chapter 3, ranges from an adherence to a strict patriarchal ethos where the husband leads in a top-down command
style to family life organized around to a give-and-take exchange
among spouses. However a family is organized, everyone accepts,
at least as an abstract principle, the importance of the husband's
place in forging a viable plural family.

The importance placed on a husband's ability to lead his family is colorfully illustrated in an exchange between a mother and
her teenage daughter. Reflecting on what made plural marriages

work, a mother informed her daughter that "in a monogamous love it is total and complete, but in polygamy it is not necessarily a good sign." Her unmarried daughter replied, "Monogamy does not work—at least that is what I have been told." To which her mother responded: "Neither does polygamy." Whereupon her daughter responded: "It isn't polygamy; it is celestial marriage. There is a difference." Her mother then asserted: "There is a problem in polygamous marriages too. The key is the man—how well he works with everyone and cooperates with his wives." The exchange encapsulates the plural family's core dilemma: who is most responsible for the coordination of a complex marriage?

In the Allred community, it is understood that the husband is responsible for promoting "harmony, love, and unity amongst all family members, including wives" (Altman and Ginat 1996:116). The Montana Pinesdale community believes that a satisfactory marriage is possible if a husband actively involves all his wives, providing "good treatment" along the way to all of them (Bennion 1998:107). The women in Angel Park, like those in the Pinesdale community, believe that a "good marriage" requires a "good husband" who is equitable in his treatment of all his wives. He demonstrates no favorites and loves his wives with similar respect and devotion. Or, in the words of one woman who seldom sees her husband, he "comes home at night." When she was asked if he loves all his wives the same, she answers in the affirmative: "he loves everyone the same." The "good husband" is thus capable, responsible, caring, and affectionate in an egalitarian way.

Not all men are able, however, to succeed in this. In families where the husband is not a wise or capable leader, his wives will try to undermine his authority. Their efforts often transform the family into competing rival subunits. In one highly dysfunctional family, I was told they considered the 1980s Zhang

Yimou–directed film *Raise the Red Lantern* (about cowife rivalry in 1920s China) an accurate depiction of their family life. In contrast, among men who are financially well off or have a college education, the marriages typically are more successful. The husbands are more at ease and comfortable in the expected give-and-take conversations that can address a wife's anxiety, fears, and existential doubts. A husband who is comfortable engaging his wives in thoughtful conversation will typically earn the appreciation, loyalty, and unalloyed love of his wives. For example, a forty-something-year-old woman recalled that "my husband helped me understand a different way to interact with my children—he has given me confidence and sensitivity toward the larger plural family and he has clarified and reaffirmed the higher ideals that make life worth living. I am so fortunate to have married him." Another wife was moved by her husband's considerate and open response to her occasional panic attacks about whether he still loved her. She acknowledged that "my husband learned I was upset, and he came to my room—and we talked and talked forever about what I disliked about plural living. My husband just listened and listened and then told me he would do better and that I should stay. I did, and it was the best decision I ever made."

A husband's diplomatic skills are evident in one wife's reflection: "My husband is a sweetheart. He is for the family, and when he needs time alone he just goes for a long walk. When he returns, he is so nice to his children, holding them and kissing them." A young wife told me that her husband was a kind man who worked hard to please all his wives, saying "my husband is fair and decent to all his wives. He takes them on outings when they are emotionally down or upset. He once took me to a nearby lake, and we talked for hours."

In well-functioning families, the husband works to resolve often-competing spousal demands. For example, an elderly Angel Park woman recalled how her deceased elderly husband attempted to be considerate toward all his wives by assisting with food preparation, caring for the infants, and working around the house. She noted one memorable instance: "one day he made bread at home and brought it to me," which she shared with everyone. "All my workmates thought my husband was the best." A young woman reported to her friends that her husband "tells me he loves me twice a day—our marriage is strong because we married for love." In another family a woman, feeling disheartened, went to her husband and, in a pleading voice, asked, "Aren't I pretty? Don't you still want me?" Her husband smiled and hugged her.

A delightful illustration of spousal friendship and love is found in the teasing exchange between a thirty-something-year-old couple from a different fundamentalist community who frequently visited the Angel Park community. On the way to a local restaurant, I overheard the following exchange:

HUSBAND: I saw a wonderful woman in the city today.
WIFE: When I return will she be living with us? (She smiled.)
HUSBAND: No, but I thought it might be nice to get to know her better. (He winked at her.)
WIFE: Who is she?
HUSBAND: That girl who works in. . . .
WIFE: Her (surprised)? Well she must have slept with fifty men.
HUSBAND: Rumor!

The husband then pulled her toward him and hugged her. She put her arms around his neck, then they kissed and looked into each other's eyes.

This is not a typical Angel Park spousal exchange, nor is it unusual. The stereotype in mainstream American culture sees the fundamentalist family as rooted in an emotional orientation that is formal, reserved, and aloof. This is an accurate depiction of the senior generation at Angel Park, which similarly stereotypes the fundamentalist family; it is far less so for the more recent Angel Park generations, those born in the 1980s and 1990s. They have adopted a less formal and an occasionally playful style of spousal interaction. In Angel Park, there is wide variation in interactions between husbands and wives. What is striking in four of the seven cases I have noted is that the husband's "lover" persona was readily adopted for his favorite wife, who received the most attention and consideration.

Mira Komarovsky's study of U.S. working-class marriages identifies two factors that contribute to marital dissatisfaction: "a sharp separation of masculine and feminine tasks and the absence of the expectation of friendship in marriage" (1967:223). I found Komarovsky's insights also apply to Angel Park husbands who embrace a rigid, firm, often aloof demeanor in creating a formalized patriarchal family. In contrast, husbands who develop a special friendship with each wife have more satisfying marriages. Striving to develop emotional intimacy with each wife presents a paradox: how can dyadic intimacy be achieved within the larger plural family without undermining the very idea of forming a loving plural family? The community's idealization of "coupleness" heightens the expectation that marriage, whether monogamous or polygamous, will be a "means of self-expression and personal fulfillment" (Lepore 2018:93).

Most men find the attempt to adopt a different persona with each wife exhausting or, in the words of one man, "an almost impossible task." A mature man who recently had taken a second wife readily acknowledged that "I thought I could focus on the new wife and reassure her until I could see both together. Now I realize I cannot. In a way each wife is an [emotionally] bottomless pit; that you need to spend quality time and see her often." A polygamous husband can be likened to a conductor who must integrate an entire ensemble, or, in the case of the polygamous husbands, all his wives, into a harmonious whole. It is a requirement easier accomplished for a maestro than it is for the head of a plural family. Men would readily concur with an old Turkish proverb: "A house with four wives is a ship in a storm" (Young 1954:152). In Angel Park it is the man's responsibility to sail the ship into calmer waters.

## EMOTIONAL EXCLUSIVITY, REGRET, AND PLURAL FAMILY JEALOUSY

A widow of Joseph Smith who later married Brigham Young declared that "a successful polygamous wife must regard her husband with indifference, and with no other feeling than that of reverence, for love we regard as a false statement, a feeling which should have no existence in polygamy" (Miles 2011:195). Most Angel Park women, as noted, do not believe love is a false emotion. While they do not experience romantic passion in the earlier stage of their placement marriages, many do fall deeply in love as their marriage develops and matures.

In response to women's often unvoiced inclination toward an exclusive dyadic love bond, community leaders routinely restate the dangers of monogamy and the benefits of polygamy. It is one of the two recurrent themes in Saturday's men-only priesthood meetings, as well as in Sunday home family services and at Sunday church gatherings. In each of these customary group settings the biblical saying is repeated so often that it can be thought of as a chant: "Hell is the fate to any woman who refuses a man another wife, and it is a selfish wife who will not accept a sister-wife into her family." Despite the continuous admonishment to embrace and accept plural marriage, many women have difficulty doing so. A twenty-one-year-old woman, on the eve of her wedding, asked her mother, "why do I have to share a man? I do not want another woman holding and kissing my man." Her mother firmly advised, "Work it out." Then she added that "it is your responsibility to help your husband create a good marriage, which means you must blend together with all his wives."

To that end, a good marriage has implicit norms that most families try to follow. It is understood that a husband and wife should not share their sexual secrets with the sister-wives. Wives expect their husband to keep their personal fears, anxieties, and hopes to himself, never revealing them to her sister-wives. In this regard, each wife seeks to establish, however momentary, a dyadic zone of personal intimacy organized around emotional exclusion rather than cognitive inclusion.

Despite religious doctrine and the constant admonishment by the church leadership, most Angel Park women strive in their own way to create a dyadic bond with their husband. Many fantasize having a deeper, warmer, more intimate and, though typically not stated to anyone else, more exclusive marital relationship. For most, it is an unrealistic hope. Still, the consistent inclination or pull toward a "monogamous heart" can be an unpleasant reality. Angel Park men often become angry whenever a wife who is not the favorite begins to push for a more exclusive relationship. A middle-aged man reflecting on his plural family's situation said glumly, "There are four families here: "Sun's," "Mo's," "Mary's," and "Gracie's." Sometimes I feel like I am living in a monogamous family." After pausing for a moment, he added, "I will not live in four different monogamous families. I go to different houses and feel we are losing our large family identity." Yet many women complain that their husband cannot live in a plural family because he also has a monogamous heart. This is not a recent complaint.

Nineteenth-century "Mormon diaries, historical records, and scholarly analyses are filled with examples of personal attraction" (Altman and Ginat 1996:96; Young 1954) as well as a desire to form an exclusive love bond. Ida Udall, living in the 1880s, admitted that she held a deep love for her husband and experienced emotional trauma trying to cope with sharing her beloved husband with another woman (1998:45). In her 1980s autobiography Dorothy Solomon (2004) granted that her sister-wives suspected that she "harbored a selfish dream of being [their husband's] only wife." Susan Schmidt (2006:139), in her autobiography, revealed that among sister-wives jealous feelings are common. As she revealed: "I had been raised in the Church prepared all my life for polygamy. Yet I was crying. Jealous! So jealous, my hands were shaking, and I wanted to physically tear into Charlotte" (141). Her experience is typical also of many Angel Park women. It is a common response: studies have documented female-to-female conflict organized around the display of indirect aggression, which is strongly correlated with the ability to access and retain a mate (Vaillancourt and Sharma 2011:569). At a biopsychological level, these contemporary yearnings for fervent or passionate love resemble those found not only in mainstream America but also in other cultures around the world (Jankowiak and Paladino 2008).

Women are caught between the commitment to practicing their religion, which demands the formation of more inclusive bonds with all family members, and their personal desire to establish an exclusive husband-wife relationship. Women struggle over the push of commitment to their community and the pull toward their own inclinations. A married woman, for example, was sitting next to a good friend when she suddenly felt that "an evil had come over me. I was in danger. My friend sensed this and held my hand. Together we overcame this force, thus experienced a love for each other, and together pushed evil's presence away." When I asked what she meant by evil, she looked at me with tears in her eyes and confessed that "I wanted to live monogamously. It was a sinful thought." The conflict is a silent and, at times, an immensely disruptive psychological force that is present in every plural marriage.

The conflicting emotions arise from two competing values—the desire to form a pair-bond and the wish to create a loving harmonious plural family. The inability to integrate them evokes a feeling of shame and its ethical twin cousin, guilt. "Why cannot I," a wife bluntly declared, "accept this life? I believe the religion is right but am troubled with my inability to handle my emotions."

The emotional pain that arises from attempts to integrate, bracket, ignore, or accept the duel between the desire for an exclusive pair-bond and the strong sense of responsibility to create and sustain a plural love account for much of the regret, disappointment, and occasional rage that periodically erupts inside the polygamous family.

## MANAGING A PLURAL LOVE MARRIAGE

Given the community's articles of faith, family discussion regularly takes understandable recourse to religious tenets designed to remind each member of their role and place in the community as well as the all-important agreement to form a plural family. To that end, husbands foster a sense of guilt in order to support and strengthen the family's cooperative spirit. Individuals are put face to face, directly or indirectly, with their failure to live up to and uphold religious doctrine, a doctrine that everyone affirms is "true" and "righteous." Frank admonishments encourage individuals to acknowledge their transgression and thus correct his or her behavior. For example, when a wife visits another home too often, a husband may assert that "a good wife stays home and carries for her children." Or, if the husband believes a wife is becoming too independent and no longer willing to work with her sister-wives, a common refrain is to question whether this behavior "is guided by the Devil." The women, for their part, will typically acknowledge the complaint and work to alter their behavior. If, however, a wife believes that her husband is mistaken, she will push back.

The following exchange captures the way husbands and wives use religious discourse to justify their position.

> HUSBAND: "You need to live in the righteousness of the Lord."
> WIFE: "How dare you disturb the spiritual harmony of the home."
> HUSBAND: "You cannot be so selfish. You need to learn how to help a man expand his kingdom."
> WIFE: "I am not selfish. How dare you suggest I am not one with the Lord."
> HUSBAND: "I'm the Lord and you are beneath me."

This kind of conversation emerges from a relationship stalemate in which both people leave the room with no resolution.

Marital disagreements often bring out strong positions, strong feelings. One husband became so exasperated with his wife's refusal to listen, he suddenly blurted out: "I wish you were my employee and not my wife." Another husband may just yell and claim that "the Devil has caught you." Another husband refers to the priesthood council's dictum: "It is critical for men to lead, and women to follow." His wife, a mature woman, nods in agreement, while muttering, "Maybe." The tension did not dissipate. There are times when a husband's criticism is effective. A young wife told me that she often ignored her husband's request to remain home so she could party with friends. She then disclosed: "I did feel guilty and thought about it a lot. I realized my husband was correct and I tried to stay with him more often."

If a wife criticizes her husband too much, he will simply leave the house and visit another wife. For example, a thirty-something man visited his second wife, who was angry that he had not seen her for more than a week, yelling at him for being inconsiderate. He initially apologized. However, she continued her complaint vehemently, and so he walked out on her and went to see his third wife. Later he divulged to me: "This will teach her not to yell at me."

Other men who have a strong marital disagreement often refuse to financially support their wife. As one man remarked: "I just did not give her any money that month—that taught her not to raise her voice at me." Other husbands, especially if they have successfully organized their family around a consensus ethos, will calmly listen and honestly discuss his wife's concerns or criticism. For example, one man with a deeply ingrained sense of Mormon history regularly read with his wives the writings of early church leaders, selected by him because they expressed the importance of practicing tolerance and mutual respect. He told me that the underlying aim was to revitalize "fairness and equal appreciation for all family members." His wives respected, admired, and loved him for his generosity and fairness, and he was thought to have a well-functioning family. Another man felt that he could satisfy the emotional needs of his wives by giving them an expensive gift every year. He later concluded that it was better to give them a series of small gifts throughout the year, which was a pleasant surprise for his wives. In that respect, women in plural marriages resemble their monogamous counterparts: each wife believes that gifts, whether expensive or not, show that she is recognized, appreciated, and loved.

Laurel Ulrich's historical research found that nineteenth-century Mormon men, "despite their patriarchal posturing's, [still] wanted to attract, not command, female loyalty" (2017:107). James Hulett's research into the nineteenth-century Mormon family similarly uncovered their love or some form of affection. Although "middle-aged women continue to be subordinate to men, in actual practice there was a good deal of rough and ready comradeship and partnership" (Hutlett 1939:250).

If a husband invokes religious doctrine to guide or change a wife's behavior, wives do not hesitate to invoke religious doctrine too. If the theological tenet of "I am your Lord" can be used to assert male authority, it can also be used, in a more personal setting, to promote intimacy and performative adoration. In making sure that her husband feels adored, a wife can enhance her emotional bond with him and thereby escape a feeling of loneliness. Such a feeling is echoed by a woman from another fundamentalist community, remarking: "The loneliest feeling in the world is to be in a marriage where your husband ignores you—there is no feeling like it." A thirty-something woman touched on the experience of this loneliness and how it came about: "The problem with my marriage is I fell deeply in love with him after we were married. My heart would just throb. I loved him so much, but he told me that I turned him cold . . . he claims I am an uncontrollable romantic. I love to touch, hug and kiss. He does not." She expanded on her married dissatisfaction: "When I reminded him of his responsibility to be fair to all his wives, he muttered, 'That is for true believers.'"

Late-nineteenth-century Mormon wives whose husbands rejected them often "resorted to neurotic compensations though retreating from family conflict through meticulous care of the home and children" (Hulett 1939:260). While some Angel Park wives are known to have resorted to this kind of behavior, the majority do not. Most assert their "agency" as active participants in their marriage, even if often rooted in antagonism. An assertive wife, who had little respect for her husband, was adamant that it is essential "not to give into him." Another wife told me that she "argued with my husband every day. I think he would not appreciate me if I did not. I want him to know I cannot be manipulated." A young wife who became her husband's favorite discovered he liked to sleep on the couch, which she found unsettling." She responded to this habit: "I put a stop to that. You want to hug your man. It is upsetting to rollover and not find him there." A man who did not enjoy being with his third wife bought her a king-size bed so that he did not have to touch her. But his wife showed determination by lying close to him. By the end of my field research, I was told their relationship had improved. He became more involved with his children and was spending more quality time with her.

Another example of a marital relationship changing over time is illustrated in the story of a woman whose husband informed her on their wedding night that he only married her because the brethren (or priesthood leadership) thought she belonged with him. Because he wanted "another body to reproduce his children." She informed me that "I accepted that, but he felt nothing for me"; she added, "it hurts to know this." I asked her to consider that, despite her earlier frustration, after seven years of marriage, he now calls her almost every day to tell her how much he misses, loves, and wants to see her. She responded with joy:

"Yes, Yes, it is all true." In assessing the overall quality of a marriage, it is important to take a longer perspective over time and not focus on a marriage's early years when there is some difficulty in adjustment for not only the wife but also her husband and thus a more acute disappointment. Over time, the disappointment may diminish and in some cases fade away.

## SEEKING THE PRIESTHOOD'S MARITAL ADVICE

Mainstream media often report that polygamous communities hold a negative view of women, at times seeing them as inferior. While this view is an accurate assessment in a few families, it is not representative of the entire community. The church leadership does not encourage or sanction this attitude. In examining hundreds of historic Short Creek sermons as well as frequently attending Angel Park church meetings in the 1990s, I found that priesthood leaders neither condoned nor supported a husband's aggressive behavior or disregard toward a wife. Instead, the leadership consistently urged men to control any anger or disapproval and work to develop a more loving family home environment.

Angel Park's priesthood council is in solid agreement with Leroy Johnson, the deceased leader of the earlier Short Creek community, who advised married men on how best to treat their wives. As early as a 1975 sermon, Leroy Johnson reminded his congregation that "you men have got to know the worth of women. There is no place in the Celestial Kingdom of our Father without a woman at your side. If you have women sealed to you, you have got to bless them. You have got to gather them around you and teach them the glories of the Celestial King-dom. They are jewels. God says that . . . we cannot fulfill our mission, neither man nor women, until we have learned how to take care of that which the Lord places in our hands" (Johnson 1990:1066).

Today Angel Park's leadership regularly and consistently prompts husbands of the need to "court your second and third wives . . . you cannot marry and forget them." In church meetings the brethren stress to husbands "the importance to bless their first wife, as it is his duty to bless his second, third, and all the others that follow." It impresses on them the essential guideline that "hus-bands should never forget that the first wife is just as important as the last. That is what makes a plurality of it" (Johnson 1990:1067). Recently, an Angel Park leader spoke to them, instructing hus-bands to not act aggressively or preemptively in a search for a wife but rather behave in such a manner that he "be invited into a family and not go around [on your own] and seek potential wives." Another church elder, in exasperation, bluntly demanded that hus-bands work out the difficulties of maintaining a harmonious household because he "did not want their wives coming to me to talk about the problem with the third wife."

Although Angel Park men are advised to "learn to be fair and share your time and attention with all your wives" (Johnson 1990:1226), the advice is often impaired by ordinary practicali-ties. The brethren make the point that "if a husband has spent too long with one wife and then goes to see another wife, he can forget that she needs reassurance that she too is special. If a man overlooks this often, unstated need, and just has sex with her, it can result in a negative reaction where the wife wonders if his interest in her is just sexual with no regard for her well-being." They explain that the most satisfying marriages are when the husband reassures all his wives." One experience is a case in point. A wife regularly became upset whenever her husband failed to kiss her goodbye, declaring that "he does not want to be here. I can see it." Her complaint often puzzled, if not irritated, her husband yet nonetheless he reassured her that she was mistaken. The brethren determined that in this case the wife's demands were excessive, preventing him from fulfilling his duties. In addition, they were pleased with the sensitivity he showed for his wife's well-being.

When a wife is dissatisfied with her marital effort, she will go to the brethren for advice and support. In almost every non-elite family I knew, a sister-wife had sought out a priesthood elder for advice because of what she perceived as unfair treatment by her husband. For one wife, her husband's own words sum up the problem: "I do not owe you anything. You just need to survive." Her experience led her to the realization that "I had no one, no father, no husband, no allies, only the priesthood to protect me. I had to react." Accordingly she made an appointment with the priesthood for advice.

In the 1950s, the brethren's advice was standard, not formed by attention to specifics such as "please try to work it out amongst yourself," "divorce is bad," or "you do not want to do this just to be eligible to remarry." The community leader usually ended the meeting with a reprimand: "You girls think you are going to get a man to yourself. Well, you are wrong—you have to learn how to share." If the woman persisted in being released from her marriage, her request was refused. In the 1990s, the leadership at Angel Park became more active and more responsive in its support of a wife in distress. One wife wanted her husband to talk with a church leader. The brethren instructed her "to bring my husband and they would talk to us, but my husband never wanted to go. I went alone and asked, 'What shall I do?' I was advised to 'hammer it out,' by myself, 'which I took to mean you are on your own.'"

In a different case, a new cowife felt that she was not being treated fairly, telling me in stark terms: "How was I to know where dishes and stuff were. I was not their lap dog. I wanted respect. Her kids watched TV and did nothing. I was told not to go to brethren—but I went the next day. They were very supportive and told me I did the right thing. I have been seeking their guidance about my marriage now for a long time—they have helped me endure. In the end, the brethren told me: 'He is my cross and part of your suffering you have to bear.' They also told me to continue to stand by my husband and be supportive, as he truly needed me to be in his life."

In some circumstances a church leader will visit an egregiously misbehaving husband and admonish him for his poor behavior toward his wife. He will be told in no uncertain terms that he is therefore "not in good standing with the Lord." In this way and in others, Angel Park's priesthood leadership today is more earnest and more personalized than earlier fundamentalist communities when it comes to supporting or protecting women from a violent or indifferent husband. A mature woman, for example, admitted that "I could not adjust to the arrival of a new wife. We had an argument and yelled at one another for weeks on end. It was a violent relationship. My husband kept saying 'work it out.' But then he gave the new wife $300 a week and she asked for more money to buy clothes for her kids. I asked him what about me and he just bit his lip and walked away. I could not take his indifference and favoritism and I left him, but not the religion, which I still believe in." The priesthood leadership supported her decision and placed her with a different husband who promised to be more considerate.

# MARRIAGE AS POLITICAL
# IDENTITY AND DIVORCE AS
# A PERSONAL DISAPPOINTMENT

In discussing women's feelings toward the plural family, I was repeatedly struck by the firmness of their defense of the plural family lifestyle. For most, polygamy is more than just a personal "right," it is also an essential part of their social and political identity. In the parlance of political science, an individual's metaphysical convictions are more essential to their self-identity than is their unreflective, albeit more frequent and constant, daily behavior that contradicts many of their convictions or is not consistent with them.

Given a woman's commitment to defending her plural marriage, caution must be taken in interpreting the meaning of a woman's complaints about that marriage. Marital complaints in and of themselves do not constitute a rejection of their convictions, the community, or the plural family system. They really are "in-house bitching," equivalent to mainstream monogamous wives complaining to their friends about some aspect of their marriage, which promotes the solidarity of friendship. When women from different families meet, they will sometimes voice their dissatisfactions more than their satisfactions and successes. They will discuss problems raising their children and difficulties finding a satisfying love. Women are quick to assert that men live only for the Principle (or to expand their plural family) but not the Gospel (how to be a better husband/father). They joke about the way men take shortcuts in dealing with family issues, preferring to solve issues with taut or brusque expressions such as "Stay home," "Go there," or "Move your butt."

Marriage in Angel Park, as everywhere else, has its ups and downs. It is not unusual for an Angel Park woman to admit that she wished she had been placed with someone else. This admission does not necessarily mean she wants a divorce or is thinking of one; it does suggest that she is unhappy with some facet of her marriage. The community does not take a woman's occasional complaints seriously. Everyone knows that wives often complain to friends and then recommit to their marriage, or that the commitment was never in question. Divorce is widely discouraged and believed by the community to be a step to avoid, which contributes to women's cynicism, encapsulated in the phrase "We put up with it."

In this context, proper performance of family obligations is more essential than maintaining a supportive nurturing marriage. Throughout the 1960s, if not earlier, and the 1980s, community members feared that divorce might condemn them to hell in the afterlife. In the 1950s, Angel Park wives, like the neglected Mormon wives of the nineteenth century, were taught to repress their feelings "under pain of incurring God's, her husband's and the community's displeasure" (Hulett 1939:260). Over time, however, Angel Park women have become less apprehensive about divorce and are more likely to break off a disappointing marriage, stating the marriage is no longer conducted in a manner that is "righteous." They believe that God would support them because of the absence of "righteousness." Similarly, nineteenth-century Mormons wives grew "so bitter they rejected the Principle and claimed to not want to see their husband in the hereafter" (Hulett 1939:287). A similar sentiment was voiced by an Angel Park wife, who said, "I wanted a divorce, as I did not want to belong to him for all of eternity."

When a woman constantly complains about her husband, it does signal a deep level of dissatisfaction and possible threat to her family's harmony. In one case, a husband refused to fulfill his family responsibilities, and all his wives publicly criticized him, diminishing his reputation. One of them told me with unshakable contempt that "there is nothing to lose. What do we have to gain in upholding his soiled image?" In another case, a husband visited a prostitute, caught a sexual disease, and gave it to his wives. His sinful act was a clear demonstration of his loss of "righteousness." The upshot was that all his wives left him.

Whenever a husband loses the support of his wives, dysfunction of the family quickly follows. If a husband does not treat a wife well, there can be a negative reaction. A thirty-something woman admitted that "I could not adapt to the new sister-wife—we never talked but only yelled at one another. My husband gave most of his income to her, and I had insufficient funds for my own children. I knew I could no longer remain in this marriage. I went to the priesthood and demanded a divorce, which they gave me." Another example is of an incoming wife who felt a loss of dignity when her sister-wife pushed her out of the house and would not let her return. Because she was too proud to tell her husband, who, she suspected, loved his first wife more, she left the marriage, taking her infant with her. She explained her decision this way: "If my husband loved his first wife more than me, then he can have her. This is easier for me, rather than groveling at the first wife's feet." This is unlike traditional African or Asian patriarchal societies, in which the man's offspring "belongs" to him. In Angel Park, as in the mainstream U.S., a woman's children go with her if she leaves a marriage.

For men, divorce is a nonissue. Angel Park men never seek a divorce. They simply stop visiting a wife in whom they are no longer interested. He thereby keeps the "abandoned" wife, which allows him to assert, as one man did, with some satisfaction: "I have X number of wives." In Angel Park, men who have three or more wives are members of the spiritual elite and believe they will be more blessed in the next life. In contrast, women's celestial benefit comes through marrying a high-status husband they will accompany in the next life. While this is a consideration not to pursue a divorce, it is often insufficient. There are factors other than heavenly rank to consider.

In Angel Park, the most salient indication that a marriage is a truly active one, not a "cold" one, is the pattern of a husband's visits to his wives. If he regularly visits his wife, the husband is demonstrating to his wife and to the community that the marriage is a viable one. This does not mean, however, that the marriage is, in and of itself, emotionally satisfying. The ideal husband assumes responsibilities, providing for and being attentive to all his wives. It is not unusual for some men to redefine this ideal and just provide some percentage of his wife's needed financial support, combined with an occasional visit. Though some husbands believe regular visitation is not as important as providing some level of financial support, I found that men who stopped visiting their wives seldom provide support. Some men believe that if they fulfill their family responsibilities, which for them consists of financial support and interaction with their children, they are still married. One husband sums it up this way: "I give her money and support my kids and interact with them. Thus, I am still married. I have a family." However their view of responsibilities does not include visitations, which are intended as a time when husbands are expected to communicate and interact with their wives, dealing with any issues regarding children and household matters. Women, as noted, often retain a different criterion. Their expectation of what constitutes a good marriage is for the husband to provide both financial and emotional support. As I will discuss in chapter 7, only the favorite wife succeeds in getting both.

## CONSEQUENCE OF MEN NOT
## FOLLOWING CHURCH DOCTRINE

Janet Bennion estimates that approximately 40 percent of the Pinesdale women were released, divorced, or simply abandoned, with about 50 percent leaving the community (1998:89). I found about the same percentage of 40 percent for Angel Park. In Angel Park, if a woman wants to remarry, she can always find a willing spouse. Women are keenly aware that men are eager to "expand their kingdom" by obtaining as many wives as possible, even if the wives are divorced. Men also understand that the church expects them to marry, since plural marriage is the essence of its polygamous creed. Still, women consider it better to be placed or to choose wisely and thus avoid a divorce so that they can "add to the Lord's flock" (i.e., have many children).

The high divorce rate in Angel Park and Pinesdale is similar to the rate of nineteenth-century polygamous marriages, a rate that is three times higher than that of monogamous families (Altman and Ginat 1996:469; Embry 1987). Historians found that the rate was highest at the beginning of a plural marriage, but, as individuals became accustomed to plural family life, the divorce rate grew much lower (Altman and Ginat 1996:470; Embry 1987). Kimball Young's analysis of offspring who grew up in late-nineteenth-century polygamous households found that 93 out of 175 families or 53 percent of the marriages were highly successful or reasonably successful (Young 1954). Although Young never defined what he meant by "successful," I assume he was thinking of families that continue to eat together, do some things together, and lend, on occasion, material and emotional support to each other. Young noted that the more well-to-do families reported the highest rate of marriage satisfaction. But here is a crucial point. If we use the community's utopian ideal that the perfect family is a plural family that has sustained a harmonious, loving environment devoid of sister-wife rivalry, there are no "successful marriages" in Angel Park or anywhere else on the planet. But if we apply a more realistic standard of marriages—a cooperative arrangement and mutual support, intertwined with both bouts of jealousy and disappointments with marital partners and an authentic appreciation of the entire plural family, I estimate that approximately 55 percent of Angel Park marriages are relatively successful. This is a typical pattern of polygynous societies around the world, in which resources are limited, whereas well-to-do families are in a better position to meet the subsistence needs of wives and offspring (Bohannan 1985:70).

I was not able to determine the percentage of married women who left Angel Park, never to return. For most women obtaining either a legal (state-sanctioned) or "spiritual" (church-sanctioned) divorce, their marriage effectively ended. Most of these divorced women either remarry or choose to remain single, but nonetheless in the community, the latter a statement of their religious faith. Young women who rejected the polygamous lifestyle and, in effect, reimagined the basis of their identity usually left the community as unmarried teenagers. I found that these young women habitually think about their former religious beliefs, their terms and implications, and the meaning of their experience of having grown up in a plural family. They have indeed left the community, yet I found in my conversations with them that "the community" remains inside them, intellectually and psychologically.

Angel Park, like nineteenth-century Mormons, is a community "in transition, simultaneously committed to patriarchy and to romance" (Ulrich 2017:307). The official position is that plural love is superior to monogamous love, while privately many women yearn for a strong, more complete dyadic bond. Or, in the words of a thirty-three-year-old woman, "True love is when you have him all to yourself." Her feeling is replicated in Irene Spencer's reflection on being a low-profile sister-wife: "I wanted things beyond the barest of necessities. Most of all, I yearned constantly to have a man of my own. I pleaded with God to forgive me and take away my selfish desires, but day after day they persisted" (Spencer 2007:336). Hulett's investigation of late-nineteenth-century Mormon wives concluded that "intellectual acquiescence to polygamy was much easier for these wives than was emotional acquiescence." (1939:387). This was vividly illustrated when I visited a family with young children. The girls who were playing with dolls had only one mother in their imagined family. For those children, the image of participating in the larger plural family comes later.

Ongoing tensions between the commitment to live God's law and to form a well-functioning plural family are often in direct conflict with individuals privately pursuing an enriched, emotionally monogamous experience. In other words, plural family members seek such an experience within their plural marriage. For most Angel Park women, the good marriage ideally includes motherhood and spousal intimacy. Whenever I asked members of the community, "Which type of family do you respect the most?" they always replied, "The largest plural families, who are willing to sacrifice their personal interests for the good of the family." Some women find meaning in renewed commitment to their religion and participate in wider community events. Others feel that they must carry "God's burden" and endure their lot until the next life, when everyone will be better skilled at living in a plural family. The church leadership is aware of this contradiction between dyadic intimacy and plural harmony; its response is to advise and encourage its members to develop the skills needed to be more successful (Altman and Ginat 1996). The ideal of salvation or entrance into heaven of the individual, the family, and the congregation living within the fundamentalist polygamous creed is Angel Park's metaphysical bedrock of legitimacy. But, for most, managing conflicting desires within the ethical commitment to the plural family is seldom easy. It remains one of life's puzzles, one that each person strives to resolve in her or his own way, although, it should be said, not without the support of spouses, family members, and the church itself. Consequently, the fundamentalist polygamous family remains a volatile center, with its own distinct challenges and stresses, where the existential problems of living remain on full display in act and in belief.

# 7

# COWIFE JEALOUSY, REGRET, AND COOPERATIVE EXCHANGES

*An Angel Park family was watching a national television show that discussed a woman who had recently died in childbirth. The television hosts offered condolences, saying that at least the deceased mother "went straight to heaven." Upon hearing that comment, an unmarried female cried out: "That is stupid—you only get to heaven if you are a sister-wife."*

*"My mother and grandmother raised me to believe in the beauty of polygamy, but a privileged one because it meant living a higher law of God, which always brought more happiness. A woman's sister wives were her best friends who would always be there for her in sickness and in health. The love shared for the same man extended to the love wives shared for one another's children. I grew up believing in the myth, my life proved it a lie" (Jessop 2007:257).*

*"I am more virtuous than she. So why am I not the favorite wife?" (a sister-wife).*

In *City of God*, Saint Augustine identified two hostile forces at war in our spirits: the love of God and the love of self (Lilla 2008:126). As previously noted, the community holds noble or harmonious love within a plural family arrangement as its ideal cognitive and ethical state of being. The noble love ideal is the essence of the United Order, which is founded squarely on the Christian ideal "Love thy neighbor as thyself." Leroy Johnson, a former leader of the historic Short Creek community, preaches: "No man, no family, no mother, no child is ready for the United Order until they have completely eradicated from their lives any differences between them and any other person, any thought of criticism. This is what it means to love one another" (Johnson 1990:1061). He further emphasizes that "our religion is the foundational idea or kind of glue that binds society together, which opens the way for cooperation and collective action to reach new heights" (Johnson 1990:1062).

Because "no one can ever be invested totally in idealized abstractions" (Noonan 2018), men and women discover and rediscover that, despite their best intentions, living in a complex plural family can, on occasion, be too complex or demanding. They will struggle over feelings and emotions they never realized they had, which can result in having to deal with responses that the community's theology strongly condemns.

Although families strive to uphold in public the community's image of a successful family, everyone recognizes that there is a range of family forms that only partially resemble the community's ideal. The primary forces that account for a family's organizational form is the quality of the sister-wives' relationship and the quality of the husband-wife bond. Both relationships are powerful forces that have the potential to shape the plural family into a hybrid that is very different from the official, idealized family form.

In this chapter I explore the difficulties that many, but not all, women experience in living up to the religiously sanctioned ideal of noble love, an ideal considered necessary in the formation of a cooperative sisterhood that is vital for the establishment of a harmonious loving family and its sustainability. I will also examine how a wife's position within the implicit family hierarchy contributes to interfamily conflict and cooperation. Specifically, I want to understand why it is difficult for many cowives to simply tolerate each other, but not be able to fully embrace the ethos of noble love, the community's religiously sanctioned ideal, deemed necessary for the formation of a vibrant sisterhood and the harmonious family. For most individuals, the creation of a loving sisterhood has proven to be more difficult than most participants initially thought.

## NOBLE LOVE: SACRIFICE AS VIRTUE

In Angel Park, unlike other fundamentalist communities (e.g., Allred, LeBaron), as noted earlier, noble love is thought best achieved, and thus experienced, when all the wives and their offspring live together in one large house. Not everyone can achieve this ideal, but it remains the community's most cherished ideal, and it is, within the community itself, the most admired form of family organization.

Within either the Big House (i.e., where cowives live together) or a small house (i.e., each cowife has her own dwelling), the ideal family strives to live according to the religious principles of harmonious, noble love. The spiritual sentiment contained in harmonious love is seen in what a first wife said to me when learning her husband had been assigned a second wife. She optimistically declared: "We will learn and both of us will become a better person."

Women seem to be more willing to accept their family position, and thus mute or temper any real or potential disappointment, if it has a religious component. To reinforce the restraint, community members in church sermons and in family gatherings repeatedly remind women that it is imperative to be willing to sacrifice their personal interests for the good of the plural family. In this context, sacrifice is a virtue and a treasured and highly respected community value. Aptly expressed in the words of a first wife: "she and I will adjust."

The "willingness to sacrifice" for a partner, stemming from intense empathy, and a "re-ordering" of one's priorities, has psychological characteristics "associated with romantic attraction" (Fisher 2002: 415–416, cited in Nelson 2021). Unlike romantic love, where a person sacrifices her self-interests in favor of her beloved, the fundamentalists' sacrifice is oriented not toward any one individual but toward achieving a cherished ideal: the loving harmonious family. In Angel Park, a wife, like elderly Korean wives, often makes daily sacrifices to maintain her marriage. The sacrifices range from "the provision of domestic support, an endurance of hardship springing from inadequate financial resources, enduring conflicts with her husband" (Nelson 2021:12), and, I will add, having to contend with difficult or antagonistic sister-wives. A woman's willingness to prioritize the family over personal interest effectively elevates her acts as well as herself into a more exalted state of being, if not in this life, then certainly in the next one. For women in the plural family, daily sacrifices are considered small gifts that enhance the plural family's well-being. A thirty-something woman told me: "I pray every day not to be selfish. I know I need to sacrifice daily intimacy with my husband to learn and experience a fulfilling family love."

Women retain their strong commitment to get the Work (i.e., polygamy) moving forward to build up the community before the Second Coming of Christ. This striving, this hope for the future, encourages a dedication to live what they believe is God's law. They know that if they remain steadfast in their devotion they will receive greater glory in the next life (Hulett 1939:49). This view was echoed in a mature woman's remarks on why she was so devoted to her religion. She gave voice to a community truism: "Once you learn the Gospel—a woman's a fool to ignore it. I want to go to heaven and see other women having babies and learn to be wives with other wives. You must adjust to life there and here too. I want to earn a high status, so I need to learn how to achieve it here right now."

Another woman acknowledged that her commitment to a family organized around noble love is both a wonderful ideal and a daily challenge. She stressed the importance of care for another woman's children the same way another woman would care for her own. "You have to love your husband enough so you can love all his children," she added, "you cannot say these are mine and those are yours—that is wrong." But her affirmation of the community's ideal was qualified with the remark that achieving the state of noble ideal is difficult: "it is very hard to love another woman's child as much as your own."

Participants in the plural family, however, often have a different expectation and level of commitment to the creation of a unified, harmonious family. The variation in family organization arises less from an individual's bad faith and more from personal, material, and psychological considerations.

The personality of a wife's family is a by-product of the kind of family the wife came from, whether her mother had a high or low position within the family, and the degree to which she is committed to, in the community's words, "live the fullness of the Gospel" (i.e., form a vibrant plural family). There is a correlation between the personality of a woman's natal family and the personality of her future family. A woman's personality—extroverted or confident to introverted or diffident—formed in her natal family is readily transferred into her new plural family. If she had an assertive role within her natal family, she would assume a similar role in her marriage. This phenomenon results in an added incentive for her. If her husband has a weak emotional bond with his first wife, the second wife, if she has an assertive personality, can become his favorite wife. Family conflict is guaranteed whenever two "alpha" or assertive females who had strong personalities in their natal family are placed into the same family. If the husband is weak, aloof, or indifferent, the women will form a rivalry that will result in the family breaking up into competing subunits, or, if the women are truly dedicated to the religion, they will find a way to "work out" their personality differences, learn to compromise, and form a less stressed plural family that could be on its way to some degree of unity.

The common cowives' personae are the low-profile wife, the power wife, and the favorite wife. These personae are also found in many nonfundamentalist polygynous families (Jankowiak, Sudakov, and Wilreker 2005). The low-profile wife, or, in a contemptuous folk jargon, "plantation" wife, is the more typical cowife persona. She has a dedicated commitment to uphold the community's cosmology and is tireless in working in support of the plural family. Most low-profile wives do not publicly object to their family position. For example, one mature woman admitted that "I love this Work. I wanted my husband to pick a sister-wife. He refused. But I have opened my house and heart to other families, and I must say I love my sister-wives' kids more than my own. I have a lot of love to give—I believe in the Principle and this Work."

The low-profile wife is most likely to admit being disappointed with her marriage compared with a favorite or power wife. "I just want to be held." Irene Spencer (2007), a low-profile wife who lived in Short Creek and then in the LeBaron Mexico community, writes about her need to feel loved and have companionship, acknowledging that her marriage was less than satisfactory: "We were lucky if we spent two nights with him a month" (2007:211). Commenting on her divorce, another low-profile wife admitted: "We got divorce over my status in the family—he could not take my sulking behavior. I knew when I entered the family I could not be the favorite wife or the bossy wife. I would just have to blend into the woods—but after a time I just could not accept that role and made life difficult for everyone."

Some low-profile wives are more reserved or indifferent in voicing their opinion. For example, when I asked one wife if she felt bad that her husband did not visit often, she replied: "No, he knows where to find me." Another cowife in a large family admitted that she preferred not spending much time with her husband. She enjoyed her children and interacting with a few of her sister-wives. For her, it was unimportant to constantly be with her husband.

The entire community recognizes that they belong to a larger plural family and therefore need to often sacrifice their personal desires in order to achieve what is for most the next life's ideal family organization. A woman in her mid-thirties explained: "I have an excellent family here—a strong husband and a will to make the family system work and prosper." Other low-profile wives reported a more difficult experience. For example, one woman was placed at eighteen years of age in marriage to a man who had a close relationship with his first wife and did not really want to marry her. He told everyone how much he "hated her." At the time, she thought his reaction was, in her words, "gross." But they tried to make a go of it and through the next couple of decades they had eight children and struggled to create a large harmonious family. The woman revealed how her own story unfolded: "I am going to love it. But I could not—I always wanted to leave but I was pregnant all the time. Then one day I decided I could not take it anymore—I drove my car to a nearby city and while shopping for my children I started to cry—a man asked if he could help. I told him my story and he gave me money to rent an apartment and looked in on me. After a while I married him, and he turned out to be nice to my kids and he treats me very good today."

A mature woman, while acknowledging her dedication to the Work and her firm belief that it is a better way of living, stressed that "I have tried to teach the religion to my children and have kept my hurt to myself." When I asked what she meant, she did not answer. Another mature woman, who had been a low-profile wife and no longer lived in the community, thought that one of the community's foundational axioms, "to give in, surrender, and sacrifice for greater reward in the next life," was "bullshit." A low-profile wife living in the FLDS community had a different complaint. She noticed her husband preferred to sleep with one wife over his other wives and that this resulted in that wife's children receiving the necessities, such as shoes and clothes, while his other wives and their families had to do without (Jessop 2007).

In all my conversations about love and marriage, the criticism of "unfairness" was the problem for those women who were the most dissatisfied living in a plural family. The thoughts of a mature low-profile woman are representative of the feeling of general discontent: "He promised to take me to St. Louis, and he took a sister-wife instead. I was so angry all I could say was: "This is not fair. It is not fair."

The opposite of the low-profile wife in attitude and style , as earlier noted, is the "bossy" or power wife persona. She controls the family's finances, and all requests of her sister-wives flow through her. Unlike Mali (Whitehouse 2023) or Imperial Chinese families where the first or senior wife is most esteemed, in Angel Park the custom is not a given. Fundamentalist communities have not institutionalized the senior wife position as leader of the other cowives. Instead, the position of favorite wife remains open and is not based on seniority but on which wife has the warmer and more intimate bond with her husband.

Given her assertive personality, the queen bee can assert herself and take charge of the family's ordinary affairs, either with her husband's approval or because of his indifference. A mature woman recalls that, during her childhood years, the family's power wife often swore at her sister-wives, saying such things as "You little piece of shit—I'm in control here." Because the mature woman's father was often away, she became the unofficial leader of the family. I was told a story from the Short Creek era where the power wife easily took charge of the family because of a weak and indifferent husband. During the Thanksgiving celebration, she set the table using a low-profile cowife's fine porcelain plates and ordered her to sit alone, next to a small table where she was served on paper plates. Meanwhile everyone else used her fine china.

Another way that the power wife of an FLDS family asserts her authority is to insist that her sister-wives and their children ask her for permission before doing something. For example, if a child asked his or her mother if they could go visit someone, the mother would immediately instruct them, "Go ask Barbara." Some women from other families consider this arrangement improper since "mothers have the right to control her own natal family." In the FLDS community that Brent Jeffs (2009) grew up in, he often observed that the other wives of his father (including his own mother) were afraid to go against Marilyn, his father's favorite wife. He recalls that "the other women would not complain about any of Marilyn children's misbehavior, they knew that this would somehow be turned into a mark against them" (2009:62). In most cases, the favorite wife is also the power wife.

Although in a few families the power wife is not the favorite wife, I noticed that there is a close relationship between being the husband's favorite wife and her ability to influence and control the larger family. The favorite wife is not necessarily the first, the oldest, the youngest, or the prettiest. She may be the most emotionally intelligent and knows when and how to flirt, become playfully resistant, and engage her husband in interesting conversation. A favorite wife's husband regards her as his best friend. For example, a husband goes to his wife's work and brings her a hot lunch that she was not expecting—it signals that he is thinking of her and is concerned about her. The gesture is received with gratitude and love. The favorite wife skillfully uses nuance, acts of kindness, and careful attention to small things that are reminders of the times they enjoyed together: "Honey, remember when we walked along Lake Michigan?" Or "Recall when you went away on that business trip and we were separated for a long time—and how much we missed each other?"

The favorite wife is aware that her husband cannot tolerate her emotionally withdrawing or distancing herself from him. Her capacity to withhold emotional intimacy from her husband is a formidable "resource of power." She validates his identity and self-worth and is emotionally supportive of him, while fulfilling her responsibilities to manage the household and its activities.

She also embraces the religion and is a force in organizing her husband's relationship with his other wives. It is her ability to mediate family problems and diffuse potential disruption that makes her an essential player in coordinating family dynamics.

Secure in her position in the family, she is an active participant in helping a junior wife bond with her husband. She often encourages her husband to dress up and treat the junior wife as special. Because she is successful at fulfilling her duties and promoting the values of family harmony and responsibility, the favorite wife receives special considerations: more time spent with her husband, greater confidence of his support for her children, his participation in more outings (e.g., shopping, vacations), and, most important, a deeper willingness on his part to develop an intimate bond.

Because of financial limitations, there is a tendency for some husbands to hold off on responding to a mother's concerns about her child's health. Men, reluctant to immediately bring a child to the doctor, typically advise waiting to see if the child's condition becomes serious. In contrast, when the favorite wife requests to seek immediate medical attention, she will receive a more ready and positive response from her husband. His quick response arises from his emotional attachment to his favorite wife. At the top of the family's hierarchy, she is able, like counterparts in other primate societies, to obtain more resources for herself and her offspring (Small 1992:70). Unsurprisingly, low-profile wives sometimes refer to her as the "favorite right," shorthand for her high position in the family, which enables her to assert her opinion and, because she is always right or correct, expecting everyone to follow.

Though the favorite wife occupies a privileged position, it is not proper or acceptable for her to publicly demonstrate or let others know of the "favoritism" she receives. To do so would be to delegitimatize the plural family's inclusive ideal and undermine any semblance of harmonious plural love. The favorite wife embraces the theological discourse that honors family cooperation while ensuring her interests are not undermined or neglected. To that end, both the husband and his favorite wife will resist any notion or suggestion of an exclusive arrangement. The sister-wives, for their part, tacitly agree not to challenge the special arrangement provided that the favorite treats them fairly and does not bully them.

Because a favorite wife has a richer emotional bond with her husband, she is more vulnerable if her husband's attention turns cool or is less responsive. He may deeply love her, but she can quickly feel unloved. For example, a husband who enjoyed hunting left without informing his wives where he was going. Since he had not seen one wife for a few weeks, she was not aware he left, but his "favorite" wife was also surprised and hurt that he did not contact her about his hunting trip. Another way the favorite wife can feel threatened is if her husband talks seriously, or even playfully, about wanting another wife. The thought that their special bond could be disrupted can produce acute anxiety for the favorite wife—more than it would for a low-profile wife who no longer seeks to establish a closer emotional bond.

In Angel Park, there are different story lines played out daily. One concerns the relationship between offspring and the father. Another is the relationship of men to their religion. A third is the husband-wife relationship. In the husband-wife story, the cultural ideal is, for many, the most desired story. It is when a family's willingness to surrender its desires to find fulfillment in daily sacrifices forges cooperative bonds that uphold the harmonious, plural family environment. Running parallel to this story is a resistant, alternative story, whereby individuals publicly embrace the community's ideal of a harmonious family while they pursue personal interests that can undermine that ideal. The favorite wife readily expresses her devotion to living the Principle and upholding the harmonious family home environment, at the same time, remaining ever vigilant for what is most essential to her: the emotionally exclusive bond with her husband. Over time, the exclusivity can undermine the belief and hope of other wives to achieve the official ideal. If belief and hope are undermined, the wives will decide to leave the family and, in some cases, the fundamentalist religion.

## THE LATE THIRTIES: A DANGEROUS TIME FOR A PLURAL WIFE

Dorothy Solomon recalls in her early life in a Salt Lake City plural home "hierarchy based on seniority among the women and not all women were happy with their position in the pecking order" (2004:201). Although most low-profile wives enter the plural family with a more compliant demeanor and a willingness to defer to their older and more experienced sister-wives, over time there can arise, for some, a lingering sense of injustice that their daily sacrifices can no longer endured. The general unhappiness often becomes more acute as a woman reaches her late thirties or early forties when she is more inclined to adopt a more assertive persona. For the low-profile wife, this is the most dangerous stage, one in which she is earnestly reevaluating her life and reconsidering her options. It is the stage in life when divorce, separation, and rejection of the polygamous lifestyle will most likely take place.

The publication of numerous autobiographies that form an escapist genre on growing up in a fundamentalist plural family provide further evidence of woman's ability to reconceptualize the plural family as an unproductive or unhealthy family system. In every one of these autobiographies, the woman announces that her primary motivation for leaving is an immense dissatisfaction and disappointment with the plural family that she feels has mistreated her. Although the various coauthors/writers try to make each woman's polygamous life appear one of abject oppression bordering on modern-day slavery, the reality is most of the low-profile wives were initially enthusiastic to enter the plural family and worked diligently at becoming a virtuous family member. It is only after a decade or more that some women, especially those in low-functioning families, begin to re-conceptualize their initial commitment from being acceptable to a horribly "forced" choice marriage that they should never have agreed to. Angry with themselves, their plural family arrangement, and what they consider "lost time" (i.e., their youth), they leave embittered with their husband and hostile to their former religion.

It is significant that escape autobiographies published on life in Colorado City (home of the FLDS), the Allred community (in the Salt Lake City region), and the LeBaron Mexico community are written by low-profile wives. No favorite or power wife, from any fundamentalist community, has yet to write an escape autobiography. Moreover, no one from Angel Park, regardless of social position or persona, has written a book denouncing the community or the polygamous lifestyle. Clearly, there is a wide range of spousal satisfaction and dissatisfaction within and between the fundamentalist communities.

## SACRIFICE: A PERSONAL, FAMILY, AND COMMUNITY VIRTUE

Women in the community are more willing to accept their family position and thus restrain any real or potential disappointment if it derives from a religious belief system or is given a religious gloss. Women are repeatedly reminded that it is imperative to be willing to sacrifice themselves and their personal interests for the good of the plural family. To this end, the virtue of sacrifice is deeply respected, admired, and treasured.

The doctrinal call to surrender the self is in order to find meaning in a larger good. From a metaphysical perspective, sacrifice means surrendering something of yourself to evolve to a higher state of being. Unlike romantic love, where a person sacrifices his or her self-interests in favor of the beloved, the fundamentalists' sacrifice is oriented less toward a specific person and more toward obtaining a cherished ideal: the loving harmonious family.

A respected member of the community philosophically noted that "life is not about happiness—terrific if you achieve it, but that is not the best life goal." He went on to add that "the greatest gift is to engage in daily sacrifice for someone's benefit." It is an attitude toward life that requires a firm commitment. Or, as a cowife said to me: "I pray every day not to be selfish. I know I need to sacrifice daily intimacy with my husband to learn and experience a greater family plural love."

It is not unknown for a woman over the course of her marriage to make adjustments that contribute to the formation of a more agreeable, united, and satisfying marriage. One woman explained at length: "I look up to my husband and still do. After ten years of marriage I find that I am not as manipulative as before. I used to be angry and aggressive and had felt little forgiveness. Now I find I have different needs and know how to better achieve them. From a religious perspective, I find working with a plural family has made me a better person." A third wife, reflecting back upon her fifteen years of marriage, admitted: "We almost separated. I wanted a man to always be with me, but he was often away. I went crazy and wanted to leave. But we talked and talked and decided to focus on the good things. I realized I was too selfish. I tried to focus on reaching a new level of consideration and experience the quiet joy of being together and appreciation for sharing our children with one another."

In Angel Park, wives often make daily sacrifices to sustain their marriage. It is a woman's willingness to prioritize the plural family's needs over her own interest that elevates her efforts into an exalted virtue. It effectively transforms her daily sacrifices into a stronger religious commitment that she understands will yield a more exalted state of being, if not in this life, then in the next. The women know that, if they are steadfast in their devotion, they will receive greater glory in the next life (Hulett 1939:49). This point, as previously noted, was echoed in a mature woman's remarks on why she was so devoted to her religion. She gave voice to a community truism (as expressed earlier in this chapter): "Once you learn the Gospel—a woman's a fool to ignore it. I want to go to heaven and see other women having babies and learn to be wives with other wives. You have to adjust to life there and here too. I want to earn a high status, so I need to learn how to achieve it here right now."

## BENEFITS OF PLURAL LIVING: PERSONAL GROWTH THROUGH COOPERATION

Community members are adamant that there are psychological benefits to living in a polygamous family. Singular (2008) aptly summarizes the prevailing folk explanation of the personal benefit of living in a plural family in which the women acknowledged that plural living "helped them come to terms with difficult feelings like jealousy, insecurity, competition and thinking that they 'owned their spouse'" (2008:56). Instead of denying these complex emotions, Singular concluded, they had to embrace them, which helped them develop into becoming a better person. While Singular is skeptical about the authenticity of a cowife's personal development, I did meet women who readily admitted to having grown personally in their marriage. For example, one woman who was married for more than ten years admitted that her husband "taught me new things, open new vistas.' She added, however, that "five years after our marriage, I taught him new things too. He has learned to be more emotionally mature. He is gaining control over his actions. More importantly, he understands my needs, I sense he tries to meet them and just acknowledge them . . . it is a nice balance we have here." Another example comes from a mature low-profile wife, who, looking back on her life, acknowledged that "I truly love polygamy. I really do. It has not been easy. But I have learned patience and come to appreciate other people's personalities" She then quoted from a section of the Gospel on the importance of sacrifice for building character and concluded her comment this way: "I have gotten so much pleasure living in this family system." Some wives find contentment in seeing their husband mature and find satisfaction in the knowledge that they assisted in his development. Another wife thought that plural marriage is emotionally exciting and that working with sister-wives made for a richer marriage. She said to me that "I would not want a man who had one wife. I enjoy seeing him grow and develop. He would become too boring and mundane and predictable if he only had me. He can learn to grow too. I like the excitement—the competition for his affection enhances my passion. But then she offered a qualification: "security is important. You need to know what the future is like—that is the important thing."

Some men also acknowledged that they benefit from growing up in a plural family. A particularly astute young man noted that he became politically aware in a plural family where he learned how to ask a variety of adults for favors such as money or candy. He openly stated that having to deal with a "variety of authority figures help[ed] me learn a useful conversational style that I applied in my business. I am convinced that without that early childhood experience I would not be as successful as I am today." A mature man recognized that plural marriage made him a better person, having learned to show patience and control his anger. He too thought this benefited his business: "I am much calmer in dealing with a customer, readier to listen to him complete his sentence before I respond." Clearly, in these cases living in a plural family contributed to an individual's personal growth; he or she is typically able to transfer that experience into newer contexts, different settings.

A cowife saw that becoming a parent allowed her to understand some of the pressure that her sister-wife experienced in trying to raise her children. In a reflective moment. she said: "Before I had children I complained about Peggy (but only to myself). I thought I could have done a better job. Been stricter and gotten 'kids in line.' But after I had kids, I realized it was difficult being a parent. You must let the little things go. It is tough to always be so strict. My experience made me understand her better, and it made me more appreciative of her efforts."

In contrast to the thirty-something women who begin to have doubts about the benefits of plural marriage, elderly women who remain in the community reconciled any previous misgivings and are more inclined to fully embrace the benefits and satisfaction of living in a plural family. Elderly women or grandmothers, unlike middle-aged women, who tend to be more skeptical, tend to adopt a more detached attitude toward their own life. The rise of the benevolent matriarch—really a transformation—contrasts with their middle-aged selves, when they still were in an unstated but real competitive game to gain their husband's approval. In their later stage of life, they felt satisfaction in the long-term accomplishment of having instilled in their children the proper attitude and understanding of the "blessing" of their religion.

It is difficult to determine whether an elderly woman's memory truly reflects what she feels or is a sentimental embellishment on a life not actually lived, though either way the emotion seems to be no less felt. A man who used to be a community member thought that "elderly women, especially if they were a wife in an elite family, had invested so much of themselves in the practice of their religion and would not want, late in their life, to be overly critical." Angel Park elderly, like women in every theologically governed system, are not inclined to oppose the system from which they gained an honorable and immensely respected position. They recognize their place and strive to maintain their honor and the much-deserved admiration of the community (Lindholm 2002:240). Another man put it quite succinctly, noting that "as a senior member in the community, they [elder women] are admired and respected for their sacrifice and accomplishment. They would not want to jeopardize that esteem."

The dignified reserve and clear endorsement of the plural life of elderly women presents a positive, public face to the community. Behind it is a discrete restraint against expressions of disappointment, hesitation, or reservation both about the lives they have led and the community's way of life as a whole. The same cannot be said for nonelite or low-profile women whose marriages are less than ideal. This was highlighted for me when I was talking with a mature woman who used to live in the community but now lives elsewhere. When I asked about her life in the community, she went on at great length complaining about her cowives. Irritated, I asked to stop talking only about the negative side of her experience and talk also about the positive things. She sighed and stated without hesitation that for her "it is hard to find any." A few months later, I asked her if she had ever received assistance from, or gave assistance to, a sister-wife. She replied: "Yes. I helped with childcare or taking a sister-wife to see the doctor, or I gratefully accepted a small loan needed to make an important purchase." It was evident that a lingering bitterness continued to serve as a hard filter in not readily recalling anything positive about plural living.

## THE NEW BRIDE AND CHALLENGE TO FAMILY HIERARCHY

Although women believe that their husbands have the right and the duty to bring a new wife into the family, many Angel Park women would agree with a fortyish wife who said straight-out that "it was very hard for me to accept other women into the family." Here is the community's fundamental paradox: it embraces a cosmology that celebrates plural love, yet many individuals struggle with fully accepting the personal limitations inherent within the plural or noble love cosmology. The limitations, anxieties, and disruptions are most acutely revealed each time a new bride enters a family. Montana Pinesdale women readily admit that when a new wife enters it is the "most difficult but [potentially] rewarding aspect of the Principle" (Bennion 1998:114). Angel Park women also agree that a new wife entering the family is a time when their personal commitment is tested, with some families pulling together and reaffirming their religious ideals, when other families, being overwhelmed with the new social dynamics, simply fall apart.

New brides are aware that they are entering at the bottom of the family hierarchy; some accept this, others do not. Those who do not accept the established hierarchy hope to replace the favorite wife by forming an intense love bond with their husband. It is not unknown for some young women to believe they will be able to replace the current favorite wife. This belief is unvoiced, although it is a powerful motivation of many. On occasion, the bride is successful.

Although research on Bedouin women found that the youngest wife usually replaced the senior wife (Al-Kremni 1999), I did not find this pattern in Angel Park. I listened to two women discussing the feasibility of a new wife replacing the favorite wife. One woman conceded that "she may be the new hot wife, and he may need time to bring her into the family, but there is no way she will become his favorite wife. Her husband is too closely bonded with her" (i.e., his present favorite wife). Before agreeing to a placement, most women are aware of the family's established positions and know whether there is an opportunity to become the favorite wife.

Although the incoming wife seldom replaces a favorite wife, she can become, at least initially, the husband's preferred romantic partner, what is sometimes referred to as a "play" partner. For every family that I was familiar with or heard about, the husband's longtime favorite wife remained his best friend, whose relationship continued to be based in a deep-seated comfort love, despite the fact that a new, incoming wife assumed, however momentarily, a romantic "play" role. Most Angel Park husbands, after a short or intermittent "smitten" phase, turn their attention back to their other wives, with the new bride becoming another wife among many. I was told of a few cases, however, in which a man fell so in love with his youthful bride that he completely abandoned his other wives. I heard of a man who took a nineteen-year-old bride as his fourth wife and informed her that he would focus his attention on her alone, provided she maintained her thin body. She did so, and he abandoned his other wives. In another case, a man had, by all accounts, a very good plural marriage, yet fell completely in love with an eighteen-year-old woman and then left his other wives to be exclusively with her. He continued to see his children, but had nothing to do with his other wives. In this way, the arrival of a new wife can be a precarious time for the entire family. I found another instance of a husband with multiple wives falling "madly in love" with a girl he was courting, the result of which was complete abandonment of his other wives to be with his new bride. He was not shy about letting it be publicly known: "I do not care what you say or do. I will not lose her. I will build a new house and I will live with her—I do not care if my other wives leave me." In the aftermath, his wives did leave him; one remarried, another decided to live by herself.

The community felt that this was a horrible outcome and felt sorry for everyone involved. A middle-aged woman told me that, when "my husband took a new bride, he became a teenager when he married that teenager. He started going crazy and spending all the money on her. This made things difficult for us, as we still had to pay the bills and other things." She elaborated that "this is not an unusual occurrence in this community. Old men marry a teenager and then go crazy." Reporting in 1954 on the nineteenth-century male attitude toward marriage, Kimball Young said that "men are excited courting a young woman."

The emotional volatility of passionate love has the potential of erupting with such force that it not only can disrupt a family but destroy it. Men are acutely aware of this possibility. If a man has several wives who have created a satisfactory home environment, and the household has also developed over time into a unified plural family, he will be hesitant to jeopardize taking a new wife. A husband disclosed to me that he was aware that a few younger women in the community were attracted to him but was reluctant to follow up on their romantic/erotic signals. He did not want to undermine the harmony of his family. His concern for its well-being stands in sharp relief to popular views in mainstream culture that fundamentalist men are only interested in "collecting wives for their own use."

While the incoming bride must negotiate her relationship with her new sister-wives, she simultaneously seeks to forge a spousal bond with her husband. Appealing to two audiences can heighten an incoming wife's anxiety and self-doubt. For example, a young woman who married into an orthodox patriarchal family acknowledged her difficulty in meeting her husband's spousal expectations. To avoid his constant criticism and to become the wife she thought she should be, she taped behavioral reminders to her bedroom mirror: "My head is empty"; "I'm empty and I'm here for you to write on"; "Whatever you want, I'll do"; "I'll wear what you want"; "You are my god."

In another family, I learned about a new wife's struggle to adapt to plural family living. In good faith, she daily recited to herself: "You learn from the Gospel the truth, a woman is a fool to ignore it"; if you want to go to heaven and see other women having babies, you must learn to live with other women"; "you have to learn to adjust to life here, if you want to have a higher status in heaven"; "I need to learn how to achieve contentment here and now."

To people outside the community, the women's efforts to submit to their husband might strike them as too severe or extreme, but this view does not account for the community's foundational value: the importance and willingness to submit to one's husband's ordained religious authority and leadership. In striving to do so, and using practical reminders, the women are simply following religious beliefs about the family's proper order.

In contrast to the ideal of orthodox patriarchy is the consensus orientation, which allows for greater flexibility in integrating a new wife into the family. For example, an incoming wife remembers with fondness her husband's patience and kindness. As a new bride, she asked if she could have time to be alone and gradually adjust to living in a plural family. Her husband respected her feelings and gave her time to adjust; after several months, she felt like she belonged and was so appreciative she readily admitted she loved her husband more and more every day.

## VARIATION IN COWIFE RESPONSE TO A NEW WIFE

A new wife's entrance into the family is the time when everyone's commitment is tested, with some families pulling together and reaffirming their religious ideals; while others just pull away, overwhelmed by the new social dynamics and their inability to effectively manage their emotional response.

A few women readily admitted that they were surprised at the level of hostility they felt toward a new wife whom they had not yet met. I found there are different ways that a wife responds to a new bride: withdrawal from the family; civil, daily interaction;

and positive, inclusive accommodation. In the case of withdrawal, the woman stays in her room, having no interaction or communication with anyone else.

The variation in responses of the cowives depends to some extent on their personalities and, if a cowife was at any time the only wife, the length of time in that situation. Some women are surprised at the emotional outburst they see other wives direct at the new wife. In one instance, a woman, who had been her husband's only wife for a significan duration, found herself holding a frying pan as she chased her new sister-wife from their home. In another family, the arrival of a new wife provoked the first wife to relentlessly criticize the new wife's real and imagined shortcomings. There was nothing that the new wife could do to appease the first wife since the latter was determined never to accept a new sister-wife. When a first wife discovered her husband was planning to marry again (his fourth wife), she not only withdrew but rejected her marriage and her religion by moving to another city. She told everyone: "I would no longer put up with this—so I sold the house and moved." Another less dramatic but pronounced reaction is a first wife's decision to completely withdraw from any interaction with her new sister-wife. Upon learning her husband had taken a new wife, she insisted he build her an apartment within the larger house so that she could live separately from the incoming wife, who would live downstairs. The husband strove to maintain the public image of a united plural family who lived together in one large house, while visiting each wife on different days of the week.

It is not unknown for cowives to form an ad-hoc alliance or to become part of a group to pursue "out-group antagonism" (Norenzayan and Shariff 2008:62). In one case, the sister-wives made a short-lived alliance against a new wife who clearly was her husband's new favorite. The sister-wives waited until their husband was away and then broke down the new wife's bedroom door and beat her up. Their aggression was effective. The new bride left the family and never returned.

Each wife, in these cases, had publicly stated, and privately maintained, that she was committed to living the Principle and therefore accepted her husband's right and obligation to marry additional wives. The wives' negative outburst and outright hostility toward the incoming wife speaks to a stark divide between an individual's cognitive awareness and ethical commitment and her often unconscious, emotionally charged reaction.

This reaction is shown in a new wife's surprise that her cowife did not believe in a "united plural family" and had no intention of establishing one. The new wife eventually became resigned to this situation, explaining her experience at length: "Right before I married my husband, he, his wife, and I went for a walk. My husband had his arms around both of us as we walked down the street. As we continued, I put my arm around my husband's waist, just below his first wife's arm, who was already holding on to him. Later that evening the first wife told me that 'When I felt her arm around our husband's waist it made my blood boil.' I was shocked at her comment because I thought she was committed to living the principle and create a harmonious large family (*a pause in her account*). This marriage has been a challenge from that day forward, because the first wife refuses to accept God's law" (Jankowiak and Allen 1995:286).

The volatility emerges from the fact that husbands and wives share a small house that can provoke discomfort and jealousy, undermining family harmony. Wives admit feeling uneasy if they overhear their husband being sexually intimate with a sisterwife. Irene Spencer, living in the LeBaron polygamous community, wrote that "I think it is terrible that I had to listen to you and Lucy making love" (2007:271). An Angel Park woman, living outside the community, reported sitting on a couch with her sister-wife and feeling uncomfortable as they listened to a husband having sex with another wife. I was often told that women felt "embarrassment overhearing another woman make love" to a husband because it is a reminder that their husband "is bonding with someone else." Many women feel, rightly or wrongly, that, if their husband is overly attracted to another woman, it means that she is no longer desired. If this happens, women, especially senior wives, can, in the words of one wife, "get pissed off." Women's hostility toward a husband's new wife can provoke spontaneous anger. For example, a senior wife who saw her husband kissing his new bride screamed, "You're too old to kiss that young girl." These examples, and many others, demonstrate that the desire to form an exclusive dyadic bond within the plural family remains as omnipresent as it is relentless.

The plural family operates within a world of "limited good," with a clearly finite number of good things available. Whenever a wife receives something of value, other wives believe they will therefore receive something of less value. In an environment of scarcity, women have an understandable desire to monopolize their husband's material and emotional resources. The domain of "limited good" in the polygamous family can lead to cowife jealousy and competition over unequal distribution of household resources (Al-Kremni and Graham 1999:3). In Angel Park the range of the cowife's responses is a product of numerous factors. These range from struggles over resources, protection and care of offspring, assertions and disagreements over one's position within the family, and a desire to monopolize a spouse's attention. In this setting, a complex family can quickly become volatile. This is especially so whenever the distribution of food, availability of finances, access to a husband, or childcare becomes a focal concern. Long-standing cooperative cowife relationships can quickly be transformed into disrespectful annoyance. For example, in one family a sister-wife who had childcare duties was heard yelling at her sister-wife: "I'll change your baby when I want" (she had not changed the diapers for a long time). She then started to cry and throw plates, shouting, "I'm tired of you not giving my kids the things they need, when I have to work."

Indirect aggression is a common feature of female-to-female conflict, and it is strongly correlated with the ability to access and retain a mate (Vaillancourt and Sharma 2011:569). Competitive rivalry can result in anger and hostility toward a sister-wife being transferred to the children. Among the Dogon in West Africa, there is a genuine fear that a cowife may poison a rival mother's children (Levine 1962; Madhavan 2002; Strassmann 2000). Angel Park women do not worry about that extreme form of cruelty, but they are conscious of the fact that their children may be neglected or abused when they are away. Their awareness of the possibility of abuse is universal within the community but in no way drastic or unreasonable. A mother's concern about the care that a cowife provides for her children is a legitimate anxiety. Sister-wife rivalry, combined with the prevalent desire for a more intimate relationship with the husband, accounts in large part for the weak development of allocare parenting (or parenting by nonbiologically related individuals), which is commonly found around the globe.

The subtle forms of resentment, which are about the pursuit of status and family honor, are often manifested in ordinary interactions. For example, a woman who oversees paying her family's heating bill refuses a sister-wife's request to use the dryer. Since she is responsible for paying the family heating bill, she felt that it was her right to use the dryer, but she seldom was generous in allowing other sister-wives the use of the dryer. Another instance of cowife antagonism happened when two wives went with their husband to the beach and a disagreement arose over who would sleep with him. In their beach tents. Because they lived in separate houses, they were accustomed to having their husband to themselves; unable to reconcile or come to some acceptable arrangement, it was decided that all three would sleep in separate beach tents. Another episode of this antagonism resulted in an argument of sister-wives about who would stay with their husband, who, at the time, was in a hospital room that had a small bed for one visitor. Cowives seem to find a special delight in critiquing each other's parenting skills. The competition, the rivalry, is another reason that many women do not want to share breastfeeding with their sister-wives. They are concerned that their babies might bond more strongly with the nursing mother than with them. Although these slights and quarrels are not seismic, there is a consensus of understanding that allows cowives to express their disagreements and grievances with each other. It serves as an outlet to tamp down tensions among them.

Because cowife relationships tend to involve the husband and two wives, "jealousy within a triad may cause one party to withdraw or two parties to gang up on the third" (Bohannan 1985:39). This takes place when the first wife creates or establishes a hostile relationship with the incoming second wife, who then forms an alliance with an incoming third wife. United against the first wife, they can isolate her influence and render her authority in the family weakened if not irrelevant. In the process, the two sister-wives typically form a warm, enduring friendship. Christine, a character in the TV series *Sister Wives*, acknowledges awareness of how a triad relationship can influence interactions, admitting that she is glad to be the third wife because "she never wanted to be alone with a husband, and the third wife balances out the tension between the first two" (Hall 2010:1, cited in Bennion 2012:253).

Jealousy was a constant theme that was recognized and recorded in nineteenth-century Mormon polygamous marriages. Hulett reported that late-nineteenth-century wives tried to suppress their jealousy "under pain of incurring God's displeasure. The wife had to resort to other neurotic compensations (such as meticulous care of the home and children) and thus retreat from [potential] conflict" (1939:260). Altman and Ginat's survey found that Salt Lake City Allred wives often turned "to prayer for solace, guidance, and the strength to help them adjust" (1996). In contrast, Pinesdale women sought out their husbands to discuss their fears or turned to family or friends for reassurance (Bennion 1998:157). In Short Creek, women reported that they use similar coping strategies. Angel Park is no different.

Many of Angel Park's cowives, nevertheless, do not react with intense negativity toward the incoming wife. Most strive to accommodate and integrate the new wife into their plural family. I found an instance of gradual accommodation in a first wife's effort to develop good feelings toward her new sister-wife. Upon learning a new sister-wife would join her family, she proudly informed friends and family that she could manage her feelings in sharing her longtime husband with his new wife. She surprised herself, however, when she broke into tears the first time she observed her husband kiss his new bride. Being devoted to the religion, she resolved to overcome her jealousy and foster a more accommodating home environment. Her purposeful flexibility interacting with the new wife contributed to the successful incorporation of the new wife into the larger family.

This is a salient characteristic of high-functioning families: the sister-wives' dedication to accommodate a new wife into the family. I once observed a high-functioning family where cowives took turns placing their child on their husband's lap to hold. Every time this happened, the husband held the child for about three minutes, kissing him or her six to eight times on the face. After a few minutes, another wife gently picked up the child and placed her own child on the husband's lap, whereupon he kissed the child. While this small family event unfolded, the wife would stand behind her husband, to be joined by his other wives, who then took turns hugging their husband. Taken together, they formed a memorable image of a close, warm, and unified family, with each wife engaged in a concerted effort to ensure that her interests received equal treatment.

A plural family is more than the sum of its competing units; it is a functioning cooperative enterprise. To focus exclusively on incidents of cowives lashing out at each other would be to understate and thus minimize the frequency of cooperative exchanges that transcend individual selfishness and go a meaningful way toward a plural family that is not only tolerable but, for some, a preferable family system.

## COOPERATION, ALLIANCE, AND IDIOSYNCRATIC ACTS OF KINDNESS

Cooperation is not the same thing as harmony. Cooperation can be a moral virtue. It is possible to work and cooperate with another wife while not necessarily being in a state of affectionate harmony. Ethnographic accounts of sixty-nine polygynous societies found compelling evidence that most cowives in a polygynous family prefer pragmatic or instrumental cooperation with one another, at the same time maintaining a respectful distance (Jankowiak, Sudakov, and Wilreker 2005). Research conducted among several African societies that compared monogamous and polygynous families found polygynous husbands and wives were less cooperative with one another, with cowives less cooperative. The behavior in polygynous households is more strategically reciprocal and less spontaneously altruistic (Barr et al. 2019). This characteristic behavior accounts for the fragility of many cooperative exchanges. Sister-wives are acutely aware of time and money that are loaned to each other. It is a source of gratitude, satisfaction, regret, and, on occasion, a motive for revenge.

Bennion noticed a similar pattern in Pinesdale where "women are forced into cooperative activities yet often house a contempt for one another" (1998:142). Angel Park women, like women in every polygamous society, engage more in instrumental exchanges based on a calculated reciprocity. If a sister asks for a favor (e.g., to borrow money or request a food item), and it is granted, she is expected to reciprocate later. Without these everyday cooperative exchanges, the plural family could not function. Moreover, the exchanges serve to enhance social bonds between sister-wives, which strengthens a woman's sense of belonging to the larger family.

In high-functioning families, cowives engage in reciprocal and still instrumental transactions (Bennion 2012, 2020). For example, a woman may have purchased children's clothes to give to another sister-wife or bought a sister-wife a cookbook or helped a sister-wife dig a ditch. Or maybe, in the words of another sister–wife, "she just baked cookies and brought them out to us when we were weeding the front yard." Others spoke of enjoyable acts of family solidarity such as "going on trips to a national park, river rafting, camping, fishing in the lakes." Other women meet over coffee to discuss religious issues and daily events. I have often observed cowives engaging in friendly conversation about a host of daily issues.

I also noticed that in high-functioning families there is usually a wife who serves in the unofficial, albeit critical, role of "emotional facilitator." She may or may not be the favorite wife. She intervenes to soothe the hurt feelings of a sister-wife or to mediate family misunderstandings. She defends her husband and his decisions and works tirelessly to keep the family together. If a problem erupts, she will customarily state that it is not important and best to ignore it. Constantly reminding her sister-wives of the vital importance of living the Principle, she reminds them of their spiritual journey and their shared responsibility to create a harmonious household. I knew of a husband who decided to pursue a new wife and ignore his plural family. His behavior, this turning away, undermined the faith of his wives in his "righteousness." It had a terrible impact: the family lost its emotional facilitator, and the community one of its own. Thus disillusioned by her husband's irresponsible behavior, she left him and the family for another man, a man she believed was "righteous." In the end, the family rapidly descended into a competition between various female heads of subunits who no longer wanted to work together to create a vibrant harmonious family.

Although cowife rivalry exists, so does sister-wife's helpful support. Whenever a family faces a health crisis, all but the most dysfunctional families come together. They help clean the house, provide encouraging words, and work to support an individual who is ill or who has a seriously ill child. This may include accompanying a sister-wife who is anxious about an upcoming procedure or operation to the hospital. A family member's life crisis energizes her sister-wives to rally around her, rallying support to her and indirectly to the plural family ideal.

One particularly compelling demonstration of sister-wife solidarity has stayed with me because it had a striking impact on the family. A cowife decided to quit a job she enjoyed assisting a sister-wife who was overwhelmed with childcare duties. Her decision and follow-up action generated a sense of guilt among her other sister-wives, which made everyone, at least for a while, strive to be more supportive in achieving a harmonious plural family. Another instance of sister-wife solidarity is the demonstration of concern for a sister-wife's children. A visiting woman saw that her friend washed her sister-wife's children's feet before her own children. This was clear evidence of the other woman's commitment to upholding the Principle. Sister-wife solidarity and personal consideration exist in only a few families. In most families, sister-wives perceive themselves as forming a separate subunit that produces, in the best of circumstances, a respectful, collegial interaction with one another.

The decoration of one woman's bedroom reflected her dyadic mind set. On her walls are hung photographs of her father alone and her father with her husband, numerous photos with her husband, along with photos of her husband together with their offspring. In the homes I visited, I never saw a single photo of a woman's mother or, more significantly, all her cowives posing together. I noticed in one elderly woman's home a photo of all her deceased sister-wives with their adult offspring. No longer potential rivals, her sister-wives are preserved as a symbol of the embodiment of noble love.

The dyadic mind set is also manifested in the patterns of sister-wife friendships, which usually occur between two sister-wives, but seldom more than two. In spite of a husband's anxiety that his wives may someday "gang up" on him, I know of no case where the sister-wives united and formed close friendships. A sister-wife's inclination to form dyadic friend-ships does not mean that her other sister-wives are disliked. In well-functioning families, some are, but most are not. A plural family's home environment is a busy world, a household on the move on a daily basis. There is not much time to chat and develop friendship because a lot of time is needed to finish one's work and then attend to childcare, one's husband, and friendship obligations. Individuals, as everywhere else, must regulate their time and decide who and what to prioritize and focus most on.

Besides age mates forming a friendship, there are examples of postmenopausal women redefining their previously conten-tious relationship with sister-wives into a more collaborative and supportive group. This arrangement emerges more fully when their husband is deceased or their children move away. No lon-ger being in direct competition allows some women to form a closer sister-wife friendship that is solidly based on mutual respect, tolerance, and appreciation.

Bennion observed a similar pattern in the Montana Pines-dale community, where cowife competitiveness for maternal and emotional resources limited or diminished a woman's inter-est in forming close friendships within the family but not out-side it. It is significant that in the families where the wives are postreproductive, or the family's husband has passed away, there is a clear tendency to form closer friendships (Bennion 1998:102). There is the suggestion that the presence of a husband alters a wife's priorities and sparks or makes for an impulse to competitiveness with her sister-wives that would otherwise not occur. As a woman said to me, "I wanted to come to love him and get involved in his work and learn to appreciate what he wants and why he likes it." She then added: "My dedication to him undermined my relationships with my sister-wives. I felt I could never trust them."

After her husband passed away, she found herself refocusing her energy and attentiveness on her sister-wives, seeing them as potential friends and not as rivals for the sake of love. In the process, she discovered greater self-fulfillment. A husband's long absence diminishes, if it does not extinguish, cowife competition, since there is nothing of apparent value to compete over. Women are then able to reset their relationships and form closer, warmer, and more meaningful friendships.

The quality of the sister-wife relationship can be as important as their commitment to living the Principle. In the Pinesdale and LeBaron, Mexico, polygamous communities, women did develop rich female supportive networks that enhanced their lives. Bennion suggests that the primary reason for women from outside the community to look to joining the community is to gain a supportive network of friends (1998, 2004). In contrast, in Angel Park, few women not raised inside the community want to marry into the community. Moreover, the Angel Park ideal family is "Big House family unity." The unintended consequence is to restrict the possibility of female networks with a woman's sister-wives or her natal family.

In the Salt Lake City Allred and Pinesdale communities, Bennion found (1998, 2012) that approximately 60 percent of cowives are related to each other by blood (sister, cousin, niece, or aunt), which accounts for closer bonding in those two communities. This kinship by blood is higher than the nineteenth-century Mormon estimation of around 25 percent. In Angel Park, the rate is much lower, around 10 percent. I did find that sororal (biological sisters) marriages, however, are more mutually supportive. The friendship bonding of fundamentalist sororal wives is consistent with cross-cultural research that also finds sororal marriages show decreased cowife conflict (Jankowiak, Sudakov, and Wilreker 2005).

Bennion's research among a Montana Pinesdale polygamous community concluded that the "powerful male world of priesthood power, authority and kingdom building does not exist without the supportive, obedient, and well-coordinated female world" (1998:9; cf. Bradley 1993). Her observation also holds for Angel Park.

While fundamentalist women acknowledge that the value of a unified plural family organized under the rubric of a fundamentalist theology is a noble ideal worthy of pursuit, there is a less than perfect consistency in their commitment and diligence to work toward that ideal. In Angel Park, conflicts between cowives are common or typical in the early years or stages of their marriages, where they involve verbal outbursts or physical violence. Women's anger and hostility stem from a deep-seated angst arising out of the competition for access to their mutual husband. Because affection cannot always be equitably distributed, there is ongoing and contentious rivalry among cowives for the family's most precious resource: "time with the husband" (Jankowiak, Sudakov, and Wilreker 2005:2).

Angel Park women, like nineteenth-century Mormon women, use a variety of strategies to obtain their husband's attention. These can range from "the use of illness, uphold his efforts to punish children, ridicule and criticism, pamper him, involve religious leaders, withdraw and hold attention, and throw a temper tantrum" (Hulett 1939:88). In one case, a wife demanded that her husband tell her each time he left her bed, even if that meant waking her up. Her adult daughter who overheard her comment approved: "Right, Mother, he should shine a flashlight into your eyes and say, 'I am going to my other wife's bedroom.'" In another household, a woman's offspring felt that she was being unreasonable by failing to take into account that her husband had more than one obligation, if not several. An adult son told me: 'My mother says she wants to work things out with her sister-wives, but she never does. . . . Mother just will not admit her husband has other wives and other obligations." His observation does extend to many Angel Park families. A husband's efforts to please his wives is a recurrent family dilemma. No matter how hard a husband tries, failure is the name of the game. The restraints inherent in a plural family customarily precipitate or engender emotions that reveal psychological needs, which results in a never-ending cycle of volatility.

Whereas some women are willing to modify their needs to contribute to the ethical ideal of a harmonious family, other women are less accommodating. Some are insistent that their husband adjust his behavior. For instance, a middle-aged woman explains how she tries to guide her husband to do the right thing: "My husband wants the Principle and talks a good philosophy. But he does not live the Ten Commandments and the Gospel of Jesus Christ. Those doctrines are more important and difficult than living the Principle (i.e., plural marriage). I accept the Principle, so I am not jealous of the lack of attention as long as he is fair in the time spent with all of his wives." In fact, she may have been one of the more jealous women in the community. Another woman, thinking about her now deceased husband, recalled that "my husband had no sense of how to blend us together," adding that "in time, through lots of failure, he adjusted." A similar point was reaffirmed by a remarried divorcee: "My second husband was wonderful—he helped in the kitchen, he cooked and did things for me. He may have not been from an elite family, but he appreciated me, and I consider us having a wonderful marriage."

Plural marriage is a nondyadic institution that holds it to be sinful for a wife to monopolize her husband's attention. The pull to form tacit bonds of emotional exclusivity is behavior church elders continuously lecture against. Women are urged to overcome this pull and focus on developing an environment of harmonious love within the plural family. The impulse to form a pair-bond is present, albeit in different proportions, in all cultures, even in societies that discourage its formation such as those organized around the institutions of arranged marriage or the creation of a polygynous family. The impulse to forge a dyadic husband/wife bond has the potential to undermine an ethos of noble.

Yet within the plural family there exists a favorite wife whose relationship status stands in opposition to the noble love ideal and can potentially undermine a plural family's working. Because many low-profile wives strive if not to replace the favorite wife then to augment relations with their husband, they continue to lobby, request, and demand more time with him. It is in the gray area of "quantity/quality" time with their husband that examples of cowife resentment are most vividly manifested.

Although there are acts of cowife consideration and kindness, most cowife exchanges remain instrumental, rather than based in mutual love or affection. More significant is the community's implicit tolerance, but not idealized approval, of dyadic intimacy, which often serves as the critical spark behind cowife competition and undermines the family's pursuit of noble love. In the words of an insightful man: "I acknowledge the theory is beautiful, but somehow everyone has trouble living it." The irony is striking: the very tolerance that the community has toward dyadic intimacy is, if not the spark that sets the competitiveness in motion, the phenomenon that exacerbates it no end. In this situation, Angel Park is not unique. Throughout history, different communities (e.g., the Kerista commune or the Oneida) have embraced some form of plural love, only to confront similar difficulties.

.

# 8

## FAMILY POLITICS REVEALED THROUGH NAMING PRACTICES

*"I asked my husband if we could name our newest son after my deceased grandfather, he agreed" (a favorite wife).*

*"My husband told me to pick a name as he could not think of any. I thought I would name my son after his uncle whom he respected" (a low-profile wife).*

There is no society where the "biological parent-child and sibling ties are not recognized and not accompanied by prescription for appropriate behaviors toward these categories of persons" (Schlegel and Barry 1991:92). A culture's naming practices can be a way to transform a biological entity—an infant—into a social persona. Exploring a culture's explanation for why they select or reject names can reveal implicit cultural values and pragmatic interests. In Angel Park, there are multiplicities of motives behind a fundamentalist husband's or wife's decision to name a child. In the plural family, a husband or a wife is concerned with the strengthening of a love bond, the need to assert family authority, or, in the case of cowives, the display of dominance over other sister-wives.

This chapter will concentrate on the politics of namesaking as a primary means for examining the interplay between the degree of affection between husband-wife, family identity, and cultural beliefs. I am especially interested in understanding the motives behind men's and women's namesaking decisions so as to provide a richer, more complete explanation for competing sex-linked spousal practices and parenting strategies. Focusing on the microdomain of naming practices can reveal the degree to which a husband is emotionally linked to a specific spouse and wives maintain a continued bond to their maternal kin, along with constituting another arena in which cowives compete for dignity and gain.

Naming is a salient activity in the Mormon fundamentalist polygamous community. People of all ages enjoy talking about it and are aware of who they are named after and why. In probing the community's understanding and valuation or devaluation of love, reasons behind naming children were freely invoked. It was not until I began the study of siblings that I was able to collect naming practices more systematically. I gradually came to understand that there is no normative expectation regarding naming in Angel Park. The folk notion is that naming is completely arbitrary and individualistic. Everyone insists that parents can, and do, give children a name they want. However, once I informed community members about a particular namesaking pattern, there was a near consensus as to its reasons. This suggests that, at the tacit level, there exists a cultural uniformity of understanding regarding the motivation behind naming practices.

Previous naming studies examined first names but not middle ones; I wanted to do both.[1] I chose not to incorporate girls' maiden names into the sample, as I wanted to understand the politics of personalization and kin affiliation. About a third of the girls in the sample did not have a middle name, because it is expected that, after marriage, a woman will use her father's surname as her middle name (Jankowiak and Woodman 2002).

## NAMING PRACTICES, COWIFE TYPE, AND QUALITY OF THE MARRIAGE

"Naming decisions are routinely viewed as private matters, but they are in fact social acts. Names are important symbols of social location, which are regarded as signifying family history, gender, and religion" (Qi 2020:21). In Angel Park there is a strong association between gender, birth order, and the frequency in which the child is named after the father or a paternal relative. More firstborn sons (60 percent) compared to firstborn daughters (36 percent) are namesakes after paternal kin, with 38 percent (n = 66 out of 172) of sons named after their father and only 14 percent (n = 19 out of 137) of daughters named after their mother. There is a close association of sons with paternal relatives (70 percent) and daughters with maternal relatives (68 percent) (Jankowiak and Woodman 2002). This suggests that the father-son namesaking bond is given greater symbolic precedence through its reaffirmation of the patriarchal Principle.

Although the findings are consistent with those of other namesaking studies, closer analysis shows that the underlying motivation for many namesaking decisions cannot be attributed to the cultural tradition or derived from a woman's strategy to address a man's concern with paternal certainty. There are other motivations present. The best explanation for the naming patterns and their variations appears to be a maternal investment hypothesis, with its emphasis on women's decision to focus on procurement of resources through engaging in a range of strategies, from becoming a favorite wife to establishing economic self-sufficiency and dominating the tacit female-centered domestic hierarchy.

Women seek to balance their duties to uphold their husband's public image while seeking ways to clarify and demarcate their individual status and their own uterine lines as distinct and valuable entities within the often-contentious polygamous family. One way that women do this is by resisting the doctrinal mandate to surrender their children into the melting pot of their husband's progeny. This struggle of women for some kind of balance is sharply manifested in the naming decisions made over the course of their marriages. As a woman in her mid-thirties noted: "We compete over everything, why not names too?

It is in the micropolitics of naming and kinship association that a wife's personality and status in the family hierarchy are revealed. In these instances, women use children to achieve several ends: To maintain the husband's attention to themselves and their children, to strengthen affective bonds with natal kin, and to demarcate themselves as distinct autonomous units within the polygamous family. Because Mormon fundamentalists prefer not to give one child the name of another within the same polygamous family (though a name can be spelled differently or inverted so that a first name is the middle or vice versa), cowives can and do use this normative injunction in a power game of one-upmanship. For example, if a wife knows that another cowife is planning to name her next child Jessie James, and if she gives birth first, she might give her child the birth name that the other wife wanted to give her baby. The wife would do this not because she was especially fond of the name but as a way to assert superiority over the cowife. A low-profile wife reported that a first wife did this very thing "in order to prevent me from using it to name my son." In another case, a sister-wife's plan to name her daughter after her best friend unraveled when the fourth wife insisted that she had always wanted that name for her child. Another possible scenario is that a first or second wife, upon discovering that her husband intends to take another wife, names her next child after him. In the politics of naming, the earlier wives have an advantage over incoming cowives, who, like a first and second wife, are interested in establishing closer affective linkages through child-naming practices, but tend to be more restricted by the declining number of unused names deemed socially salient (Jankowiak and Woodman 2002:247).

Women's increased interest in establishing symbolic bonds with their natal family is evident in the way naming practices have shifted between the founder generation and other subsequent generations. In the founder generation (i.e., born prior to World War II), most were raised in monogamous Mormon households that tended to name their firstborn son after paternal kin only 50 percent of the time. This frequency is less than the 1940s American national average of 60 percent. In contrast, 80 percent of all firstborn sons born after 1950 in Angel Park were namesaked after paternal kin.

The cultural explanation, with its normative emphasis on social continuity, cannot account for the post–World War II shift in the namesaking pattern that found firstborn sons were not named after their father. The increased emphasis on paternal son namesaking arises out of living privately and publicly within the polygamous family system, which produces an institutionalized anxiety that causes women to become overtly competitive with one another in the family. This family reality was not present in the founders' generation, which grew up primarily within a monogamous family environment. The increased emphasis on paternal naming preference is a pragmatic response to the social conditions typical in a Mormon fundamentalist theocratic community.

Alice Rossi's study (1965) of white middle-class women living in the Chicago area found 61 percent of all children were named after kin, with 65 percent of sons and 22 percent of daughters. Rossi identified a strong maternal bias in the middle and latter birth cohorts. She believes that this pattern arose out of men's growing indifference to participation in the naming process. In Angel Park, there is also a middle cohort effect, whereby sons are namesaked after both paternal and maternal kin, while daughters continue to be overwhelmingly namesaked after maternal relatives. But, unlike Rossi's American monogamous data, in Angel Park women's later reproductive years, or those in the eight through thirteen offspring births, namesaking patterns revert back to a paternal-son linkage, albeit to a degree less pronounced than that found in the early birth cohort (Jankowiak and Woodman 2002). Unlike their monogamous counterparts, polygamous women do not appear to become more comfortable, confidant, or content over time with their status in the marriage. I suspect the motivation of the reversal back to a paternal-son emphasis does not arise from a psychological concern in reassuring a husband that the child is his, thereby strengthening the "public's perception of genetic relativeness" (Johnson, McAndrew, and Harris 1991:11). Rather, for most cowives the primary motivation arises out of a yearning to celebrate something they have dedicated much of their earthly and spiritual existence to: a deep commitment to the fundamentalist religion. Also present is another, more individualistic or personal motivation: the defense of their family status against the potential threat, actual or imagined, of a new wife coming into the household. For example, first wives from the founder generation (married prior to 1950) who did not have a son named after their husband tend to change their attitude as they approached the end of their reproductive careers, particularly when an additional wife had entered the family. In this context, women's motivation for namesaking is directed more toward the incoming new wife than toward her husband. In this way, paternal namesaking may serve as a kind of closure to a woman's reproductive career, which began, and ended, by highlighting the father-son relationship.

A wife's personality and position within the larger family also accounts for the variation found namesaking practices. Both the favorite and the assertive wife are much more dominant players in the family than the low-profile wives. The favorite wife, whose status depends on continuation of the emotional bond she formed with her husband, defends, advances, and upholds her husband's self-image as the patriarchal head of the family. To that end, she actively supports the naming of her sons after her husband or his paternal kin. Her concern has less to do with parental investment and more to do with mate investment. She offers her sons as an extension of honor to her husband; in turn, she expects that he will honor and adore her. Her husband, out of loving reaffirmation, often gives the child a name that is affiliated symbolically to his mother's kin. For example, one middle-aged man with four wives acknowledged: "I do not know why I always give into Susan (his favorite wife), it seems that my other wives do not have the same ability to get me to agree with them." His comment is representative.

In contrast, the queen bee or assertive wife, at least at the start of her reproductive career, breaks with the more typical namesaking emphasis on the father-son association. Over 42 percent of an assertive wife's sons are namesaked after her maternal kin (eleven of twenty-six). The queen bee wife is not interested in seeking greater paternal investment from her husband. She is more concerned with making a political statement, albeit symbolically, that she will be a "force" who continues to demonstrate her authority and superiority in the polygamous family. At the end of her reproductive career, the assertive wife renews her dedication to the Principle and prefers her sons to be named after a paternal relative.

The low-profile wife, on the other hand, is already out of the running for the most valued place within the family hierarchy, yet still strives to demonstrate her commitment to her religion by namesaking her children after her husband's paternal kin. In this way, the low-profile wife, like parents of adopted children (Johnson, McAndrew, and Harris. 1991), utilizes kin names to reaffirm paternal bonds and continues to assert her dedication to the cosmology by having her husband name her sons (forty-eight of fifty-four) while she names her daughters (sixty-six of eighty-five) (Jankowiak and Woodman 2002:290).

Names, then, can be the currency by which autonomy is asserted and religious commitment is reaffirmed. Women who are active participants in family affairs are more content than those whose husbands rigidly adhere to the patriarchal ideal of absolute male authority. This interpretation is supported by the analysis of name choice, kin affiliation, and the quality of marriage (e.g., content or discontent). The most important factor that determines a wife's relative contentment in the family has to do less with whether or not she occupies a favorite or assertive role than with whether or not she feels she is in a partnership. If more than 50 percent of a wife's children's names were associated with her kin, she was relatively content in her marriage. It is evident that many fundamentalist families do not rigidly adhere to the patriarchal ideology where the husband decides everything, which leads, at least for many Angel Park women, to a more satisfying marriage.

Fundamentalist women are active participants in the family's naming process. The fact that 45 percent of all children in my sample are named after maternal kin indicates that women are viewed as key figures, both practically and symbolically, in these communities. Excluding Native American cultures, which are organized around principles of matrilineal descent, the maternal namesake association in this polygamous community may be the highest percentage found in any American subculture. The degree to which women are valued, despite efforts to render them culturally insignificant, was further revealed in a content analysis of the community's calendar, which found that 45 percent (n = 64 of 160) of all dates of birth noted are of local matriarchs or famous historical women (Jankowiak and Woodman 2002). Nonetheless, when a child is named after maternal kin, it is overwhelmingly his maternal grandfather. It is rare that a child be named after his or her maternal grandmother or maternal aunt. This preferential pattern is consistent with the glorification and adoration of the father that continues for men and women after marriage.

Thirty-five percent of naming decisions are cooperative efforts. This suggests that husbands and wives discuss naming, and that a husband agrees with or defers to his wife's choices. In this way, wives are involved in the naming decision more than 60 percent of the time. As more wives come into the family, men become more flexible in holding to the patriarchal ideal and more inclined to delegate the naming decision to the new incoming wife. This pattern stands in opposition to the mainstream media's assertion that fundamentalist women are blindly obedient to their husband's absolute authority and dominated in all situations

(Jankowiak and Woodman 2002:295). Anthropology has repeatedly demonstrated that "women are social actors in their own right who try to achieve their own goals within certain constraints imposed upon them" (Meekers and Franklin 1994).

What is the man's motivation for allowing his wife to participate in the naming of his children or to choose the name outright? In the polygamous community, it is incumbent on men to orchestrate cooperative behavior. Granting women some control over the naming process is a relatively easy way to appease, reassure, and otherwise honor them. Still, it is not clear whether a husband's motivation to name a child after a wife's maternal kin is part of his overall mating or parenting strategy, a means to maintain familial cohesion, or merely indifference. It is clear, however, that, from women's perspective, the association of daughters with their maternal kin holds a deeper symbolic value.

This pattern suggests that, while daughters are not theologically as valued as sons, they are still immensely valued by their mother. The strength of this natal link further suggests that there may be a second degree of maternal investment strategy within the community. Women invoke a broader strategy that includes using sons and daughters to establish wide-ranging linkages to all kin. This may arise out of concern for future support for children or may arise simply out of the love and continued affection that a mother feels for a particular relative. In the latter, the bond being established is not between the offspring and his or her maternal relative but rather between the mother and her natal kin.

Another factor behind women's namesaking of daughters is the opportunity to create a sense of personalization that is critical for the establishment of individual borders and psychological health. For women, the opportunity to select a nonkin or "nice" name constitutes another way in which she strives to demarcate her uterine family. Nice names, like maternal kin names, serve to establish a border necessary to maintain a woman's sense of autonomous identity within the cauldron of polygamous family life (Jankowiak and Woodman 2002). Or, in the words of a mid-age-thirties woman: "My choice, my identity, my nod to who I am. I am Grace from Jack."

Because there is no evidence that naming increases sentimental bonds between a child and his or her namesaked relative, I suspect that the use of names is more an index of a matricentric focus than a desire to establish a natal (or maternal) alliance. For most Angel Park women, namesaking their children is seldom, if ever, about alliance building, but instead about natal affection, ego enhancement, and identity assertion. For women, the dichotomy of competing solidarities is mediated by symbolically giving their sons to the father and, in turn, symbolically to their religion, while retaining daughters for themselves.

There are at least two overlapping themes in the polygamous communities: homage to the husband/father and admiration for the mother. The competing, albeit unvoiced, systems enable women to potentially manipulate the symbolic system of naming to their own benefit. Given the community's unique cultural and economic contexts, women were less focused on men as a source of mere survival. Many wives use their husbands as a reference point from which to declare their commitment to the fundamentalist theology, a commitment over and above their attachment to the man himself. At the same time, they seek to maintain affective bonds within the natal family. Here cultural contexts encourage the reduction of women's dependence upon men, and both the religious ideology and competitive polygamous environment contribute to wives becoming autonomous agents. This is evidenced by naming practices that link children to the mother rather than to the father.

The variation in naming practices reflects a woman's social position within the larger polygamous family much more than it adheres to a normative, albeit theologically driven, ideal. A wife's marital position (first, second, third, and so forth), and the quality of her marital bond (queen bee, favorite, or low profile), along with a child's place within his or her mother's birth order (top, middle, or bottom cohort) affect the frequency with which a child is named after his or her father, a paternal relative, or a maternal relative.

Names function, as Lévi-Strauss asserted, "not only to identify and individuate but also to classify" (Arno 1994). In Angel Park, women pursue a broad-based strategy to elicit support from both maternal and paternal kin. Women are, at times, concerned with establishing namesake linkage between their husband and his offspring(s), although less interested on other occasions in establishing a symbolic link with that relationship. The fundamentalist patriarchal Principle serves as the foundational myth ensuring that the community's predominantly paternal child-naming pattern will establish a link between each wife's first-born son and his father (55 percent), while also linking her first-born daughter with her mother's kin (45 percent). After a time, the maternal bias is diluted with the arrival of additional wives and a woman's increased reproduction.

The fundamentalist cosmological model serves as a primary guide and motivational force for the creation and retention of patriarchal naming, especially when it involves sons. When a woman feels more secure and valued within the family, there is a greater likelihood that she will use nonpaternal names as a source of her children's names. A wife's social position (power, favorite, low profile) within the family also influences the naming preference, and, as a result, naming patterns reveal the success or failure of a wife's competitive struggles with other cowives for power, status, autonomy, and love. To that end, women, unlike men, pursue a broader parental investment strategy that includes paternal and maternal kin, with daughters serving as a route to honor filial obligations to one's natal family while simultaneously contributing to the creation of psychological boundaries between a mother's uterine family and that of her cowives.

Although previous studies focused on naming sought to establish an underlying biological basis for paternal certainty concerns (Johnson, McAndrew, and Harris 1991), a careful analysis revealed additional, albeit often competing motives that arise out of female competition for dignity and gain among themselves in the polygamous family. In this way, Angel Park's namesaking patterns do not simply reflect official cultural prescriptions or address men's paternal certainty concerns. There are variations, and these variations are shaped, in large part, by a woman's personality, relative social and familial status, and the degree of emotional bonding she has developed with her husband.

# 9

# THEOLOGY AND MOTHER CARE
## Full-Sibling and Half-Sibling Bonding

*"I never knew a happy plural family. Mother and Jasmine fought all the time—it affected the ways the kids got along" (a former member of the community).*

*"I recall growing up with lots of siblings. We played ball, went on outings, and just enjoyed being together" (a male still living in the community).*

In a monogamous society, a mother may have offspring from different men, which makes the mother, and not the father, the primary focal point linking all her children together into a viable kinship unit. In contrast, the fundamentalist polygamous family is linked through the father's procreation, which serves as the unifying symbol that defines the family's public identity. The father is the pivotal axis around which wives and their children form their kinship identification.

In a very practical way, however, the polygamous family is held together as much by the effort of the cowives to support a cohesive center that maintains the father's public image. This pattern of organization was typical of the 1970s Taiwanese wives (Wolf 1972) and 1950s Nigerian mothers (Bohannan 1985) who fostered a clear preference, often unvoiced, for their own "uterine" family, forming a subunit within the husband/father big family. In many ways, the emotional intensity of the mother-child bond, combined with the preference to identify more with the mother than the father, presents an additional challenge to creating and sustaining a loving unified family.

In this chapter, I will discuss the relative success that Angel Park families have in achieving this cherished theological ideal. Specifically, how influential is patriarchal theology in sustaining full and half-sibling solidarity? I want further to determine if an offspring's primary, and, accordingly, the strongest, identification is with the father or the mother. If it is the father, no significant difference should be found in the interactions of full sibs and half-sibs. Sibling bonds of fellowship should depend more on personality than on whether or not they share the same or a different birth mother. Given the fundamentalist belief in a patriarchal-governed theology, a person's primary kinship should be to the father, not the mother.

## PREFERENCE FOR FULL-SIBLING OVER HALF-SIBLING SOLIDARITY

Research conducted among blended monogamous U.S. families has repeatedly found that they seldom form effective family units. The review by Monique Diderich of the literature of stepfamily relationships found stronger "solidarity between full siblings than among half siblings and stepsiblings" (Diderich 2008:6). Her research has been replicated in other studies of non-Western polygamous societies, which also found differential affection and attachment between full siblings and half siblings. Studies of sibling solidarity in the Tibetan polyandrous (i.e., one wife and multiple husbands) family, for example, have found that, when a stepmother replaced a deceased wife, she often favored her own children, which, in the long run, undermined the principle of sibling solidarity and thus the capacity to sustain the plural family (Levine 1988).

The capacity of the Tibetan family to function as a viable unit also depended upon whether the "brothers" were descended from the same or different mothers; if not the same, it would "weaken support for the ideal of fraternal solidarity" (Levine and Silk 1997:210). Specifically, Levine found that sons from different mothers were "less likely to remain in a simple polyandrous arrangement and more apt to take more than one wife for themselves" (Levine and Silk 1997:210, cited in Durham 1991:80). The degree of fraternal and sibling solidarity is determined more by having a history of growing up with the same birth mother. This raises an intriguing question: Can a society's theological axioms contradict the developmental or parenting practices that connect the child more to the mother than to the father?

Angel Park's official culture actively promotes full- and half-sibling solidarity through an ideal that literally says "we are all true brothers and sisters," an ethos that quite self-consciously strives to downplay the genetic differences present in every polygamous family. As previously discussed, cowives who are often in competition for their husband's attention tend to use their children as a way to demonstrate their commitment to their husband and consequently reaffirm for themselves the commitment they have to their religion. This behavior can be consciously calculated, or it may stem from nothing more than unexamined habit. By advancing the attention of her children toward their father, a mother hopes to demonstrate her worth among competing cowives.

When a child's mother focuses her attention on her husband, it serves as a proper, if not widely admired, role model for her children to emulate. As an ideal, she will instruct her children to love, cherish, and adore their father; at the same time, she will strive to fulfill the father's expectations of her as a wife. This effort, discussed in chapter 2, along with the child's own desire to earn his or her father's respect, enhances the father's stature and esteem. Overall, the cultural emphasis on the spiritual and administrative authority of the father serves to promote family solidarity. It is in "the name of the father" that cowives and their offspring are told to overcome their rivalry and come together as a cohesive family unit. Fundamentalist husbands are unwavering in their view that all their children should see themselves as being part of a large single family and "should not refer to or even think about siblings of a different mother as [being] 'half' brothers and sisters" (Altman and Ginat 1996:396).

I attended numerous Sunday church services where I regularly witnessed a strong emphasis on the importance of family solidarity,[1] which is also a recurrent theme in private home services among family members. Adults could readily recall the emphasis that their teachers (those who live in the community) put on the importance of family cooperation. And, yet, whenever I asked someone what their birth order was within the large family, everyone, regardless of age or gender, responded with their birth position (e.g., first, second, and so on) in relation to their birth mother, immediately followed by their position within their father's or the big family. Only fathers provided their birth son rank within the family; mothers never did. For example, one man, in his thirties, epitomized this tendency when he noted, "I am my mother's first child, my father's eighth child, and I am my father's third son." When asked to draw "their family," the majority of participants, from fifteen different polygamous families, included every comother and father, as well as full and half-siblings. Only three (13 percent) drew their birth (maternal) family. When asked about other family members, each listed, without hesitation, his or her remaining half-brothers and half-sisters and their names and ages.

Significantly, everyone drew his or her birth family first and then added his or her comother and her offspring. This exercise shows that they have a clear image and clear remembrance of their relatedness within the larger family unit. In effect, at the normative level, the cultural ideal of family solidarity is overwhelmingly present, with offspring cognitively prioritizing their place first with their natal or birth family and then out from there to include everyone else in the larger family (Jankowiak and Diderich 2000:134).

## ADDITIONAL EVIDENCE OF FULL-SIBLING PREFERENCE

Self-identifying first with the mother's birth order, rather than the father's birth order is one, albeit a cognitive, indicator of natal affiliation. Another factor is the way that financial support and domestic service are distributed among kin. According to Spigelman and colleagues, remittance of a family member is a strong indicator of negative feelings toward the excluded family member (Spigelman, Spigelman, and Englesson 1992). Given the community's subsistence level, money is always, in many families, in short supply. Thus who lends money to whom can be a powerful index for assessing their level of closeness. In a survey I did about the giving and lending practices over the course of an individual's lifetime, only eight of twenty-nine (27 percent) individuals reported giving money to a half-sibling. For everyone else, money was deemed such a precious gift that it was reserved only for full siblings with whom close bonds have been developed.

The degree of full-sibling solidarity can be also found in the preference for natal family siblings whenever a babysitter is needed. I found that married siblings overwhelmingly preferred having younger full siblings babysit their children rather than younger half-siblings. For example, in seven out of eight instances, I found a full sibling was asked to babysit; only one asked for a half-sibling. I suspect that the reason comes out of a feeling of comfort; having spent more time with full siblings, it was easier and less worrisome to ask them for support. Research conducted in other cultures has consistently found that "half siblings do not provide infant care of equal quality to that provided by full siblings" (Mulder and Miller 1985:257).

Another reason is that full siblings feel closer emotionally to their mother's natal family offspring. When asked to name the sibling they felt the closest to, an overwhelming 74 percent (n = 52 out of 70) selected a full sibling. Given the close proximity of being raised in the same household, numerous daily interactions (e.g., watching television, snack/dine together), combined with their birth mother's involvement, it is not surprising that full sibling emotional solidarity is so pronounced.

I found evidence of the preference by observing birthday celebrations and wedding receptions. On eleven birthdays, fifty-four of seventy-nine (or 68 percent) brothers and sisters attending were full siblings of the person celebrating a birthday. Moreover, at seven wedding receptions, which tend to be more community-wide events than birthdays, thirty-two of the fifty-six (57 percent) siblings who attended were full siblings.

If the father was alive, adult full siblings and half-siblings continued to meet at his home. However, once the father passed away, adult full siblings and half-siblings were less inclined to eat together, but instead chose to hold "family" gatherings around their birth mother. An informal query, conducted over a five-year period (1993 to 1998), found that adults, once married and thus moved out of the house, seldom attended a half-brother's or half-sister's family gathering. If a half-sibling did attend a comother's dinner, it was usually by invitation, implying that someone within that family had established a close friendship with a half-sibling or a comother. According to Furman and Burhrmester (1985), similarity in age and gender promote relationships that resemble friendships. Their finding also holds for Angel Park, where half-siblings continue to associate with one another through their teenage years. In this way, half-siblings attend family functions more out of friendship bonds previously established, whereas full siblings attend because of a variety of reasons that range from deep affection to not wanting to disappoint their mother. Adult interviewees were firm in their assertion that they too felt warm emotional bonds with their half-siblings (Gyruis et al. 1986).

Full-sibling preference and identification does not mean that half-siblings seldom formed close bonds with other half-siblings. Twenty-six percent (eighteen of seventy) of those interviewed said that they felt closer to a specific half-sibling than to a full sibling. For example, one family played, without second thoughts, in a competitive local baseball league where most of the team was composed of full and half-siblings. I also saw firsthand that warm sentiments were extended toward all family members (e.g., long-distance calls in which everyone talked to the caller, expressing sympathy for a family member's illness or injury).

Big family solidarity is found in the thoughts of a twenty-five-year-old man on growing up, telling me that "we did not necessarily get along with each other when we were younger, but as we got older we started to work things out. We realized we were brothers and sisters and not from separate families but united together in one large family." Another youth spoke in clear agreement: "Once you grow older and mature, as far as I can tell, disagreeableness toward [half-sibs] no longer exists." He added that "I do not have stronger feelings toward my other mothers' children than I do for my mother's children." Another especially reflective youth said that his childhood was filled with "brothers fighting," acknowledging that "you want your own way, you don't get your own way, that's all about growing up and learning to become a good person." However, he qualified this, adding that "having so many brothers and sisters makes for a more fulfilling life. It helps you with personal growth." Another youth recalled that "my comothers were constantly competitive—I think that influenced us kids as we became intensely competitive too." Others recalled frequently visiting a comother if she "was decent and nice to them" or on an equivalent basis. A twenty-six year old fondly went to her comother's room when she was nine years old to study. The chief reason, she said, was because "I felt comfortable around her and I was always invited into her room."

Despite genuine fondness for some comothers and their offspring, however, the overriding preference is for closer bonds with full siblings over half-siblings. One young man tried to clarify in what way his feelings for full siblings differed from those he had for half-sibs. He confirmed that he felt closer to some comothers' children than to the children of other comothers, noting that "I am closer to Barbara's kids—if I had to pick who to associate with, more Barbara or Harriett, I would pick Barbara. But there is a special something, a feeling of closeness, of belonging that I have for my mother's kids that I do not have for Barbara's kids—maybe it is a DNA thing."

It was clear to me that Angel Park residents can readily make a cognitive and affective distinction between their mother's offspring and the offspring of their comothers. The residents there, like offspring in monogamous families, know to whom they are related and are able to easily discuss their relative position within their father's line and within their mother's line. Contrary to the official religious position, most individuals' primary self-reference was to their birth order or to their place within their natal family, followed, as we have seen, by their place or birth order in their father's larger family. When I sought clarification, my queries were met with surprise, with those I spoke with noting that their self-reference appeared inconsistent with the official position. No one ever disagreed. Like many cultures where the official mores are one thing and the reality of everyday life another, surprise was not followed by denial. Nor was the disparity particularly troubling to anyone. Most remained content to not contemplate it, leaving only me, the anthropologist, to reflect upon the disparity.

Residents told me without hesitation that if anything happened to their other brothers and sisters they would feel "a great loss." To the follow-up question, "So, OK, but who in your heart do you feel closest to, your mother's children or your comother's children?" Inevitably, and without fail, all acknowledged that they felt closer to their full siblings than to their halves. A thirty-something female elaborated: "I feel I can curse my siblings from my mother's family, but must be more reserved, careful in fact, when voicing displeasure at my half-sibs." A mature man concurred, pointing to a pronounced bias toward your own children. He explained: "In church people are always preaching, maybe because no one does it. Blood ties are stronger than social ideals. Sister-wives should love everyone the same. People should not emphasize blood or birth children. But I've never seen it. I've lived in many homes and I have never seen it." He concluded by saying that "it is not natural to ignore your biological offspring." The gamut of affection, restraint, indifference, and resentment is ubiquitous in American polygamy, as it is in the American blended monogamous family.

What is the driving cause of the hierarchy of feeling and affection? Is it an artifact derived from the children's own unconscious predisposition? Or is it shaped in some way by the dynamics of the polygamous family? I could not determine whether or not children's perceptions of genetic differences arose from parental clues or implications or from the different treatment by comothers. What could be determined from observations, and from the accounts of the adults who grew up in a plural family, is a strikingly clear awareness of the different treatment received from their birth mothers as opposed to their comothers. Adults were unambiguous about this different treatment. For example, a mother stated directly: "I have to protect and guard my family," meaning her natal family. When there is a fight or disagreement between children from different birth mothers, invariably fundamentalist mothers, unlike Chinese villagers, who seldom take their child's side, take the side of their offspring. If challenged, many mothers, but not all, assert a defensive demand: "Who are you to tell me about my kid?" This is not recent. The research by Hulett (1939) of children raised in late-nineteenth-century Mormon polygamous families found a similar natal bias. "Children got caught up in the interplay or rivalries that they considered to be normal. Their mothers appealed to them for support in contests within the family" (1939:392). Clearly, among Mormon fundamentalists, there has always been a pronounced natal preference that continues to contribute to the development of a stronger, warmer identification with the natal family.

In Angel Park, whenever discrepancies arise between the official ideal and actual behavior, a common refrain, often said in exasperation, is "The Mothers." It is expected that the mothers, who must strike some balance in the competing demands for individual attention and the value of expectations of their religious belief, will succeed more often than anyone else does. Mothers are caught within a cultural paradox: they have a genuine devotion to their religion and a deep attachment to their children. Try as they may to embrace a life of self-sacrifice for the greater good, many find themselves, on at least occasion, slipping into a monogamous kind of orientation.

Some fundamentalist fathers are concerned that their wives may steer the children toward themselves rather than center on them as the head of the family. In these instances, the fathers in Angel Park will reorganize the duties of their wives so that it becomes difficult for the wives to exercise as much influence on the children. One method is to pass along care of the baby from the birth mother to another mother, who, after a period of time, turns over care of the baby to another mother. The goal is to show the child through all-care parenting (the term for child-rearing by the community) that he or she has "mothers," not one mother, and the father as a result becomes the focus. This type of family organization is not representative of Angel Park families. The practice underscores the concern and anxiety some men have had that the children may bond more with the birth mother than with them.

It remains to be seen whether or not children who were independent of adult intervention and guidance would naturally form bonds of full-sibling solidarity. I could not determine if a child's different feelings originate from inclusive fitness (or a preference for kin with whom he or she shares a closer genetic relationship) or occur as a by-product of patterns of emotional affection set in motion in early childhood through early mother-child intimacy. For example, all children eat and play together in a common family room that may or may not be supervised by their birth mother, while an infant will sleep with his or her birth mother. Young children (three to nine years old) often spend time in their birth mother's bedroom. Children from different birth mothers often pass the middle of the day in close proximity, while being close in the early mornings and late evenings with their birth mother and, therefore, with their other full siblings. However, I did notice that every time a child who was playing fell or cried out, it was the biological mother who ran to the child's aid and comfort.

There are other factors that influence a child's perception and sense of identification within the family. Parental favoritism and scapegoating are two of the more obvious forms where a variance of sentiment is manifested within the monogamous family household. This is also found in the polygamous family. Because children are conscious of other siblings' actions as well as the adult caretaker's favoritism, they are acutely aware of the difference between themselves and their siblings (Dunn and Plomin 1990; Gyruis et al. 1986). This can serve to reinforce a cognitive sense of separateness (Musun-Miller 1993). For example, a twenty-something woman recalls telling a comother whom she disliked: "You cannot hit me, as you are not my mother."

In terms of social comparison, children are highly attuned to differences or discrepancies in treatment, no matter how subtle or indirect (Festinger 1954). The issue here is not the actual frequency of favoritism but the perception of it. The literature on child perception has found that, as early as thirty months old, children are able to make comparisons. They work out the attention that they receive from their mother as compared to the attention that their siblings receive (Dunn and McGuire 1994;

Koch 1960). Every adult I interviewed between the age of twenty and fifty-five vividly recalled one or two childhood instances where a nonbirth mother showed favoritism (e.g., giving more candy, cookies, or a larger slice of cake or letting house rules slide for their children but not for comother's children). Moreover, birth mothers established borders by taking their children to their bedroom and reading to them, watching television together, or talking with them. While other children are not necessarily excluded, more often than not they gather in the evening around their own birth mother. All these small, yet noticeable, activities convey clear differences and thus contribute to the formation of a strong natal identity within the larger family.

Anthropologists who have studied sibling solidarity in non-Western cultural settings have found that the normative ideal of solidarity is often counterbalanced by the equally pervasive pattern of intrafamily hostility (Goldstein and Beall 1982; Levine 1988; Peristiany and Pitt-Rivers 1992). Because the family is often a contentious zone of competing interests and pragmatic alliances, individuals readily differentiate between natal and non-natal subfamily units, which contributes to the promotion of full-sibling identification and, thus, solidarity. But competition and solidarity are not necessarily contradictory. They are two often competing motivational forces that shape a family's organization and ambience. In spite of this competition, or maybe because of it, full siblings grow closer to, and not more distant from, one another (Jankowiak and Diderich 2000:136). In this way, domestic conflict serves to establish and maintain the identity and boundary lines of intrafamilial groups that can be reactive whenever there is present challenge or danger to the larger social group (Coser 1974). The often-contentious sibling relationships found in a polygamous family are strikingly similar to those found in a monogamous or blended family (Diderich 2008), which suggests that, regardless of family organization, sibling interaction is seldom entirely smooth, cooperative, loving, or sweet (Jankowiak and Diderich 2000:121–139).

In spite of the force of religious ideals, and notwithstanding the continued close physical proximity of half-siblings in the polygamous family, there is a pronounced clustering of feeling and affection in the polygamous family that is organized around birth mothers. Other researchers working in different fundamentalist communities have reported the presence of "powerful bonds between a mother and her biological children" (Altman and Ginat 1996:321).

The difference between full and half-sibs in Angel Park is consistent with the degree of familiarity and felt closeness between identical twins who were raised in separate households but later rejoined together. In every case, the behavior and attitude of the newly rejoined twin were closer, more in sync, with that of his or her biological twin than with the nonbiological sibling (Reiss et al. 2003; Segal 2012). From an ethnographic perspective, this is not unusual.

There are many claims to an individual's affection and loyalty in a polygamous family. In one context, everyone comes together in the name of the father, but in other settings full siblings meet to honor their birth mother. For example, Mother's Day is a huge day celebrated with arrangements of flowers and meals, while Father's Day is simply ignored. As in other cultures, whenever a family is threatened or challenged, everyone, regardless of birth order, comes together in support. In these situations, sibling competition is suspended while the larger family asserts a united front. At other times, when big family unity is not imperative, full siblings and half-siblings are more interested in advancing their own interests than promoting family solidarity.

# 10

## THEOLOGICAL PARENTHOOD AND THE MAKING OF THE GOOD POLYGAMOUS TEENAGER

*"My father told me that maybe the women we are meant to marry live in a different polygamous community and we have not had the chance to meet them" (a twenty-something man).*

*"I like many features of the life, but I did not like all the hypocrisies" (a youth who no longer lives in the community).*

Every society, in its own way, strives to transmit the beliefs, values, and life orientations essential to its cultural survival. Because religious communities draw upon an inclusive cosmology, that cosmology serves as the primary lens through which people perceive and evaluate each other's behavior as good or bad. It further provides parents with a conceptual framework for identifying the cultural standards or values their offspring need to make the right choice as to whom to listen to and whom to seek out for advice. Parents need their cosmological framework so that they can give accurate advice, constructive discipline, and when necessary point their children to the right spiritual advisers. For religious subcultures, whose values often stand in opposition to mainstream society, successful transmission can never be assured. To that end, religious communities must remain vigilant if they want a child to develop into a "good person" who shares their values (Henrich 2016:36). In this chapter, I will focus on socialization practices found in Angel Park in order to probe how parents' attempts, in their own words, "raise up the good child" into becoming a "respected and esteem adult." I want to understand how religious ideas along with often unvoiced secular American cultural values shape the criteria parents use to assess who is and who is not a "good person." Whatever our understanding, even if it deepens over time, they—religious ideas and cultural values—are often at odds with one another and continue to be so.

My focus is the teenage years—the time when youth are more prone to doubt, if not reject, parental instruction and question, if not defy, community ideals. It is a time when neither is simply accepted. Exploring which ideals and cultural practices are more readily challenged provides insight into the cultural contradictions and structural restraints individuals face in their journey into adulthood.

## RAISING A RESPECTFUL PERSON WHO ACHIEVES COMMUNITY IDEALS

Given the uniqueness of the polygamous family system, it is easy to overlook the commonalities that fundamentalist Mormons share with mainstream American culture. Forged out of the nineteenth-century American frontier experience, fundamentalist Mormonism embraces many American middle-class values: a basic frugality of means, emphasis on controlling one's destiny, a striving for upward mobility, and a belief in individual responsibility. In this way, the fundamentalist community resembles something of the "old middle-class republic with its independent citizen adventurous and yet rooted in family, home, and community" (Bellah et al. 1991:66). The cultural idea is to raise healthy, morally upstanding, hardworking people who are committed to upholding the religion. The community prefers to stress "self-mastery rather than self-discovery because human beings are born with sin, infected with dark passions and satanic temptations; only self-mastery could provide some control over them" (Brooks 2008). They are in good agreement with northern India's morality, where it is thought that a good person "should not do what he likes but should conform to public morality and respect" (Parish 1994:82). Because Angel Park is a fluid community, with individuals often visiting other regions for work or just to sightsee, people are acutely aware of an underlying tension between the local emphasis on order and security and mainstream society's fascination with change and innovation (Schwartz 1987:72).

Although Angel Park acknowledges that individuals have agency or personal autonomy, mainstream American society's most esteemed value, it is not the community's only one. Angel Park, like eighteenth-century America, continues to value self-sacrifice, obedience, good manners, self-reliance, and being well behaved, which are seen as virtues, not values. Taken together, these virtues provide members with a fixed moral compass necessary to create the proper orientation that makes life worth living.

## VARIATIONS IN
## PARENTING SOCIALIZATION

In spite of the community's glorification of the patriarchy, the expression of male authority, there is a range in men's approach to their organization of the family and how best to raise the community's offspring. In Angel Park (as previously noted), there are three leadership or management styles: a stern authoritarian style, an easygoing diffuse one, and one of indifference to any and all family leadership obligations.

Like nineteenth-century Mormon polygamous fathers, contemporary fathers inclined toward an authoritarian approach have a clear idea how best to organize their family, which is to stress obedience (Hulett 1939:281). For example, Brent Jeffs, who grew up in different polygamous communities, in his autobiography recalls his father continuously stressing that obedience is owed to him and to the priesthood leaders. He writes: "Every Bible story became a tale of how the obedient were blessed and the disobedient were cursed" (Jeffs and Szalavitz 2009:102). His father often bragged that his thirty-four children together were quieter than two kids alone. In contrast, other fathers, due either to being away for long periods of time or feeling overwhelmed by pressing family responsibilities, withdraw psychologically as heads of the family and relinquish its oversight to their wives or to one individual wife who takes responsibility for managing the larger plural family (Hulett 1939:290). The easygoing father, like his nineteenth-century counterpart, remains active and engaged in daily family affairs while also preferring to delegate parental authority to his wives. This type is more likely to appear in middle age when a man is more confident in his ability and more pragmatic in family affairs. Middle-aged, easygoing fathers, are seen walking a child to school or accompanying them to a school performance.

Whichever family management style a man adopts, wives report that many fathers admit to having a difficult time with their teenagers. Some offspring fought their father, while others ran away. Wives noted that their husband was "good with young ones. A middle-aged mother recalled that her husband "often played with his children, slapped them when they were bad." But she notes, "You cannot do that with teenagers, you have to talk to them. This was something he had trouble with." A thirty-eight-year-old father of eight admitted he "loved kids, especially the young ones. It is good to have them around the house. Afterwards they can go their own way."

Every father, regardless of his management style, repeatedly reminds his offspring, especially teenagers, of the essential difference between "natural man" and the "socially mature man." Natural man has innate drives such as sexual desire, status competitiveness, and individual aggression. It is critical for an individual, male or female, to master these natural drives. It is through controlling that he or she learns how to live the proper moral life necessary for becoming a good person. One young man vividly recalled his teenage years, when his father would often take him aside and remind him of the necessity of such mastery. His father warned him that "failure to do so meant you failed to master yourself which can also mean you are not worthy to remain in the community." The experience of felt guilt combined with the implied threat of social ostracism serves as a powerful restraint on behavior.

Angel Park has made self-sacrifice one of its primary virtues. Fathers routinely refer to and talk about the need for sacrifice whenever their wives or children request something they cannot readily provide. It is thought that in order to create and maintain a harmonious family each member must "pursue the good in common" (Bellah et al. 1991:9). This pursuit customarily requires making some kind of sacrifice for the plural family's well-being. To that end, fathers regularly admonish wives and children about the importance of making and sustaining a deeper, more spiritual commitment to the family. Many younger men and women readily recall being deeply moved by this ideal and motivated to achieve it. Moreover, they often and easily recall how much they respected their father for his strong religious convictions, combined with the daily sacrifices he made to support the family. For example, a young father stated that the "purpose of polygamy is to raise up for God righteous children." He elaborated on his conviction: "without righteous principles, children do not have a clear path to salvation. They can easily lose their faith and be lost to the outside world. Parents have a responsibility to teach, educate their children to follow God's rules." He used the term *righteousness*, and I asked him what it entails. Smiling, he explained, "it is easy and it is difficult—To be righteous is to follow God's laws—you should have sex with only your wives, you should produce children who want to obey God's laws, you have to hold regular Sunday (or family) meetings—you need to guide your children and provide valuable instruction so they know what to do." I asked him how he responds when a child, especially a teenager, misbehaves. "You need," he said, "to discipline them; you can hit them until they do the right thing" or "you can seek priesthood guidance, and they can pray for their son or daughter." He reluctantly added that "if they refuse to adjust and become the Devil's child, then you have to reject them, otherwise they will infect the entire family."

An example of a young person's religious dedication spurred on by the memory of his father's admonitions is heard in the words of a nineteen-year-old male: "My father would lecture us for six solid hours on the importance of making a total commitment to living together in the larger plural family. He would quote scripture and sermons and tell us stories of redemption and triumph." I noted that six hours seemed like such a long time and wondered if he might have gotten bored. With no hesitation, he said, "No, it was the best time." Afterwards he admitted that he tried to live up to values of cooperation to be a better person when interacting with his half-brothers and sisters and their mothers.

To that end, fathers often share their revelations with the family. These acts are understood to show their connection with the spiritual world, which further legitimizes their familial authority. All these routine activities contribute to promoting the social solidarity of the family. They also serve to uphold a nineteenth-century Victorian image of family life, with its "upstanding father, and a warmly embracing mother" (Fass 2016:10).

If teenagers, male or female, do not admire, respect, or fear their father, they normally reject his counsel. For example, one thirty-year-old woman remembered her father telling her "to stop putting makeup on." But she refused, saying, "I just ignored him, and he yelled at me, but I continued to ignore him. I did try to be more reserved when he was around, however. But in the late evenings I would secretly leave to meet with friends at parties where I would wear loose clothes, makeup, and do whatever I wanted. I was free." Her attitude is typical of those youth who feel a "real ambivalence toward fathers who had been aloof, authoritarian figures for most of their lives" (Foner 1984:116). Fathers are not troubled by this common offspring response. For most, the creation of a "Daddy bond" is not their primary goal. Rather they want to establish a proper relationship organized around respect and deference.

There is a gender difference in the way some fathers advise, counsel, and discipline their sons, with greater expectations for their sons than their daughters. Mothers, however, tend to be more tolerant of a son's challenging behavior than a daughter's. After puberty, girls are more closely monitored. Often-unvoiced, the family concern is about sexuality and its control. Given the community's puritan mindset, sex is regarded as an essential force, but a dangerous one. The regulation of youth's sexuality, especially that of females, is a paramount concideration. One example is a typical exchange that mothers have with their daughters. When a teenage girl wants to go for an evening stroll, a mother will say, "please hold on, and I will go or one of your brothers or sisters will go with you." When this happens, the girl is, in almost all cases, no longer interested in going. This tight restriction does not hold for boys, who are allowed to travel outside the community, even if just to hang out with friends. Given the mindset, an insightful observer of the community's faith-based norms noted that "males think they can define reality and say 'my demands and expectations are reasonable.'" Females, in contrast, in the admission of a twenty-six year old, perhaps cynical: "We are taught to be insecure. We are urged to go along humbly accepting our fate. That is how they control us."

Because adolescence is a time when youth become aware of "alternatives, there is a shift in social and emotional orientation, away from almost exclusive dependence on the family . . . with an attachment to peers and adults outside the family" (Schlegel 2013:305). For example, a twenty-year-old woman acknowledged how she learned to manipulate the community's gendered system. "I learned," she said to me, "how to play with my mother." She described how she and several of her friends managed this: "first, you act just like mother wants you to, and she will give you everything. She wants a nice little girl, so I behave in front of her that way. I am the model wife: I stay home, have children, and am obedient. I say this, but I want to go places and do things, I do not want to be fenced in. I am honest, I don't know what I want. I do not want to be placed [in placement marriage]. I want to do things." Later she confessed that she was part of a defiant group of youth who, during the evenings, would periodically sneak out with other girlfriends and an occasional male classmate(s). Much like other American youth in the 1980s, she rebelled; without telling anyone in her family, she drove to a nearby town, playing loud music on the way. She told me: "we just had fun. Some of the girls would buy beer and cigarettes. . . . We wanted to be bad." Many, but not all, young men rebel in similar ways.

Elizabeth Wall, who grew up in a different polygamous community, remembers that "faithful [sons] were expected to serve their fathers in a humble manner, greeting them by saying things like: 'I am here to do your will. What do you want me to do? I want to be a humble servant of the prophet.' . . . But my brother listened to a deep inner voice that told him that this type of behavior just wasn't right." She adds: "As hard as Dad tried through, example and scripture, his sons struggled to live the principles of our strict faith" (2008:80).

## MOTHERS PARENTING STYLE: AFFECTIONATE TO INDIFFERENCE

Although men are the patriarchs of their family, most families, outside of a ritualistic setting (e.g., Sunday service and priesthood meetings), are organized around the mother. While women are deeply committed to upholding patriarchal values and, with it, male privilege, they are also the repositories of the pragmatics of everyday nurturing, a nurturing that is more situationally based than theologically directed. Their primary goal is to raise decent, loyal, respectful children who want to live the Principle (i.e., establish and maintain a plural family). To that end, mothers strive to keep their family together, despite the various challenges they will face.

This arrangement ensures that there will be stronger emotional ties between mothers and their children than between fathers and their children (Parker, Smith, and Ginat 1973). Janet Bennion found a similar trend in the Montana Pinesdale community, where "boys suffer from the absence of fathers which challenged their ability to find solid role models and affection" (2012:183). A father's absence also troubled Brent Jeffs, from the FLDS community, remembers how his father, who seldom visited his family, would confuse him with one of his brothers, which left him feeling betrayed and angry. To compensate, he tried to form, without much success, a closer relationship with his mother.

A person's birth order or relative place in their birth mother's family significantly impacts their personality. I found that offspring unconsciously tended to define themselves in opposition to a same-sex sib who was closest to them. For example, if a nine-year-old girl had an older eleven-year-old sister who was "parent pleasing," she often adopted a "parent-displeasing" behavior. If the next sib was a girl, she adopted, in opposition to her older sib, a parent-pleasing behavior. This behavior pattern is similar for boys too. Frank Sulloway (1996), in his groundbreaking study of the birth order effect of being open- or close-minded to social change, found a similar tendency whereby sibs defined themselves as being more liberal or conservative depending on what posture their closest, albeit older sib, had adopted. Youth who adopted a parent-displeasing posture were the most rebellious in their teenage years.

In Angel Park, polygamous families are de facto matrifocal units embedded within the overarching ideal of a patriarchally governed plural family. Although women endorse and uphold in public discourse their husband's position as the family's spiritual and administrative authority, in practice most focus on their own matrifocal unit. In some cases, it feels like a retreat. Most Angel Park women, like women in other polygamous cultures, do not oppose the system from which they gain an honorable position (Lindholm 2002:240), that is, a position of meaningful status. They believe their ideal place is in the home and derive esteem from upholding the family system.

Mormon fundamentalist women, like eighteenth-century New England women (Ulrich 1982:45), are idealized as an affectionate archetype whose presence and actions modify some of the overt rigidity found in a patriarchal system that stresses discipline, obedience, and deference. The quality of the mother-child bond, however, depends on a woman's personality, her work schedule, and the number of her children. A few women are simply indifferent to the daily responsibilities of childcare. Others were committed to closer relationships, but their work schedule often prevented them from being present. Some others noted that, of all their children, they were closer to their last-born because they had more time to interact with him or her. My sibling relationship survey found that the mother-child bond was strongest between the last-born children (Jankowiak and Diderich 2000). As one middle-aged mother said, "I just had more time with the last two children." I also found that women who were college educated tended to have a closer relationship with their children. They were, in general, more open to talking, often engaging their children through the use of clever analogies and thoughtful suggestions. For example, a young man told me that he grew up in a family that encouraged conversation as well as discussions about theology and other matters. He felt that he could talk with his father or mother about issues, and they never criticized him for asking questions about the meaning of life, God's purpose, or whether the polygamous system is a fair system. He reported that he often had long talks with his mother (and, to a lesser extent, with his father), and "enjoyed discussing theology with both parents." In other families, mothers were less knowledgeable about theological matters and at times apprehensive of entering into open discussions about theology. However, in these families, mothers maintained their focus on the children and remained actively involved in their development by offering encouragement, advice, and, at times, financial support. What they desired above all else was for their offspring to remain in the community, and if this was unfeasible they tried to maintain frequent contact with them.

Mothers strive to raise a moral person and a good person (one and the same in fundamentalist religion) through modest living. A forty-five-year-old woman recalled how "my mother would try to be happy even when we had very little to eat. She would just make jokes and encourage us to sing happy songs." Mothers customarily give love and demonstrate generosity to help their children identify with proper values. A mother of seven teenagers felt strongly that loving support was essential to guide teenagers into adulthood, explaining it this way: "Kids need to see they belong. They need to realize they have love and a place and a future." Many mothers discipline their offspring by invoking religious axioms and expressions. For example, a twenty-eight-year-old female recalled how often religion was invoked around the house: "my mother would casually ask if my behavior was the result of the Devil influencing me. I hated when she did this, but I did modify my behavior." Smiling, she added, "at least for a while."

Significantly, community members recalled the highly competitive nature of their family life in which they, like Flora Jessop in the FLDS community, "fought for everything" (2007:388) and only "the strong survived" (Jessop 2009:179). Wanting to change their child-rearing practices, a number of Angel Park's parents admitted they did not want to raise their children the way they were raised. For example, a wife acknowledged her husband used to beat his sons the way his father beat him. But he then realized he would turn his family against him and he stopped. Another wife admitted that, like her mother, she would scream at her children until she realized, "I had lost it. I went to my room and cried. I now try to be more evenhanded with my children." She adds: "My husband helps out too; we have a much better family environment."

Both males and females model themselves on their father's and mother's everyday behavior and will bring their assimilation of that behavior into their own marriages. If their mother or father was passive-aggressive in seeking resources, they are similarly inclined. Further, when the family environment is contentious, and openly hostile, individuals are prone to negatively critique the community's cultural practices. On the other hand, if their mother or father customarily sought to be a conciliator and bring cowives together, they also adopted that approach, even when they lacked their parents' skills to be successful. The pull of influence is so strong, so dominant, that children will emulate the same parenting despite it going against the grain of their personality.

## PUBLIC EDUCATION AND CULTURAL TRANSMISSION OF RELIGIOUS VALUES

If fathers are the public voice of community values, the local public and privately operated religious schools act as a secondary institution that further serves to reinforce the community's core values. Because the overwhelming majority of the teachers, administrative staff, and students are from the community, the typical restraints on actively and forcefully voicing theological convictions in a public school are overlooked. Youth recall that they were often lectured in classrooms about the importance of living God's law to form a plural family. They are regularly reminded that the Devil is constantly active in the world and always trying to seduce them away from their religion. Many young people remember schoolwide assemblies where they were warned against romantic love because of its implied expectation of and desire for exclusivity. Romantic love would only intensify the jealousy that they would likely experience when they joined a plural family. They were instructed in the need to adapt to the limited time with their husband as well as the competing needs and expectations of other wives. To successfully do this, they were encouraged to make a renewed dedication to live God's law and complete his Work. Everyone believed that the Devil would try to undermine the ability to live up to religious ideals, which in many resulted in palpable fear. Taken together, schoolteachers, administrators, and parents formed a unified cluster, or group, in stressing the importance of upholding Mormon fundamentalist doctrine. To date, their efforts are highly effective, as evidenced by the fact that the community continues to see a great majority of daughters marrying into a plural family (Quinn 1991).

Although schools are the guardians of the community's stated values, youth learn from their peers that there are other, often unvoiced, values or modes of thought that can oppose those values. In bringing youth from different families together in one place on a routine basis, high school offers and provides, for some youth, support for the outward expression of alternative values. In 1999, the leadership of a rival sect, the Fundamentalist Church of Jesus Christ of Latter-day Saints, fearing its youth would become spiritually "contaminated" or "sullied" through contact with unbelievers or sinners, decided to pull their children out of the local public school in favor of homeschooling. In the process, the community maintained a firm hold on its historically based insistence that there are only two stages of life: childhood and adulthood. In contrast, Angel Park's leadership continued to promote the benefits of extended education, which, albeit tacitly, also recognized adolescence as a distinct life stage.

Although community leaders, teachers, and parents set goals and boundaries, siblings also act as a significant socializing agent, though they themselves are loosely supervised overall. In this setting, children tend to raise each other (Weisner 1982). Older siblings neither indulge nor coddle younger siblings. They are allowed to explore, but the strong preference is for younger children to stay within their own family compound and play there. The dynamic of this child-rearing is conducive to the formation of an implicit hierarchy where the older children influence the younger, who are more inclined to look up to older children than to their parents for guidance and direction. In this way, they learn valuable behavior that allows them to culturally survive through imitating the behavior of same-sex siblings. For example, a youth recalled that when he was five years old he was hit by his nine-year-old brother for being "pushy" (that is, not knowing his place): "I learned my place and the importance of not challenging those who are higher in the pecking order." Another youth fondly remembers spending good times with his family: "we would make our football teams from the larger family; we would go to the barn and hang out—that was the fun years." In loosely managed polygamous home environments, adult offspring recall it as being a "living hell." Others just remember "Pa and Ma fighting and fighting and fighting." A thoughtfully reflective young man noted: "I am glad I was raised under the conditions of crying, complaining, whining mothers—I hated living there and vowed never to create that type of family. It was the best thing for me in retrospect." In this setting, children learn that life is a struggle and that competition is more "the law of the land" (their term for American legal jurisprudence) than cooperation. The reality of family conflict, and especially sibling rivalry, goes against the community's cherished ideals, which heightens a teenager's suspicion that the community's ideals may not only be unattainable but also less than desirable.

## SOCIAL STRUCTURAL REALITIES AND THE REJECTION OF THE PLURAL FAMILY

Mormon fundamentalist youth have mostly internalized and accepted the community's core values and its life orientation. A twenty-two-year-old male's life goal is highly representative: "to live in spiritual peacefulness, marry, have children, a family, and to support that family." It is the life goal that Angel Park's parents strive to instill in their offspring. To that end, everyone endeavors to raise a "good child" who has the awareness, ability, and dedication to achieve the community's highest ideal: living a decent life through the creation of God's ideal family, the polygamous family. The community recognizes that not everyone has the talent or dedication to achieve this ideal. It is well known that many are called but few receive God's blessing, and there is the understanding and expectation that most efforts to form a plural family will fail.

Angel Park youth are aware of the community's expectations and subsequent critical judgment if they cannot achieve its most cherished ideal. They take seriously the belief that rejection of community norms will "result in their going to hell because God has rejected you." Whenever youth secretly gather together, the issue of whether or they want, or are able, to form a plural family is a recurrent topic. These gatherings are ad hoc, always secret, and take place at midnight outside the community.

Men and women from different school cliques and families attend these sessions. With them, they create an antistructure or nonhierarchical liminal zone where the use of drugs and alcohol are intertwined with intense discussions about their parents' behavior, cowife interaction, the validity of their religion, and what makes life worth living. A twenty-eight-year-old woman recalls: "when I was fourteen years old, we would meet secretly and discuss sexual attractions and what it meant to be a moral person—our talks lasted the entire night." She adds, "We discussed our love crushes we had or what we observed of our friends." At these gatherings, youth are not above expressing their personal exasperation, often making fun of religious ideals and what they consider parental hypocritical behavior. One angry female told her peers of an incident in which her mother asked what she was going to do for the day, and she yelled out, "I will stay home all day and praise the Lord." Her peers laughed and identified with the experience. Another youth reported that he enjoyed pointing out to his parents their hypocritical behavior, which he noted, with a smile, "always upset them."

The community strongly condemns these midnight gatherings. In the 1980s, youth developed a code whereby they would call each other on the landline, and if a mother answered, or listened on the extension, they would discuss clothes to wear going to school. The mother thought this was just school chitchat. When the youth became aware that their mother was not listening, they shifted to discussing where to meet for the evening gathering. In the more conservative 1980s the "most grievous sin was to be accused of masturbation or looking at some girl, to lust after her" (Bistline 1998:86). Bistline, a longtime

FLDS community member, thought the worst mistake the leadership made in the early years (1950–1980s) was not to have dances where youth could associate. He notes that leadership was so concerned about boys and girls meeting and forming love relationships that they decided it was best not to allow any opportunity for the opposite sexes to meet. The weekly church sermons are filled with lectures to avoid social interaction. The community prophet repeatedly stated: "You girls and boys know when you do wrong and when you do right. You boys know when you hear the servants of God say to leave the girls alone (Johnson 1990:1020). In the 1990s, I attended a church service where the leader once again lectured community youth to stop trying to date the girls and wait to be assigned. He then noted that mature males knew more about dating and had more resources than they had, so young males should not even try to engage in a competitive competition for a female's attention.

It Is not unknown for youth to become romantically involved and want to marry their age mates. If such marriage occurs, it results in another woman being removed from the marriage pool. Angel Park is keenly aware that frequent peer group gatherings are a threat to their placement marriage family system whereby the religious elite marries a person or selects one to marry "their heavenly mate." The tacit opposition of Mormon fundamentalist communities against male adolescents is derived from the reality that there is always an insufficient number of females to support a polygamous community. Their ambivalent attitude toward unmarried youth is typical of polygamous communities around the world where "old men often have hostility toward young unmarried men" (Foner 1984:33). In turn, young men often are "bursting over with envy and resentment toward the older [men who are] in control" (Foner 1984:22; also reported in

Schlegel and Barry 1991). A priesthood leader articulated the intergenerational tension at a Sunday meeting when he reminded the unmarried youth at the service that mature males knew more about dating and had more resources than they had, so young males should not even try to engage in a competition for a female's attention. A few families have teenage sons who challenge their father with the words "I can take you." This always results, in this type of family, in the sons trying to physically throw down their father in an aggressive wrestling match. Although this behavior is NOT representative, it does reveal an often-unvoiced intergenerational antagonism. Another example of intergenerational tension, due, in large part, to the skewed sex ratio, is symbolically played out every Thanksgiving when the married men play a pickup football game against the unmarried youth in what locals refer to as the Turkey Bowl. In the game, onlookers report that the bachelors are noticeably more physically aggressive than the married men.

Although the official cosmology demands obedience and respect for authority, many community youths are in open defiance of that cosmology. For some, their disagreement is theological, but for many others it is about adolescent search for identity. A twenty-eight-year-old male revealed his struggle in his search for existential meaning, noting: "The religion did not scare me; in fact, I liked it. For me it was striving to create an identity that was my concern. Where is my place? This question haunts me and my friends." I found his personal journey highly representative. It should not be surprising to learn that unmarried youth identify with the phantom in *The Phantom of the Opera*. Angel Park youth, like Montana youth (Bennion 1998:86), often turn to alcohol and illegal drugs to cope with their anxiety. In the 1970s, Angel Park was an insular community, and youth apparently seldom thought about leaving and had to be pushed out. Today, on the other hand, youth discuss leaving among themselves.

Angel Park's tacit intergenerational antagonism over access to females was common among Plains Indians. Hämäläinen reports that the more successful some Lakota Sioux men became, the larger the pool of men who struggled to marry at all. "It was a dangerous social pathology that threatened to divide the Lakota men into fully franchised and marginalized individuals" (2019:183). The Lakota pattern continues to be found in most American fundamentalist polygamous communities. It drove the Lakota, and, two hundred years later, Angle Park youth, "to see one another as [more often than not] rivals rather than comrades" (183).

When the intergenerational competition becomes more explicitly voiced, it signals a disenchantment with the person's belief system, which makes the continued adherence to that system more fragile and suspect. John Saul reminds us that a culture's ideology is, "like theater, dependent on the willing suspension of disbelief. Once the suspension goes, willingness converts into suspicion—the suspicion of the betrayal" (2004:41). Although Mormon fundamentalist youth retain a deep-seated commitment to their faith, many, especially during the adolescent years, simultaneously harboring a suspicion that the plural family is an institution with serious problems. Youth who are from a low-ranking family are seldom given a wife; thus most leave the community to find a mate, which inevitably results in her refusal to move to the polygamous community. Once a youth has left the community, there is a revision in how they conceptualize their childhood. Having an intimate understanding of the plural family's difficulties, they come to define themselves in opposition to the community's faith-based norms. However, when a youth comes from an elite family, or part of an elite family, he recognizes that he will indeed be assigned a mate and tends to be less drawn to leaving the community. The ability of elite families to hold on to their sons results in "clan cannibalism," whereby elite males attract daughters from nonelite families who prefer to marry into the more elite families. This pattern of incorporating low-ranking females into higher-ranked families over time results in the high-ranking families becoming "larger, more powerful, and to reproduce more successfully overtime, while low-ranking families . . . become smaller, less powerful, and reproduce less successfully" (Levine and Silk 1997:381).

Whatever the quality of a youth's home life or his father's social rank, there are other social structural factors that contribute to a limited marriage market. It is telling that the community adopts a blind eye to this reality: the shortage of females. In avoiding the structural deficiency inherent in a plural family system, the community finds solace in its nineteenth-century metaphysical perspective, which puts the inability to find a mate on the individual's lack of character or weak moral fiber. For the community, the youth who leave represent God's rejection of them as suitable candidates for living in "God's chosen community." In the common parlance of the community, a youth is either a "good" person or a "Devil" person. The distinction is common in many fundamentalist communities, which habitually, constantly, draw lines between the "elect" and the "damned" or unsaved (Williams 1991:811). A youth's departure is regarded as a simple example of one "losing the spirit of the Lord" and therefore "losing the spirit of the Work."

Females, in contrast, have no worries about finding a spouse. They are concerned about the quality of their future husband—whether or not he is a decent man and he is too old. This does not mean that some females do not have occasional existential doubts about the viability and suitability of forming a plural family. Unlike males, however, they have a certain safety: they can always return and be immediately honored for doing so. Nonetheless, many females struggle with the existential decision to stay or leave. A number of them admit having been "wild" as teenagers and, in their words, "sinned often." Some girls will leave the community and take up with a boyfriend, drink in excess, and, surprisingly, join in sex parties, only to discover in their early twenties that they truly belong in the community and that leaving was a mistake. For example, one young woman wrote a letter to her mother praising the polygamous family, admitting she became close to being damned but now wishes to return to become a plural wife, stating that she feels refreshed and fulfilled in the prospect of doing so. She thanked her mother for her love and for never abandoning the hope that she would return. In Angel Park, prodigal daughters are warmly invited back and immediately placed in another family. There is less desire, less willingness, to accept youthful prodigal sons, who, unable to find a wife from the community, must thus go outside it, seldom returning. When the community does welcome a male back, he is always middle aged or older, and if he finds a wife it is often a postmenopausal widow who expects him to be her protector and benefactor.

The critical issues that polygamous parents must deal with include: 1. children's lack of nurturing or bonding with siblings, 2. cowives' aggression directed toward their children, and 3. doubts about their offspring's ability to live the Work. Although parents respond in their own way to these issues, they often do so in a different voice, rooted for the most part in gender. Men, as the real or symbolic head of the family, tend to talk in moral axioms and religious dogma, whereas women respond with greater variation, making pragmatic adjustments that take account of situational factors. This is due, in large part, to mothers being more involved with their natal offspring through interaction on a daily basis. This is not unique to Angel Park but can be found in other polygamous communities, where "women often have stronger ties of affection to children and grandchildren than men do" (Foner 1984:115). It is not new to present-day reality. Nineteenth-century diaries are filled with entries of women thinking about the strength of their involvement with their offspring (Ulrich 2017).

No one in the community publicly rejects the official doctrine of plural love. It remains an ideal worth striving for if only in people's imagination, almost everyone believes. For most, it is an ideal best left in the abstract realm, while one works at doing one's best in day-to-day life. Most men tend to ignore the contradiction and think of plural love as a goal they can someday achieve: if not in this life, then in the next life. The fundamentalists' communitarian impulse is for everyone to live in the spiritually unified and socially harmonious plural family. To do so, however, requires overcoming structural tensions and restraints common to plural family living. In addition, there are demographic factors that are often too powerful for most males to overcome. This is common to every polygamous community. For example, Bennion (2012) reports that 65 percent of the males in her Montana community left over the inability to find a mate. Eckholm reports that in a nearby city private groups have formed a center designed to help banished boys (primarily from FLDS community) adjust to life outside the community. There are one hundred boys at the center, with 70 percent having been expelled from the FLDS community, but not the Angel Park community, which refuses to engage in this practice (Eckholm 2007:9).

Every family in its own way strives to raise a good person and must consider more than just a straightforward application of church doctrine. The demographic realities ensure there will always be a skewed ratio of more males wanting a wife than there are potential wives available. This skewing further accounts for young males' acute anxiety over whether they can marry and thus remain in the community. It is the sociological factor that leads youth to engage in serious, often internal reflection on the viability of their religion. As a result, successful adolescence socialization depends upon more than effective parent-child interaction, a necessary but insufficient condition for producing what the community deems its major spiritual and cultural ideal: the production of men and women not only capable of but in fact forming a plural family.

# 11

## THE LONELY WORLD OF POLYGAMOUS MEN

*"A man must learn to live and uphold God's law; to do less is a sign of failure"* (a man with numerous wives).

*"I pretend not to see anything and leave everything alone"* (a man's philosophy toward family management).

*"You do not understand what is involved living in a plural family"* (a man speaking to the media).

A recurrent media image of the polygamous family holds it as a bastion of male privilege where men are the primary beneficiaries of the plural marriage system, while experiencing little stress or burden in providing for their family. This image is completely at odds with men's actual lives. I found that many men are psychologically tormented whenever they failed to live up to their religious convictions and failed to meet the expectation of forming a harmonious loving plural family. The deeper the religious devotion of a man, the greater his anguish will be if he does not succeed in providing proper care for his plural family. The goal—the challenge of the goal—is not a matter of singular events or the ordinary defeats of everyday life. It is a life-long aspiration, an unceasing struggle to meet the responsibilities that every husband as a provider and as a parent will face over the course of his marriage.

Although the community's core values often stand in opposition to personal emotional needs and pragmatic interests, men remain steadfast in their commitment to shape and direct a family that is integrated and balanced. In this chapter, I want to explore the financial and existential pressures placed on polygamous males. I will probe the reasons why so many men are in emotional turmoil over their inability to achieve their life goal: creating a harmonious loving family. I will further explore the ways in which they struggle, set aside, and deny their family's shortcomings, thus lessening their chances of maintaining their faith and living a rich meaningful life.

## DUELING VALUES: INDIVIDUALITY OR PATRIARCHAL ABSOLUTISM

Angel Park and Pinesdale (Montana) women agree that it is more difficult for men to live the Principle, the creed, than it is for women. The primary reason is that men carry greater and more diverse responsibilities that they must fulfill to remain good citizens of the church. To most men these responsibilities feel like weights are bearing down on them, which results in numerous arbitrary or unsystematic ways of meeting family and church obligations while also rejuvenating themselves as distinct individuals (Compton 1997:417).

Thomas O'Dea (1957) was the first to point out that there is an implicit contradiction within Mormon theology: an emphasis on self-actualized individualism with an insistence on patriarchal absolutism. If obedience, servitude, and self-surrender are the essential virtues, how can individuals cast off restraints to develop themselves? If self-development is also a virtue, how can individuals adapt to religious authority?

Contemporary fundamentalists differ from mainstream Mormons only to the degree to which they acknowledge or accept a person's right to disagree. The fundamentalist communities of FLDS and Kingston, located in the United States, and Bountiful, located in Canada, restrict individual expression in favor of absolute obedience. The more open polygamous communities of Allred, LeBaron, Pinesdale, Centennial Park, and Angel Park embrace the American cultural ethos that values the cultivation of personal autonomy and self-fulfillment. They do not believe that the highest moral purpose is "unfettered individualism where man exists for his own sake, in the pursuit of his own happiness" (Putnam 2020:187). They also do not believe that the best life is one where you "celebrate, assert, and advertise yourself" (Brooks 2016:499). Rather, fundamentalist communities believe that it is virtuous and worthy to embrace in-group norms such as duty, obligation, and sacrifice (Inglehart 2020). They readily agree that what is best for "the greater Us, is what is best for the smaller You" (Greene 2013:23). The recognition and embrace of a "greater Us" is not as totalizing or complete, however, as it may seem.

There is an inherent contradiction in an fundamentalist cosmology that values both individual self-reliance and in-group harmony. Many of the conflicts, expressed and unexpressed, that occasionally erupt in the plural family arise from the uneasy relationship that individuals have in trying to blend the two oppositional values into a manageable whole (Putnam 2020). To establish a stronger degree of interfamilial cooperation, it is essential for the collective interest to triumph over individual interest. In effect, participants "must willingly agree to pay a personal cost (i.e., give up something) to the benefit of others" (Greene 2013:23). This orientation generates, in turn, an underlying public morality that values altruism, unselfishness, and a willingness to sacrifice for the greater good (23).

Fundamentalists believe they are engaged in a moral struggle with themselves for greater insight and self-improvement that will lift them up to a level of worthiness to enter heaven. In this endeavor, character enrichment is essential. A thoughtful man, reflecting on his own path of character improvement, said to me: "I know I have sinned and, to overcome my selfishness, I must become a soldier in the army of the Lord, who will help me battle the Devil and become a more righteous and worthy person." Or, in the words of a thirty-something man: "I have a lot of growing up to do. I see my weakness. I love the idea of creating a loving plural family. I accept the things it stands for." A test of the importance of character development is a man's response to being assigned a wife. In one case, the man at first had no interest in developing a bond with her. He preferred video games and playing softball with his friends. He talked only of himself and how good he was at this or that . . . But five years later, he changed. Whenever he and his wife went somewhere, he held her hand. He ceased to hang out with his male friends, fully embracing his family responsibilities. People who knew him noted that he had become more righteous in his approach to life. When I got to know him better, I asked about his past, and he willingly shared his journey into what he considered the development of a new character from within himself. He acknowledged that he had become humbler. He stopped beginning every sentence with "I." He no longer criticized his wife and began to pay real attention to her requests. He found satisfaction in assisting her in ordinary tasks. As his love for her increased, he worried whether or not he would be able to integrate a new wife into the family. He feared that taking a second wife would disrupt the bond he had developed with his first wife. Since he was raised in a large family, he knew that adding new wives could be a source of family disruption. He was devoted to his religion, however. He understood the importance of learning how to bring multiple wives together into a harmonious whole. After prolonged reflection, he believed that he would take a new wife if the church felt he was worthy. His story highlights the reluctance of many husbands to take a new wife just for the sake of having another wife. His initial skepticism and apprehension lay aside the preconception of mainstream culture that polygamous men are customarily eager to obtain additional wives.

Because an individual's salvation rests on an act of faith and commitment to the development of a more virtuous character, Angel Park men and women are self-reflective about how best to become a better person. For most, their religious values provide a baseline from which they quantify and put into perspective their sinful acts and their virtuous behavior. In the community, it is a recurrent theme in most of my conversations. A youth explained, "You have to progress [i.e., in personal development]. I do not care how long you live, you have to be constantly learning new things." A mature man stressed to me how essential it is to embrace one's responsibilities, since "they are the foundation of your character." He elaborated: "I pay my tithing, sometimes my family funds are low, and I am not sure if I should give to the church, but then I recall that paying your tithe first good things will happen. I find that to be true; I obey the word of wisdom and lead my family in prayer. I advise my wives to be righteous and my children to live up to our values. The Devil and the outside world are always trying to undermine us, so we must be strong in our beliefs." Considering further, he added, "Most importantly, I feel I must set a good example of how to live a righteous life." Given their convictions, the majority's internal dialogue is framed within a theological context that encourages self-reflection on the best methods, in the words of a longtime church member, "to overcome my weakness, my imperfections and be prepared for the glorious resurrection." I found that every member of the congregation engaged, at one time or other, in this kind of critical self-reflection—although some members are more devout and aspirational than others.

During the first few years I visited the community, I was struck by the intensity of its religious convictions. The first two hours of every conversational exchange I had with them focused on their religion and their place within it. Gradually I realized what was being conveyed to me was the unmistakable serious- ness of the connection with their religion and their identifica- tion with it. I think these spontaneous self-reviews of the rela- tionship to their faith underscores their intense introspection and concern for character development. Their readiness to share their experiences and feelings tells me that their faith, and its mean- ing, are far more important than any inhibition or reluctance they might have in disclosing their inner thoughts to an outsider like myself.

Angel Park men and women are cognizant of their difference to others. They are aware how mainstream culture, or, in their phrase, "out in the world," views the plural family. The aware- ness of their marginality extends and deepens an internal dia- logue over what it means to be human and, more important, how to become a good person. The presumption that the plural mar- riage lifestyle is spiritually superior enhances esteem for the com- munity's men while providing a criterion to assess their personal lapses and failings. It also accounts for a relentless self-criticism as well as criticism of others in the family that can result in a view or acknowledgment of being unworthy. "The problem in my home is," a man disclosed to me, "that we do not love one another enough, we aren't close enough, we cannot forgive one another—this is our weakness."

Because sustaining cooperation is "the central problem of social existence" (Greene 2013:20), there is always "some tension between self-interest and collective, between Me and Us that is [continuously] in danger of eroding" (Greene 2013:21). The fundamentalists are not alone in their struggle to maintain a cooperative spirit within a plural family structure that is filled with self-reflective individuals. In this setting, the husband is more responsible for resolving tensions that arise within the family. It is a task that requires everyone's support, but, whether he receives or does not receive the family's full support, it is the husband who, in the end, is either admired or disdained, appreciated, or derided, for his ability or inability to form and maintain a harmonious family.

Because men operate and administer the "priesthood," the divine spiritual authority, it is understood that they have a special responsibility to guide their family in the ever-challenging task of family governance. The fundamentlist husband calls on his religious vows, designed to remind everyone to respect and help each other. Likewise, his responsibility to financially provide for and fulfill his wife's emotional needs is understood. This responsibility is not simply a spousal and family one but also a metaphysical obligation that is a ceaseless and, at times, disruptive psychological force forever tugging at a devoted man's consciousness, leading to the question "am I worthy?" The extent to which this responsibility and obligation make up a polygamous man's identity, and constitute his inner self, remains a subject that calls for future study and investigation. Nevertheless, the burden of his religious obligation is invariable and fixed. One wife recalls, for example, the overwhelming guilt that her husband felt when he could not successfully shape or guide his family. An adult offspring told me that his father used to remark that his wives "say they work things out, but they never did." The phrase "work things out" is the common expression. One evening, his father described the advice he gave to his wives: "Now don't go to your room, you stay in the kitchen and learn to associate better." His favorite wife, more influential, looked at him and walked back to her room. He never commanded her to return. Afterward, he retreated to his own room." When I asked a mature man who had numerous wives what pressures he felt when guiding his plural family, he vociferously responded: "You ask what pressure? Three words: emotional! economic!! and pragmatic!!"

A review of polygamous literature from around the world found that there is a heavy financial burden inherent in most polygamous families (Jankowiak, Sudakov, and Wilreker 2005). For most, the plural family is closely correlated with a lower quality of material well-being. Janet Bennion also found that Pinesdale men could not "feed and clothe all their children, much less their wives" (1998:72). In Angel Park, many men feel an intense strain and constantly worry over their lack of wherewithal to support their family's unforgiving needs (e.g., mortgage payments, sudden mental emergencies, dentist bills, wedding anniversaries, children's school supplies, clothing, and so forth). They find the bills that sometimes seem to be for just "this or that" unrelenting. As one man summed it up: "I feel like I will never get ahead. Then a car breaks down." Some men wonder whether only well-off families should practice plural living. This notion when expressed is always met with a sharp rebuke: "So only the wealthy can practice our religion?" The rhetorical question shifts the conversation to a neutral or uncontroversial subject while leaving unresolved the genuinely relevant question of how an honest but not wealthy man can satisfactorily provide for his plural family. Although men tend to push aside the issue and thus avoid asking the question, I was aware of some men who are unable to free themselves of the anxiety of not being able to provide for their family.

Providing for one's family also includes a metaphysical component: men's obligation to be a moral leader of and for his family. A longtime member of the community confessed to me that he was most troubled by his family's "not being able to come close enough—it seems we do not love one another enough." He elaborated: "I feel responsible for this, but do not know how to make it better." Another man, reflecting on the dynamics of his family, thought they were "united but often could not forgive one another; it is our weakness." The most disheartening aspect of the problem was his: " I see this as my weakness—my inability to bring the family stronger, more righteous and one with the Lord."

Michael Quinn (1991) observed that fundamentalist men's social status or ranking within the community is linked to their success in three areas: attracting and holding onto wives, producing righteous children, and forming a relatively harmonious family. Quinn believes that there is an unspoken yet nonetheless seriously competitive tension among men about attracting the largest number of wives and producing the most children. This status competition for more of both can collide with the religious values that stress formation of a modest and virtuous character. There is an underlying expectation of humility and gentlemanliness on men's part. The tension between the two values presents a moral dilemma over which path to select. Everyone knows the community holds a deep admiration for the reproductive success of its founders (i.e., the original heads of present-day large families) who often had ten or more wives, along with thirty to sixty offspring and hundreds of grandchildren. Participating in the competitive arena of mate selection intensifies a man's pressure to not only care for his existing family but also to continue to expand it. The desire "to grow" one's family has a materialistic downside. A man with numerous wives admitted, for example, that "sometimes I wonder how I am going to provide for all these children, then morning comes, and I renew my faith and conviction that my religion is correct. This is the Lord's expectation and I continue in the Work." His introspective acknowledgment of the often-dueling burdens that men face is representative.

Besides religious values, men are also influenced by the community's admiration for the ideal of the "good husband/father," one who not only financially provides for his family but can effectively unite it. The inability to do so produces regret, guilt and, for some, an existential angst that seems to never go away. The distraught emotion that men of Angel Park often feel is frequently shared by Palestinian polygamous men, who admit to being "stressed out" trying to balance their ethical commitment with their financial obligations (Nevo, Al-Kremni, and Yuval-Shani 2008). Concurring, Bennion has observed that Pinesdale males are in a continuous state of anxiety over the "enormous responsibilities that stretch their energies, finances, sometimes beyond endurance, especially if they are also required to donate a high percentage of their income to the Church" (1998:143). Clearly, men, around the world, can be not only emotionally overwhelmed trying to support their growing plural family but also deeply troubled over their inability to fulfill their religious commitments.

Some men just walk away. By chance, I met a man who no longer lived in the community. One day he decided to leave his family and drove to a large city; he never saw his family again.

During our chance meeting, he informed me that he had lost himself trying to fulfill his family obligations, saying, "I realized very early I did not have the ability to manage my family. I did not take the lead; I wanted out. My wives pleaded with me for directions, but I said no way you can work it out, but neither they nor I could work it out. I told them I did not want to; I do not want the responsibility. I hated my kids—I just left and never returned. I am sure it works for those who believe and work at it but for me there was the religion, which sounded real and right, and then I confronted my reality, which was failure." After a long pause, he added: "I chuckle whenever I hear monogamous men wishing for another wife . . . if they only could have their wish granted they would discover the truth of our religion. It is the men who suffer the most."

Besides having to render material support, men are often overwhelmed in trying to reassure the wives of their love. The community's folk ideal holds that the best marriages are formed when the husband develops a bond that is best suited to each wife. To achieve this, a husband will adopt a different persona, or personal approach, for each wife. These personae vary greatly, but many involve interacting as a sensitive counselor, pragmatic psychologist, stern theologian, and thoughtful lover, or some combination of them all. But men find adopting a different persona with each wife to be exhausting, an almost impossible task. This near impossibility is echoed by a man who had recently had taken a second wife: 'I thought I could focus on the new wife and reassure her until I could see both together. Now I realize I cannot. In a way, each wife is an [emotional] bottomless pit where you need to spend quality time with each of them." Angel Park men agree with Palestinian men who acknowledge the Quran, which states that a man who wants to form a polygynous marriage must treat all his wives "absolutely equal—it is a stipulation that many have noted is practically impossible to meet except by a saint" (Lindholm 2002:232).

Kody Brown, the lead actor, and husband, in the popular TV series *Sister Wives* would agree. Although the Brown family receives a significant monthly payment for the TV crew's access to their lives, the plural family, after twelve seasons, is no longer willing to sustain, in public, a harmonious front. Increasingly the media reports a growing rift between Kody and his four wives. Christian now wants to divorce him, while Janelle and Meri are considering leaving too. Only his fourth wife intends to remain. Moreover, Kody admits he is disinterested in an emotional relationship with three of his four wives (Mauch 2022). Like Angel Park husbands, Kody Brown is emotionally exhausted and burned out managing his plural family.

Because most plural wives expect, at least initially, to develop a special relationship with their husband, their relative satisfaction or dissatisfaction will to some extent determine whether or not a family operates harmoniously, which will affect a husband's emotional well-being. Part of men's angst derives from their accord with their nineteenth-century Mormon counterparts that "God required wives to submit to their husband, [while] He also expected husbands to love and care for their wives, as Christ did the Church" (Ulrich 2017:40). To achieve the ideal, men need their wives to cooperate and hold together to sustain a unified plural family. For example, I went to a family dinner where the husband who sat between his wives put his arm around both while he spoke of taking one wife on a trip and the other wife on a different trip. What struck me about this exchange was the wives' reaction. Both stared straight ahead, then quickly glared at each other; not a smile was given. Their husband at once realized that his effort at expressing family unity had failed, then pulled his arms back, overwhelmed with his failure to display to a visitor the unity of his family. Later he confided to me: "it is such a burden being attentive to everyone." His observation about the seemingly endless challenge of creating unity is not usual. Another example of this disappointment in the LeBaron community is a husband who repeatedly told one of his wives: "This is hard on me, too. Don't think it doesn't tear me up to see you unhappy. I'd never do it if God hadn't commanded it . . . I can't even keep two wives' content, let alone three" (Spencer 2007:167). Often during incident of family disunity, men experience the same kind of anxiety and sometimes angst that leaders in other areas of life experience. In the case of polygamous husbands, they have persistent doubts that they are not worthy of forming a harmonious family or do not have the capacity or skills to do so.

One deeply religious man believed that, if he was fair and righteous in leading his family, his wives would willingly cooperate and work together in the joint task of creating a workable plural family. When he married a new wife he discovered that "each family has its own history—I was naive—at first I wanted to combine my wives together and create a new history together. But we are unable to—primarily because they are unable or refuse to work together—so, I now have two families and drift between them." His realization of the difficulty with previously formed families is not unusual. Part of the difficulty stems from the family not living together. The available houses differ in size. Wives who live in a separate house develop a different family history than those who live together in a large house. A husband whose wives do not all live together suffers in his sense of belonging, lessening his chances of the complete connection needed for a successful marriage and harmonious household.

Every Angel Park man that I knew who shuttled between households did not have his own bedroom but stayed in his wife's bedroom. This pattern of moving from bed to bed accounts, in part, for their being less psychologically invested in their homes. A plural wife told me that "my husband sometimes forgets where he is or who is the person next to him. He often forgets where he left his clothes" (Udall 1998:2). Brent Jeffs, living in a different community than Angel Park, recognized the emotional toll his father experienced moving between his wives' households (Jeffs and Szalavitz 2009). I spoke with one husband who disliked the arrangement of having to go from one house to another. He thought that all his wives should live together in one big house. The shuttling back and forth produced an emotional detachment in which his wives would treat him like "a visiting relative home for a few days" rather than as "the master of the family." Angel Park men, like those in Allred and FLDS who rotated between households, feel little or "no emotional attachment to their home" (Altman and Ginat 1996:258). Given the difficulty of achieving a sense of belonging, Angel Park men believe it is better to live together in one big house. In contrast, the LeBaron community believes that each wife needs her own house and discourages them from living together. The community leadership there believes that a wife is more content having her own home because it relieves some of the pressure on her husband to satisfy her wants. In the LeBaron community, it is understood that the "best" marriages are those where the wife is the more satisfied spouse. Another factor that contributes to men feeling at times overwhelmed is the lack of privacy or personal space. Although the common places of public understanding stress the value of in-group harmony, fundamentalists are more like mainstream American culture that socialized its youth to be independent, discouraging interdependency. This makes the need of polygamous men for privacy or occasional solitude a pressing issue. One mature man with several wives told me that "sometimes you can be overwhelmed by the whole situation."

A mature man complained that "*I can never be alone*—it is so time consuming being with my wives and children all the time. Do not get me wrong, I love my wives, but sometimes I just want to be alone." Some men seek solitude by going on long walks or hiking in the mountains. Others retreat into their "man cave" to play computer games or watch TV, while avoiding interaction with their children and wives. The research of Altman and Ginat (1996) found this a common response of men in living another fundamentalist community.

Another source of stress is not being able to truly relax even within the domain of intimacy. Men fear, as one man told me, that "what you tell one wife (in secret) will always come back to you in the future. You must always be deliberate, careful in your choice of words." He elaborates for me: "This is what is meant for a man to sacrifice and build character." Typically left unspoken is the pressure or need to always remain guarded in expressing fears, doubts, concerns. The good husband must keep his own counsel and not seek emotional support from his wives, who may use their disclosures of emotion as information that in other contexts undermines his family authority.

In the effort to reduce family pressure, husbands often respond to their wives' complaints with indifference or denial. The common response—often a refrain for some men—to "work it out" may be a wise or effective approach in resolving minor family disagreements, but it also allows men to ignore or avoid the larger issue: not facing up to the structural and personal difficulties in trying to live God's law. Some men will do almost anything to escape the drama of plural family living. Women, for their part, routinely talk about the details of family living. Husbands detach themselves from the daily grind of plural family management and typically leave such problems as a child's illness, absence of sufficient food and proper clothing, or a car in need of repair to their wives. Husbands can look past these problems because they know their wives will solve them. Husbands will rationalize their lack of participation, often making remarks such as "women engage in silly quarrels." In some cases their explanation is more elaborate. One husband caught the feeling of it all when he told me: "I'm so sick of listening to other women bitch about other women's kids. I just do not want to hear about it." There is a layered burden in everyday living where husbands can feel overloaded with problems and responsibilities. Some can grow more and more removed from their families. In any case, polygamous families adhere to the same traditional division of labor between husband and wife that mainstream American culture did in the first half of the last century.

The pressure of plural living sometimes can break out into spousal abuse. A wife's resistance or defiance can present a challenge to a man's ideal as a good provider and leader of his family. In these situations, he will take on an inflexible authoritarian persona or retreat entirely from the family with feelings of anger, resentment, and disillusionment. I knew several men who were adamant about not physically abusing any of their wives. One man explained his perspective: "I never, never hit my wife. That is pure physical abuse. I don't believe in that. Just because men are responsible—he is the caregiver and protector and not someone who takes or uses physical force to impose his will on someone else." The church leaders, as noted, often criticize its members for not being able to control their anger and abusing their wives. The leaders take an active role in addressing the problem by providing counseling for married couples as well as individuals as needed. I found that the more educated a spouse, especially husbands, the more comfortable he or she was in talking about whatever concerns they had and, in the case of husbands, talking through a wife's complaints rather than using physical force.

A man's ability to learn and become smarter from interacting with his family is not typically a simple or easy progression, but for many men it can happen. The ability to adapt or modify one's behavior is one of the reasons why husbands who have a business and are college educated are more successful in creating and maintaining a highly functioning plural family. These men are comfortable listening, engaging in conversation, and compromising as well as rendering sound advice. Families that are headed by men who are not at ease communicating with their wives and children do not function on a consistent basis, often experiencing ongoing problems, unlike families that work together in a cooperative way because the husband is relatively more sensitive to his wives' emotional needs. Unafraid of losing authority over the family, they can engage in pragmatic adjustments. For example, a wife recalled that as her husband aged he became more at home with himself and his role and less strict with his children. She described it this way: "My husband changed, he was less worried and uptight and could smile more. I could feel the pressure leaving his body."

Men take their obligations and the responsibility of integrating a new wife into the plural family seriously. One mature man recalled the experience of being assigned a twenty-year-old woman as awkward and anxiety producing. He told me that he had to learn "new ways to communicate and to develop new ways to respond so I can better comfort her." He understood the need to protect her against possible abuse from sister-wives while at the same time working to prevent them from reacting and withdrawing from the family. It was a balancing act to have to work with everyone, a time-consuming process that turned his family into an arena of discussion and negotiation. In the end, his labors proved successful, finding just the right touch to integrate the new wife into the family. His behavior is typical of well-functioning families, often involving a route to success that required flexibility and care. But this is not typical of dysfunctional families, where a man may take one or more wives at the same time and then pull back and tell everyone to "work it out." Whenever this kind of behavior occurs, the family becomes the site of resentment and frustration, which finds an outlet in public gossip, eliciting ridicule at the man's inability to form a harmonious family. In that kind of situation, where the husband feels overwhelmed by his duties, he will walk away or pretend, albeit unsuccessfully, that everything is fine. His general denial and success at avoiding criticism are always short-lived, since the community's commentary about lack of skills is relentless.

Men think that their wives have it easier since they can withdraw from family life, while their husband, the mediator in all things, should not, as it is considered a breach of responsibility to not comfort and talk through family issues. The withdrawals can last a few minutes, a couple of hours, or months on end. One man told me that what bothered him the most was not being able to satisfy the needs of all his wives. I found that he had many wives who needed his presence, often at the same time. With some exasperation, he said, "it troubles me so much that the kids need me, my wives need me—who should I see first. How can I reassure them? This bothers me a lot. Alas, other men just walk away angrily, commanding: "Deal with it." Others will simply go into their bedroom, while others will seek out their favorite wife, pulling away from the continual onus of managing the larger family and seeking sympathy and understanding from their favorite wives.

Angel Park women readily state that in their view it is more difficult for men than women to live the fullness of the Principle or achieve the religious goals of being just, kind, and creating a harmonious plural family. Pinesdale men report being frequently frustrated in their roles as father and husbands. In trying to juggle the several relationships and provide for so many people, many found the experience overwhelming (Jankowiak 2008). Janet Bennion estimated that 65 percent of the women she knew were satisfied with plural living, whereas 72 percent of the men were dissatisfied (2012). I found Angel Park men shared many similar concerns with the Pinesdale community, but the percentage of satisfied women is lower. Dawn Porter, a journalist, who visited different fundamentalist communities, found that husbands also felt weighed down trying to cope with their wives' emotional uneasiness. She described one case where a husband would return home from work and, before going inside, sit in his car thinking: "OK, which one is going to be mad at me now?" (Porter 2008). I knew of a similar case where an Angel Park man with two wives acknowledged becoming "overwhelmed by the whole situation . . . I sometimes wondered about this life and then I recall my children and what they mean to me and then I just soldier on."

A man's offspring are aware of their father's burden and its impact on his well-being. One said, in a gentle and affectionate tone, "My mother always defended Dad. She would say: 'you do not understand the pressure he's under.' Or would say: 'When you are older, you will understand his reasons.' My mother never criticized Dad in front of me. She always stood up for him." He elaborated: "When I left the community and later returned I asked my father how he can handle all his family obligations. He sighed, 'You have to keep your faith. You have to believe this is the way God wants you to live.' He then smiled and added: 'if I lived a different way, I would never have had you.'" Another woman told me about a man who had several wives and over fifteen children: "He had an epiphany. He called his family together to inform them that he did not want any more children. He knew he could no longer meet his financial and instructional responsibilities. He realized he had made a mistake in forming a plural family, but they would remain in the community as an independent family that is no longer affiliated with the church. For emphasis, he said: 'Plural family may work for some, but it does not work for me or this family.'" "I think," she continued, "that he must have been suffering a long time trying to decide what to do." Though this is an extreme case, the pressures being the same for husbands as for wives as they mount; suffering is clearly not a female monopoly. It can be a hard lifestyle for everyone.

## DYADIC LOVE AND THE GUILT CONSCIOUS

The Angel Park family is organized around religious values of humility and gratefulness and consequently the rejection of any form of selfishness, pride, and arrogance. The values serve to promote harmonious plural love within the family. Although harmonious plural love is the official ideal, it is vulnerable to sexual and romantic desires. Men, in particular, fear these desires because to act on them is to undermine their ability to be effective leaders of the family.

In Angel Park, whenever men discuss the possible benefits of placement marriage, the one they stress most is the avoidance of emotional entanglements. The assumption is that an emotional connection is unlikely to develop because they have no prior relationship with the woman they will marry. What is truly significant is how frequently they do not get the anticipated benefit. As it has a way of sometimes doing, reality intervenes, and one gets the opposite of what one had hoped for. In their case, most of these men do develop an emotional connection, a connection that some grudgingly acknowledge and others silently embrace. This is not a recent phenomenon. The connection presents a serious challenge for the plural family. Lawrence Foster's historical research discovered that romantic love often undercut and disrupted the nineteenth-century Mormon plural family (1991:187–189). I also found romantic love to be a continued source of family upheaval and personal guilt.

In Angel Park, each person must reconcile in his or her own way the often deeply troubling emotional experience—initially both desired and feared—that is associated with being passionately in love. Many men dismiss or downplay the value of emotional love, believing that it is, at bottom, an illusion and not the firmest basis for a marriage. The strength and consistency in which this belief was expressed initially persuaded me that fundamentalist men seldom felt anything that resembled passionate love for a spouse. More in-depth probing, however, found that two-thirds of the men I interviewed had been rejected as young men in high school. Some had secret crushes. All of them had hopes of being placed with a particular woman. Most were not. The leadership is unaware of these love crushes because they are held in secret. For the young men, the experience of rejection was so distressing that they decided to never become emotionally involved again. I asked one man on his wedding day whether or not he was in love with any of his wives. He said that he was not and then disclosed that, while in high school, he had fallen in love with two women who rejected his overtures. He told me that "it hurt so much I decided never again to let myself experience that feeling." Twenty years later, he found himself in a deep and, at times, passionate love with one of his plural wives. Despite the surprising turnaround in his marital experience, and that of others, the anxiety of being hurt emotionally is common in Angel Park (Jankowiak and Allen 1995:283).

I was told about a man, for example, whose wives thought he was too cold, aloof, indifferent, and embittered to love anyone. They believed he "did not know how to express love." But after losing several wives, a neighbor observed that "he is worried about losing his last one. I think he is afraid of being alone. It scares him. I noticed he is more attentive to his last wife—fear can change a man. I suspect he no longer sleeps well at night (laughs). Maybe he thinks his wife will not be there when he wakes up." When I shared this account with another married man, he did not react, but acknowledged, "We know our wives love us, and yet if we do not return it or do it poorly or inconsistently we can undermine the entire family. I think and worry about this a lot."

Men's anxiety over the possibility of losing emotional intimacy through abandonment is revealed in the following account. A middle-aged woman recalls the anxiety of her beloved husband and his words on their wedding night: "Have you ever wanted something your whole life and, when you finally have it, you feel that it is going to be taken away from you?" No," she replied, "I guess I have not lived long enough to desire something that much." Then he told her that he was "so afraid of losing me because he loved me so much." That night she promised never to leave him. Twenty years later her husband, bedridden from old age, could no longer control his bowel movements. Whenever she grew weary of the tedious duties involved in bathing, feeding, and cleaning him, she remembered her wedding night promise never to leave him. She reaffirmed that promise this way: "I stayed with him because in the end I realized that I loved him. I know right now he is preparing a place for me on the other side and, when I die, he will come and take me back with him, but only if I am worthy" (Jankowiak and Allen 1995:286).

Mormon fundamentalist men's reaction to the loss of love, whether through death, divorce, or abandonment, resembles their American mainstream male counterparts, who tend to slowly recover from emotional separation. Men's capability for extended dejection due to the absence of romantic love is illustrated in the following account. A middle-aged woman unexpectedly met the son of a former high school classmate who had asked to marry her years ago. Much to her surprise, she discovered that the man had, for more than twenty years, harbored a love crush, which he only recently revealed to his young son. When the son met her, he remarked without any forethought: "So you are the woman that my father always talks about. He was so crushed when you married that older man" (Jankowiak and Allen 1995:285).

Another example of men's propensity to quietly endure emotional loss is found in the torment of a man whose second wife left him to join another polygamous community. When I asked him about it, the man did not want to answer because he was afraid it would cause him to relive the experience emotionally. However, his son told us: "My father was depressed for months. He lost the woman he loved." Another wife revealed that her husband was devastated when his third wife left the family, remarking: "When Sam's third wife left him for another man who had been secretly courting her, it affected his health. He cried for three straight weeks and simply deteriorated into an invalid. We buried him six months later" (Jankowiak and Allen 1995:286).

For Angel Park women, the absence or presence of romantic love, much more than role equity, constitutes the primary measure of the quality of their relationship. It also accounts for some of the heightened guilt and shame that men and women often feel in striving to live up to the principle of plural marriage. If a husband can avoid pursuing personal interests only and in turn struggle (or, in the word used by several husbands, make a "sacrifice") to uphold the religious principles, the household's ambience will be relatively harmonious and content.

Because the plural family, like a well-functioning society, thrives on trust (Fukuyama 1995) or the belief that its norms are not only fair but followed, the dyadic love bond is a potential threat to the trust that binds the plural family together. The polygamist husband understands that, if he becomes too attached to a particular woman, it may result in both disruption of family bonds and damage to his reputation within the community. Most men can ignore the negative gossip that is sometimes voiced in other families. But the real damage is personal and internal. The burden of management falls predominantly on the man. Men know that, if the family has the reputation of being disharmonious, it may be more difficult to attract a future wife. Given the unmistakable understanding of the possible consequence in forming an exclusive love bond, it is revealing that it remains a constant recurrence.

The power of love is so strong that when it is rejected it can push some men to respond irrationally. I was told of an instance where a man's favorite wife left him. He began hating her and paradoxically hating the children (a primary reason for forming a plural marriage) he had with her. After she left, he told them how much he hated them. He soon left the community and never returned. To the people who knew him, he was, in their view, always in some sort of psychological turmoil and never could reconcile his religious conviction and family ideal with the realities of his lived experience.

## SHAME AND HONOR: STRIVING TO BE A GOOD PERSON

Because the community strongly encourages ethical introspection and highly values the aspiration of becoming a more complete moral person, men are more prone to experience guilt and shame if they fail to live up to or fulfill what is for them a deepseated moral foundation. The yearning for emotional intimacy or dyadic exclusiveness compels many to acknowledge, if only to themselves, that they cannot love everyone with the same intensity. Therefore there is a ranking of preferences. The preferences are often not that closely weighed and assessed because the person has already had experiences with the other, and the experiences are felt and remembered without a deliberating process. Husbands typically do not struggle intellectually with the rankings; they can fall into place without much forethought.

It is the pursuit of emotional preference or intimacy that accounts for much of the anger and psychological turmoil in plural families. Both stem from the guilt, and the anger and turmoil will turn back on the guilt, deepening it and thereby fueling a deeply disturbing cycle. My survey found that most polygamous men refer to and reflect on the value of harmonious love while living on a day-to-day basis in a monogamous love relationship with their favorite wife. Harmonious love has a longer arc of importance for husbands, whereas the experience of love with a favorite wife is immediate and does not prompt doubts about its impact on the people involved. It is the difference between abstraction and concrete personal experience, and both can have equally compelling impact and importance. I also found a few cases where men who were first-born sons rejected or resisted a dyadic love bond in favor of an aloof demeanor and emotionally reserve posture, which resulted in a life of loneliness and bitterness. The resulting dissatisfaction became readily apparent to their children as they came into adulthood. In the five homes where this was the reality, all the men's offspring openly acknowledged how lonely their father's life seemed in his plural family. Further, a profound sense of shame is concealed or secreted beneath the surface of many men and women's public presentations of propriety (Fessler 2004; Johnson 2017). For example, a young man, who had recently taken a new wife, told me straight out: "Sometimes I want to always be with my new wife, but I know that it is selfish, so I try to be with other wives. But then I feel abused for not seeing the wife I prefer and feel I am not living the fullness of the Gospel (i.e., polygyny)." On reflection, he added, "Sometimes I dislike myself for not being able to uphold my religious convictions."

It is an undeniable and unmistakable dilemma for men. They embrace the polygamous principle and its call for plurality while simultaneously seeking to hold onto or rekindle a romantic passion once felt toward a particular spouse. Although elevated love, the love esteemed by religious doctrine, is understood to be the ultimate value, passionate love remains a powerful force in the community. The reality is that most of the community's polygamous families seldom achieve a genuine long-lasting harmony; families remain, typically, a hotbed of competing interests that periodically rupture the already worn balance that unites a man, his wives, and children together in their religiously inspired cultural system. The clashing of values has resulted in a moral dilemma that never seems to be satisfactorily resolved (Brooks 2016). Although the community's public voice holds elevated love to be the superior value, passionate or exclusive dyadic love remains the preferred private option, even when denied. Sometimes the denial covers a strong desire for that love. The tensions that are expressed in struggles to reconcile this seemingly unreconciled moral dilemma is the source of much of the drama found in Angel Park homes. In this way, polygamy, for many residents of Angel Park, has become the embodiment of their religious convictions, anchored in an ethos of self-sacrifice that sustains their efforts to achieve a humble spirit. For most, there is no greater sacrifice than that involved in resisting the need to merge with another in an exclusive emotional and physical bond. The continuous struggle to achieve and maintain a life of humble self-sacrifice is, for most residents, evidence of their worthiness to achieve God's plan for humanity. It is also a statement of the strength of their beliefs.

## STRESSFUL LIFE AND MEN'S HEALTH

The cumulative effect of the daily pressures on a man's health is seldom discussed. Research has established that the ability to be emotionally intimate with another person is a strong predictor of health and happiness. When individuals are uncomfortable with intimacy or commitment they can easily feel discontented and immensely dissatisfied with life (Hendrick and Hendrick 2002:23). For Angel Park, I found this to be true too. I suspect that one of the more common responses to the pressures embedded in plural living is excessive drinking. In Angel Park, alcohol consumption is very common. It is not unknown for some men to drink in their workshops or overconsume when they come home. Irene Spencer (from the LeBaron community) recalls how her husband tried to manage his emotions through the overconsumption of alcohol, which he took "before he came to see any of us" (2007:28).

The pressure of complex family living can affect a person's mental health. The research of Nevo, Al-Kremni, and Yuval-Shani (2008) among Palestinian families found that polygamous women experienced more mental health issues than their monogamous counterparts. Other research conducted in Saudi Arabia where polygamy is legal discovered that polygamous men have higher blood pressure, higher rates of diabetes, and higher rates of coronary artery disease than monogamous men (Daoulah 2015). Dr. Amin Daoulah, who conducted the research, speculated that there is a persistent financial burden and emotional expense in caring for so many households. Although I did not obtain Angel Park health statistics, I would not be surprised if the health records of the fundamentalist community proved to be similar. In 1999 there were only ten Angel Park men over the age of forty-nine who were active in the church. The other men had either died or moved away.

For most Angel Park families, the forming of a harmonious plural family is more an aspiration than an actual lived reality. This is not an easy lifestyle, with men experiencing a range of emotional stress: acute anxiety, vengeful pride, violent anger, existential guilt, deep regret, and occasional jealousy. I suppose that, once seen from inside the polygamous family, its dynamics look and feel like those of any other family type or structure, though with a greater multiplicity of relations, tensions, and layers of circumstances and the more complex challenges that ensue. Seen from outside, the polygamous family looks distinctly different and, no doubt to some, odd or foreign. A prominent elder of a polygamous community once spoke the essential truth to those outside trying to look in. The occasion was the 2007 arrest of the infamous Warren Jeffs for marrying an underage girl, which produced a tremendous swirl of negative press around the issue of polygamy. When that prominent elder leader was asked by NBC reporters about his way of life, he responded with the disgruntled tone of an instructor: "You do not know what it means to live in a plural family." In short, what I, an outsider, learned is that the polygamous life puts (some would say "imposes") demands on every person in that life, and perhaps more so on men than women.

# CONCLUSION

## Themes and Trends

*"I tell all my wives: If you can't get along in one family, I will build everyone a separate house and I will not visit you until you want to act as a family" (a community member).*

S ince the Middle Ages, people have erroneously misunderstood the primary motivation for the establishment of a polygamous family. Contrary to the prevailing folklore, the polygamous family was never principally designed to satisfy male sexual desire. On the contrary, it is the institutionalization of a marriage and family system designed to increase reproduction to achieve an exalted spiritual state of being. It stands in contrast, therefore, to the monogamous family system, which is ideally anchored in the intimacy of a couple, complemented by active coparenting of the mother and father. The polygamous family system values and promotes the development of warm supportive relationships with all family members. Its structure is distinctly more collective than individualistic.

Every family is different. Because a person's place and understanding of family life is shaped by his or her position within the family, any investigation into the plural family requires probing the way fathers, wives, cowives, and offspring understand their place within the larger family structure. There are variations within variations. Still, there are prevailing themes and commonalities typical of most polygamous families. It is a misconception to think that most fundamentalist families live in bad faith and/or assert and affirm religious doctrine and moral standards they do not believe in—I found this not to be so.

Every community "exists on secrets and privacy" (Bailey 1994:55). Angel Park is no exception. To understand the community, it is essential to recognize the strength of individuals' dedication to core theological tenets, along with the pragmatic ad-hoc rationalizations that protect or advance individual interests, which at times may not be consistent with their religious beliefs. It is the interaction between moral conviction and private desires, albeit often denied, that shapes the cultural ambience commonly found in many polygamous families. These contradictory pressures account, in large part, for much of the family conflict and individual existential angst. In exploring the Angel Park complex family, I found the following underlying patterns, recurrent themes, and readily identifiable core features.

The father is an idealized and *adored* figure, but the mothers are more deeply loved and remain the central focus in organizing relationships between the children and themselves and relationships between the children and their father.

In contrast to the patriarchal ideology, most families have an unofficial mother-centric focus. It produces in the children a stronger bond and more intimate solidarity with their natal family than is found in the children's father's larger or "big" family. This does not mean that offspring do not identify with their father's larger family. They do value that identification. Rather, it indicates that there is a ranking of affective loyalties that begins with the natal mother-offspring bond that then extends outward to include other half-siblings and their mothers.

Despite the community's emphasis on upholding "big family" solidarity or harmonious love there is an emotional gradation in full-sibling and half-sibling self-identification. Full siblings are more closely bonded and identify with their natal mother's offspring or their full siblings than they do with their other "mothers" and their half-siblings.

Women are the primary agents behind the push toward a more exclusive couple-centered or dyad love intimacy. For example, most women prefer to celebrate their anniversary date and birthday with only their husband but not other sister-wives.

In Pinesdale (Bennion 1998), where many who did not grow up in the community and only later, in their more mature years (mid-forties), made the decision to join, cowives do sometimes form close friendships. I found in Angel Park, however, that few cowives were able to do so. At first this seems odd. Why would women who were raised in the community bond less closely than women who were raised outside the community in a monogamous family? I suspect the primary reason is personal choice. Pinesdale women, as adults who have lived in a monogamous marriage they found less than satisfying, made a decision to seek out and try living in a different family organization. Because it is a choice made only after living in a different family system, they are aware of the benefits and costs of life inside a plural family. In contrast, Angel Park women know no other family system. Although they too have the choice to agree or disagree to a suggested marriage, they have less opportunity to know themselves or what they want from a plural marriage. Having been raised in a plural family that is often rife with cowife competition and smoldering resentment, they understand that their marriage will probably mirror their mothers, and thus they may adopt a reserved and detached posture toward their sister-wives, who have also assumed an equally guarded persona that seems not to lessen over time.

Mutual suspicion contributes to the creation of a family environment where wives are content to either ignore each other or adopt a cordial quasi-colleaguelike attitude in their daily interaction. In larger families with numerous sister-wives, friendships do emerge, but these seem to be limited to those between two individuals, seldom extending to three or more cowives. Friendships between three cowives occur only when they are biological sisters or the by-product of an alliance formed to protect themselves against the wrath of another cowife.

Men do embrace the religious ethos and strive to love all their wives equally, but more often than not they fail in their effort. For most men, there is an acute existential struggle to achieve their exalted goal: creating a harmonious, loving plural family. Husbands more than wives experience acute guilt if they do not uphold the community ideal of plural and equal love and succumb to yearnings for a dyadic bond with one wife. These failures within plural or inclusive marriage demonstrate the sharp and critical difficulties these marriages frequently hold for the individuals living in a plural love society.

The community's young unmarried men are the most disadvantaged demographic category, a structural tension common to every polygamous community, which arises from an insufficient number of women who are interested in remaining in or joining the *work* (the term for creating and sustaining a polygamous family). The decision of young men to remain active in the church or to leave depends upon whether they can find a girl from the community to marry them. When young men remain unmarried, they find themselves in potential or outright conflict with the community's married men. In these cases, there is a subtle, often unvoiced but sharply felt, tension between the generations that is manifested in a variety of contexts. In contrast, the shortage of marriage-age women contributes to the enhancement of the marital value of middle-aged women.

Contrary to popular opinion, polygamous men do not have "out of control" libidos that compel them to take new wives for the sake of partner variety. I found that in high-functioning families husbands are cautious in accepting or inviting a new wife into their home.[1] Husbands are acutely aware that marrying another wife could undermine the delicate balance sister-wives have established among themselves. Although men may be tempted, most are reluctant to actively seek or accept a new wife without careful and extensive reflection, which often involves consultation with their wives and the priesthood council.

Religious salvation through reproduction, not sexual desire, is the paramount motivation for men wanting to form a polygamous family. The core motive is less about sex and more about paternity. The value placed on paternity is intertwined with social status, which is manifested in the religious ideal that a man with three or more wives is "more blessed" than men with less than three wives because the man with three or more can gain "entrance" into the next exalted level of the religious elite. Three wives are the threshold.

The cross-cultural literature is filled with accounts of cowife jealousy and open hostility. William Irons (1988) suggests that women tolerate to varying degrees living in a polygynous marriage. If a woman gains some benefit from being associated with a wealthy man's resources, or has an opportunity to form valued female coalitions, most women will find satisfaction in plural marriage.

Angel Park women's willingness to cooperate arises from whether there are sufficient material resources available to provide for themselves and their offspring. A corollary to this factor is her husband's ability and willingness to love and communicate with all his wives. Marital problems come about when one of these factors is absent. In that event, the family can easily break apart into a Hobbesian world of competitive individualism and fanatical self-serving rivalry.

The creation of a plural family does not always result in men or women finding psychological satisfaction. In fact, my contributors note that, in their respective societies, many husbands become easily "stressed out" as they strive to fulfill their family obligations.

The community's gradual quasi secularization brings opportunities and challenges. Working outside the community is something that the community increasingly gives much-appreciated acceptance to, while there is serious concern that it may lose more offspring to outside influences. This is especially so when applied to female choice. The increased presence of mainstream society's legal institutions provides Angel Park women with more resources of outside support than at any time in the community's history.

The recent decision by attorneys general in intermountain states to prosecute reported abusive behavior, but not polygamy itself, is evidence of further integration of many fundamentalist polygamous communities into modern life. The interjection of state authorities provides fundamentalist women with a new "resource of power," one where outside legal authorities actively support women in their effort to protect themselves and their children. Women no longer fear that contacting the state police will result in harming the community. Because women are now able to access social programs more than they used to, they are less tolerant of domestic abuse and less likely to quietly accept the loss of child support. But drawing in or involving outside forces does have the potential to further secularize the community, which has long striven to remain an enclave closed to the outside world. The outside world almost always creates a tension where a benefit to the community also brings with it a threat to the community.

Given the community's small population, it is understood that frequent intermarriage between families can result in genetic complications. A medical researcher, engaged by the community, confirmed the validity of the concern. The community fathers thought it advantageous to attract other families into the community, adding a different genetic pool of potential wives. This challenge has occurred among the FLDS community, which has the highest rate of fumarate deficiency in the world. It would not be surprising to find other polygamous enclaves that also have the same kind of complications, and perhaps at the same rate.

There is also the issue of emotional health. As earlier noted, a study on the mental health of Middle Eastern women found that Palestinian women in a polygamous marriage had more mental health problems than women in a monogamous marriage (Al-Kremni 1999; Al-Kremni and Graham 1999; Nevo, Al-Kremni, and Yuval-Shani 2008). Since I did not apply mental health instruments in my study, I can only speculate. I suspect that the strength of Angel Park women's religious commitment can mute, at least for a while, any disappointment and for a time reduce the severity of the emotional angst they may experience living in a plural family. If a woman believed she had entered a religious or spiritual contract with God, combined with her husband's striving to be "fair" in the distribution of material and emotional resources (the latter a significant factor in accounting for her emotional satisfaction or dissatisfaction), then she and her family may fashion a highly functional plural family. If either is absent, without real substance, or inconsistent, that family had low functionality, which intensified a woman's jealousy, anger, pain, and loneliness. Consequently, husbands also suffered. This increased when men took their ethical responsibilities seriously and tried but failed to provide financially and emotionally support their wives and offspring. Clearly, the polygamous family has a profound psychological impact on both sexes. This should not be surprising. Many monogamous marriages can also operate in a spectrum, from highly functional to seriously dysfunctional. The fact that there are some low-functioning monogamous marriages does not invalidate monogamous marriage as a viable marriage system. Similarly, the existence of low-functioning polygamous marriages does not invalidate polygamous marriage as a viable marriage system. Polygamous marriage in and of itself should not be viewed as unviable. The fundamental and more meaningful question is: why do some families manage to become more highly functioning than others?

In agreement with Bennion's findings (1998, 2004, 2020), I found that high-functioning families have sufficient financial resources to support the entire family, treat each other with mutual respect, promote cooperative exchange between cowives, and have an "enlightened" husband who routinely interacts and thus engages his family through regular dialogue. In these families, college education is a reliable predictor of greater, more supportive dialogue between cowives and between a father and his entire family including his wives. In addition, an "emotional support" wife who also is in regular dialogue with her sister-wives, reminding them of the importance of sacrifice and the value of cooperation, further supports the husband's position within the family.

Low-functioning families' dissatisfaction arises from lacking sufficient financial resources, less involvement of husbands, and indifferent sister-wives focused on the enhancement of their own interests rather than the larger family's interest. In these families, men and women are no longer, if they ever were, willing to sacrifice their own interests for the good of the wider family.

Besides material and social organization factors, the ability to sustain a working commitment to family harmony depends on how individuals, especially husbands, can manage their emotions within the domain of love. The impulse to form dyadic love is relentless. This impulse forms almost a subtext that operates within the more formal theological framework organized around the promotion of duty over emotional desire. The core existential dilemma embedded in the Mormon fundamentalist polygamous lifestyle is an individual's inability to overcome his or her yearning to form a dyadic love bond. The illicit love bond can readily be seen in a few places: in children's names, in full siblings' declaration of exclusivity, and in the creation of a dyadic bond between the favorite wife and the husband. Both the declarations and exclusive love bond are not announced or stated in public but are clearly seen in ordinary, everyday behavior.

The Mormon fundamentalist ideal of plural or multiple love bonds is similar to the contemporary cultural phenomenon of polyamory (or the ability to love more than one person) found across the world. Both strive to avoid creating or establishing emotionally exclusive dyads. The community readily acknowledges that the best family is where everyone takes pleasure in one another's well-being and finds joy in witnessing their love for their husband. But this is an ideal seldom realized in actual life.

Successful polyamorous unions are grounded in greater material affluence, linked to a personal commitment sustained through informal but ongoing conversations. In effect, polyamorous unions function as ad-hoc therapeutic groups when three or more individuals gather to discuss their relationship with each other and the benefits of their mutual love. Significantly, the issue of reproduction and care for offspring is not a matter of contention for sustaining most polygamous unions. In a polygamous family, each wife is primarily focused on providing care for her offspring. Plural wives do not have the opportunity to engage in regular in-depth conversations with family members. For most of them, focusing on their natal family is the primary way in which they organize their time and thus their relationship with their children and their husband.

Given the polygamous proclivity to form exclusive dyadic bonds, we are left with a critical question: can contemporary polygamous families endure over time? Their success will depend to a large extent on whether their members can uphold another equally salient and very human capability: sustaining a commitment to a cosmologically inspired ideal that says plural love is superior to monogamous love. This presents something of a paradox; humans are both a pair-bond species that desires to form dyadic unions, even when these are not culturally sanctioned, and one that shows an adaptive cognitive capacity to create alternative ways of living.

Angel Park is an intentional community that celebrates its faith or religious conviction as well as its commitment to the *hope* in creating and sustaining a high-functioning harmonious family. An insightful community member acknowledged, "The only way our system can survive is if we believe it can work—either now or later." It is everyone's desire and hope that they can overcome their more self-centered impulses and, through an "act of will," achieve what is to them God's ideal family. Unlike early American utopian experiments in family living, which lasted less than five years, Mormon fundamentalist polygamous communities, albeit small in numbers, have continued in some fashion or amalgam for more than 150 years. This suggests that whatever impulse and practical realities individuals face, there will be some who continue to live in a nonmonogamous family.

The relative continued success of plural family arrangement underscores the power of human imagination to form or shape an ethical ideal out of a commitment to marriage. Robin Fox (1993) argues incorrectly that polygyny is as desirable a form of marriage as the monogamous marriage, and that serial monogamy, which he characterizes as involving frequent divorce, separation of children from their parents, and the multiplication of stepparent relationships that may result in child abuse, is largely absent in polygamous families (see Bruce Whitehouse 2023 for an in depth discussion of polygyny in Mali). I found that these behaviors and issues are as present in plural marriages as they are in monogamous marriage and show no sign of diminishing. In this way, polygamous and monogamous marriages can be remarkably similar. What is admirable about American plural marriage is the idealization of marriage and its consequent power to create, sustain, and strive for a more expansive form of love.

And yet I am left with a sense that, however, noble an individual's commitment to his or her religious ideals, most community members are more disappointed than satisfied in that they have not experienced or created a culturally sanctioned harmonious big plural family. But that does not mean they do not experience a measure of satisfaction living in the community or creating loving bonds within their respective natal families and selective kin from other mothers.

Most have.

For most, the creation of the more idealized and thus exalted plural family remains a powerful, inspiring idea that is beyond the reach of most participants. Although it is more of an abstract ideal, most members believe in it and are proud to embrace it. They believe that, if they do not achieve the ideal family in this life, there is the next life when they will have the emotional tools and practical experiences to be more successful in restraining their personal desires so that they can not only live in a complex family system but also support and contribute to it. In this and in so many other ways, one of "the most interesting family experiments in American history has not really ended" (Bohannan 1985:83).

# NOTES

## 1. PLURAL MARRIAGE AND WHAT IT MEANS TO BE HUMAN

1. The community refers to its style of life as *polygamy*, rather than *polygyny*, the latter being the more academic term. Polygamy refers to having multiple spouses simultaneously, which can be either one man with several wives or one woman with several husbands. Polygyny refers to marriages with one man and multiple women. Mormon fundamentalists prefer using the word *polygamy*. They also use a variety of words to refer to plural or polygynous marriage. These range from "Plural Family," "The Work," "The Principle," or "Celestial Marriage" (Bennion 1998). In the following pages, I will defer to the community's preferred terms of *polygamy* or *plural marriage*.

    Polygyny has been studied primarily from a structural perspective, which seeks to understand its evolution as a form of adaptation to certain ecological restraints. With the notable exceptions of Young (1954) and Bohannan (1985), analysis of an individual's experiences in a polygamous household is, for the most part, overlooked.

2. "Monogamy in Animals," Wikipedia, November 16, 2006.

## 2. FUNDAMENTALIST POLYGAMY

1. Gordon Mathews, personal correspondence, May 1, 2022.

## 8. FAMILY POLITICS REVEALED THROUGH NAMING PRACTICES

1. Although anthropologists have explored women's efforts to maintain affective ties with their kin (Watson 1984; Fortes 1969; Wolf 1972), there are few parental investment studies that have probed for the motivation of women's choices.

## 9. THEOLOGY AND MOTHER CARE

1. To identify potential behavioral patterns, I sought to understand how siblings and their parents interacted in a variety of social settings, which ranged from church service to giving financial and domestic service support to attending a family member's "course of life" celebrations (e.g., birthdays and wedding receptions). Taken together, I was able to reach some conclusions as to the relative strength, vitality, and identification that siblings have for each other.

   Thirty-nine individuals were asked: "Did you ever borrow or give money to a brother or sister?" If the answer was yes, he or she was asked: "Is this sibling from your birth mother or from a different mother?" For babysitting preference, eight adults were asked: "Does a younger brother or sister ever babysit for your family?" If the answer was yes, they were asked: "Is this sibling from your birth mother or from a different mother?"

## CONCLUSION

1. High-functioning families is a distinction first introduced by researchers studying Palestinian family organization (Al-Kremni and Graham 1999; Nevo, Al-Kremni, and Yuval-Shani 2008). Janet Bennion successfully applies the distinction in her analysis of Mormon fundamentalist polygamous families (Bennion 2012, 2020). I have also found the distinction useful in my own work.

# REFERENCES

Agar, M. 1996. *The Professional Stranger: An Informal Introduction to Ethnography*. London: Emerald.

Al-Kremni, A. 1999. "Women of Polygamous Marriages in Primary Health Care Centers." *Contemporary Family Therapy* 21 (3): 417–430.

Al-Kremni, A., and J. Graham. 1999. "The Story of Bedouin-Arab Women in a Polygamous Marriage." *Women's Studies International Forum* 22, no 5: 497–509.

Altman, I. 1993. "Challenges and Opportunities of a Transactional World View: Case Study of Contemporary Mormon Polygynous Families." *American Journal of Community Psychology* 21, no. 2:133–161.

Altman, I., and J. Ginat. 1996. *Polygamous Families in Contemporary Society*. Cambridge: Cambridge University Press.

Arno, A. 1994. "Personal Names as Narrative in Fiji: Politics of the Lauan Onomasticon." *Ethnology* 33, no. 1: 21–34.

Atran, S. 2004. *In Gods We Trust: The Evolutionary Landscape of Religion*. New York: Oxford University Press.

Bailey, F. G. 1994. *The Witch-Hunt, or the Triumph of Morality*. Ithaca, N.Y.: Cornell University Press.

Bair, D. 1995. *Anais Nin: A Biography*. New York: Putnam.

Balzarini, R., C. Dharma, T. Kohut, L. Campbell, J. Lehmiller, J. Harman, and B. Holme. 2019. "Comparing Relationship Quality Across Different Types of Romantic Partners in Polyamorous and Monogamous Relationships." *Archives of Sexual Behavior* 48, no. 6: 1749–1767.

Barash, D. 2016. *Out of Eden: The Surprising Consequences of Polygamy*. Oxford: Oxford University Press.

——, and J. Lipton. 2002. *Myth of Monogamy: Fidelity and Infidelity in Animals and People*. New York: Henry Holt.

Barker, J. 2018. "Happy Birthday Karl Marx: You Were Right." *New York Times*, April 30: A1.

Barr, A., M. Dekker, W. Janssens, B. Kebede, and B. Kramer. 2019. "Cooperation in Polygynous Households." *American Economic Journal of Applied Economics* 11, no. 2: 266–283.

Barret, G. 2000. "Utah and Its Polygamist's Race Against Time to End Abuses." *USA Today*, February 2, D10.

Bellah, R., R. Madsen, W. Sullivan, A, Swidler, and S. Tipton. 1991. *The Good Society*. New York: Knopf.

Bennion, J. 1998. *Women of Principle: Female Networking in Contemporary Mormon Polygyny*. New York: Oxford University Press.

——. 2004. *Desert Patriarchy: Mormon and Mennonite Communities in the Chihuahua Valley*. Tucson: University of Arizona Press.

——. 2012. *Polygamy in Primetime: Media, Gender, and Politics in Mormon Fundamentalism*. Waltham, Mass.: Brandeis University Press.

——. 2020. "The History and Culture of Mormon Fundamentalism in the United States." In G. Shepherd, G. Shepherd, and C. Cragun, eds., *The Palgrave Book of Global Mormonism*, pp. 677–702. New York: Palgrave.

——, and L. Joffe, eds. 2016. *The Polygamy Question*. Logan: Utah State University Press.

Bistline, B. 1998. *A History of Colorado City*. Colorado City: Colorado City: Ben Bistline.

Bohannan, P. 1985. *All the Happy Families*. New York: McGraw Hill.

——. 2010. *How Culture Works*. Detroit: Free Press.

Boserup, E. 1970. *Women's Role in Economic Development*. New York: St. Martin's.

Bradburd, D. 1998. *Being There: The Necessity of Doing Field Research*. Washington, D.C.: Smithsonian Institution Scholarly Press.

Bradley, M. 1993. *Kidnaped from That Land*. Provo: University of Utah Press.

Brisen, E. 2013. *Brigham Young*. Washington, D.C.: Regency History.

Brodie, F. 1984. *The Devil Drives: A Life of Sir Richard Burton*. New York: Norton.

Brooks, D. 2008. "The Art of Growing Up." *New York Times,* June 6.

———. 2016. *The Road to Character*. New York: Random House.

Cannon, J. 1992. "My Sister, My Wife: An Examination of Sororal Polygyny in a Contemporary Mormon Fundamentalist Sect." *Syzygy* 1, no. 4: 315–320.

Chisholm, J., and V. Burbank. 1991. "Monogamy and Polygyny in Southeast Arnhem Land: Male Coercion and Female Choice." *Ethnology and Sociobiology* 12, no. 2: 91–113.

Chmielewski, W., L. Kern, and M. Klee-Hartzell. 1993. *Women in Spiritual and Communitarian Societies in the United States*. Syracuse: Syracuse University Press.

Clark, A., and I. Clark 1991. *Fathers and Sons in the Book of Mormon*. Salt Lake City: Deseret.

Collins, J., and T. Gregor. 1995. "Boundaries of Love." In William Jankowiak, ed., *Romantic Passion: A Universal Experience?*, pp. 72–92. New York: Columbia University Press.

Compton, T. 1997. *The Sacred Loneliness: The Plural Wives of Joseph Smith*. Salt Lake City: Signature.

Coser, L. 1974. *Greedy Institutions: Patterns of Undivided Commitment*. New York: Free Press.

Cragun, R., and M. Nielsen. 2011. "Social Scientific Perspectives on FLDS Raid and the Corresponding Media Coverage." In J. Cardell and L. Burton, eds., *Modern Polygamy in the United States*, pp. 209–235. New York: Oxford University Press.

Daoulah, A. 2015. "Polygamy Increases Risk of Heart Disease by More Than 4-Fold." *Science Daily*, April 28, p. 1.

De Munck, V., A. Korotayev, and D. Khaltourina. 2009. "A Comparative Study of the Structure of Love in the U.S. and Russia: Finding a Common Core of Characteristics and National and Gender Difference." *Ethnology* 45, no. 4: 337–357.

De Munck, V., A. Korotayev, J. De Munck, and D. Khaltourina. 2011. "Cross-cultural Analysis of Models of Romantic Love Among U.S. Residents, Russians, and Lithuanians." *Cross-cultural Research* 45, no. 2: 128–154.

Diderich, M. 2008. *Sibling Relationships in Step-families: A Sociological Study*. Lewiston, N.Y.:Edwin Mellen.

Dunn, J., and S. McGuire. 1994. "Young Children's Nonshared Experiences: A Summary of Studies in Cambridge and Colorado." In E. M. Hetherington, D. Reiss, and R. Plomin, eds., *Separate Social Worlds of Siblings:*

*The Impact of Nonshared Environment on Development,* pp. 111–128. Hillsdale, N.J.: Erlbaum.

Dunn, J., and R. Plomin. 1990. *Separate Lives: Why Siblings Are So Different.* New York: Basic Books.

Durham, W. 1991. *Coevolution: Genes, Culture, and Human Diversity.* Stanford: Stanford University Press.

Eckholm, E. 2007. "Boys Cast Out by Polygamists Find Help." *New York Times,* September 9, A1.

Ellsworth, M. 1992. *Mormon Odyssey: The Story of Ida Hunt Udall, Plural Wife.* Urbana: University of Illinois.

Ember, M. 1985. "Alternative Predictors of Polygyny." *Behavior Science Research* 10:249–228.

——, C. Ember, and B. Low. 2007. "Comparing Explanations for Polygyny." *Cross-cultural Research* 41, no. 4: 428–440.

Embry, J. 1987. "Burden or Pleasure: A Profile of LDS Polygamous Husbands." *Dialogue: A Journal of Mormon Thought* 20, no. 4: 158–166.

——. 2011. *Mormon Polygamous Families: Life in the Principle.* Salt Lake City: University of Utah Press.

Fass, P. 2016. *The End of American Childhood: History of Parenting from Life on the Frontier to the Managed Child.* Princeton, N.J.: Princeton University Press.

Fessler, D. 2004. "Shame in Two Cultures: Implications for Evolutionary Approaches." *Journal of Cognition and Culture* 4, no. 2: 207–262.

Festinger, L. 1954. "A Theory of Social Compassion Process." *Human Relations* 1:117–140.

Fisher, H. 1993. *Anatomy of Love: The Natural History of Monogamy, Adultery, and Divorce.* New York: Norton.

——. 2004. *Why We Love: The Nature and Chemistry of Romantic Love.* New York: Henry Holt.

——. 2019. "Sex, Love, and Attachment: An Interview with Dr. Helen Fisher." *BrainWorld,* February 14.

Fletcher, G. 1993. *Loyalty: An Essay on the Morality of Relationships.* New York: Oxford University Press.

Foner, N. 1984. *Ages in Conflict: A Cross-cultural Perspective on Inequality Between Old and Young.* New York: Columbia University Press.

Fontaine, M. 2013. "America Has an Incest Problem." *Atlantic,* January 24, p. 13.

Fortes, M. 1969. *Kinship and the Social Order: The Legacy of Lewis Henry Morgan*. Cambridge: Cambridge University Press.

Foster, L. 1991. *Women, Family, and Utopia*. Syracuse: Syracuse University Press.

Fox, R. 1993. *Reproduction and Succession*. New Brunswick, N.J.: Transaction.

Fukuyama, F. 1995. *Trust: The Social Virtues and the Creation of Prosperity*. New York: Free Press.

Furman, W., and D. Buhrmester. 1985. "Children's Perceptions of the Qualities of Sibling Relationships." *Child Development* 56:448–461.

Giddens, A. 1992. *The Transformation of Intimacy: Sexuality, Love, and Eroticism in Modern Societies*. Stanford: Stanford University Press.

Goldstein, M., and C. Beall. 1982. "Tibetan Fraternal Polyandry and Sociology: A Rejoinder to Abernethy and Fernandez." *American Anthropology* 84:898–901.

Greene, J. 2013. *Moral Tribes: Thinking Too Fast and Too Slow*. New York: Penguin.

Greenhouse, C. 1986. *Praying for Justice: Faith, Order, and Community in an American Town*. Ithaca, N.Y.: Cornell University Press.

Gyruis, P., L. Kozma, Z. Kisander, A. Lang, T. Ferencz, and F. Handel. 1986. "Beyond Sibling Rivalry: An Empirically Grounded Theory of Sibling Relationships." In P. A. Adler, P. Adler, and N. Mandell, eds., *Sociological Studies of Child Development: A Research Annual*, pp. 105–122.

Hardacre, H. 1991. "The Impact of Fundamentalism on Women, the Family, and Interpersonal Relations." In M. Marty, S. Appleby, H. Hardacre, and E. Mendelsohn, eds., *Fundamentalisms and Society: Reclaiming the Sciences, the Family, and Education*, pp. 129–161. Chicago: University Chicago Press.

Hämäläinen, P. 2019. *Lakota America: A New History of Indigenous Power*. New Haven: Yale University Press.

Handel, G. 1986. "Beyond Sibling Rivalry: An Empirically Grounded Theory of Social Relationships." In P. A. Alder, P. Alder, and N. Mandell, eds., *Sociological Studies of Child Development*, pp. 105–122. Greenwich, Conn.: JAI.

Hardy, Carmon. 1992. *Solemn Covenant: The Mormon Polygamous Passage*. Urbana: University of Illinois Press.

Harrell, S. 1997. *Human Families*. New York: Routledge.

Harris, H. 1995. "Rethinking Heterosexual Relationships in Polynesia: A Case Study of the Mangaia, Cook Island." In W. Jankowiak, ed., *Romantic Passion: A Universal Experience?* pp. 95–127. New York: Columbia University Press.

Hatfield, E., and R. Rapson. 1996. *Love and Sex: Cross-cultural Perspective.* Lanham, Md.: University Press of America.

Heaton, T., and C. Jacobson. 2011. "Demographic, Social and Economic Characteristics of Polygamist Community." In C. Jacobson and L. Burton, eds., *Modern Polygamy in the United States,* pp. 151–162. New York: Oxford University Press.

Hendrick, S., and C. Hendrick. 2002. "Linking Romantic Love with Sex: Development of the Perceptions of Love and Sex Scale." *Journal of Social and Personal Relationships* 19, no. 3: 361–378.

Henrich, J. 2016. *The Secret of Our Success.* Princeton, N.J.: Princeton University Press.

Hirsch, J., and H. Wardlow. 2006 [1986]. *Modern Loves: The Anthropology of Romantic Courtship and Companionship Marriage.* Ann Arbor: University of Michigan Press.

Hulett, J. 1939. "The Sociological and. Social Psychological Aspects of the Mormon Polygamous Family." PhD diss., University of Wisconsin.

Illouz, E. 2012. *Why Love Hurts: A Sociological Explanation.* Oxford: Polity.
——. 2019. *The End of Love: A Sociology of Negative Relations.* Oxford: Polity.

Inglehart, R. 2020. *Modernization and Postmodernization: Cultural, Economic, and Political Change in Forty-three Societies.* Princeton, N.J.: Princeton University Press.

Irons, W. 1988. "Parental Behavior in Humans." In L. Betzig, M. B. Muller, and P. Turke, eds., *Human Reproductive Behavior,* pp. 57–78. Cambridge: Cambridge University Press.

Jacobson, C., and L. Burton. 2011. *Modern Polygamy in the United States.* New York: Oxford University Press.

Jankowiak, W. 1995. "Introduction." In W. Jankowiak, ed., *Romantic Passion: A Universal Experience?,* pp. 1–20. New York: Columbia University Press.

——. 2008. "Co-wives, Desires, and Conflicts in a USA Polygamous Community." *Ethnology* 52, no. 3: 163–180.

———. 2019. "Theological Parenthood, Demographic Restraints, and the Making of the Good Polygamous Teenager." In Brien Ashdown and Amanda Faherty, eds., *Parents and Caregivers Across Cultures: Positive Development from Infancy Through Adulthood*. New York: Springer.

Jankowiak, W., and E. Allen. 1995. "The Balance of Duty and Desire in an American Polygamous Community." In W. Jankowiak, ed., *Romantic Passion: A Universal Experience?*, pp. 277–295. New York: Columbia University Press.

———. 2006. "In the Name of the Father: Theology, Kinship and Charisma in an American Polygamous Community." In A. Lehmann, J. Meyres and P. Moro, eds., *Magic, Witchcraft and Religion: An Anthropological Study of the Supernatural*, 6th ed., pp. 382–391. New York: McGraw Hill.

Jankowiak, W., and M. Diderich. 2000. "Sibling Solidarity in a Polygamous Community in the USA: Unpacking Inclusive Fitness." *Evolution and Human Behavior* 21, no. 2: 125–140.

Jankowiak, W., and E. Fischer. 1992. "Romantic Love: A Cross-Cultural Perspective." *Ethnology* 1:149–155.

Jankowiak, W., and H. Gerth. 2012. "Can You Love Two People at the Same Time? A Research Report." *Anthropologica (Canadian Anthropological Journal)* 54, no. 1: 78–89.

Jankowiak, W., and X. Li. 2017. "Emergent Conjugal Love, Mutual Affection, Female Marital Power." In G. Santos and S. Harrell, eds., *Transforming Patriarchy: Chinese Families in the Twenty-first Century*, pp. 185–205. Seattle: University of Washington Press.

Jankowiak, W., and A. Nelson. 2022. "Archaeology of Love: A Review of the Ethnographic Exploration of Love Around the World." In David Buss, ed., *Handbook on Human Mating*, pp. 51–57. Oxford: Oxford University Press.

Jankowiak, W., and T. Paladino. 2008. "Introduction." In W. Jankowiak, ed., *Intimacies: Between Sex and Love*, 1–22. New York: Columbia University Press.

Jankowiak, W., M. Sudakov, and B. Wilreker. 2005. "Co-wife Conflict and Cooperation." *Ethnology* 44, no. 1: 81–98.

Jankowiak, W., and L. Wolfe. 2021. "What Polyamorous and Polygamous Relationships Tell Us About the Human Condition." *Culturico*, June 21, A1–2.

Jankowiak, W., and Woodman. 2002. "Paternal Reassurance or Material Reassurance? Parental Investment in an American Polygamous Community." In P. Davis and H. Hocomb, eds., *The Evolution of Minds: Psychological and Philosophical Perspectives*, pp. 271–292. Cambridge, Mass.: Academic.

Jeffs, B., and M. Szalavitz. 2009. *Lost Boy*. New York. Broadway.

Jennings, C. 2016. *Paradise Now: The Story of American Utopianism*. New York: Random House.

Jessop, C., with L. Palmer. 2007. *Escape*. New York: Broadway.

Jessop, F., and P. Brown. 2009. *Church of Lies*. New York: Jossey-Bass.

Johnson, D. 2017. *God Is Watching You: How the Fear of God Makes Us Human*. Oxford: Oxford University Press.

Johnson, J., F. McAndrew, and P. Harris. 1991. "Sociobiology and the Naming of Adopted and Natural Children." *Ethology and Sociobiology* 12, no. 5: 365–375.

Johnson, L. 1990. *The L. S. Johnson Sermons*, 7 vols. Hildale, Utah: Twin Cities Courier Press.

Jones, D. 2000. "Group Nepotism and Human Kinship." *Current Anthropology* l36, no. 5: 730–738.

Josephson, S. 1993. "Status, Reproductive Success, and Marrying Polygynous." *Ethnology and Sociobiology* 14:391–396.

Judson, P. 2016. *The Habsburg Empire: A New History*. Cambridge, Mass.: Harvard University Press.

Kanazawa, S. 2001. "Why Father Absence May Precipitate Early Menarche: The Role of Polygyny." *Evolution and Human Behavior* 22:329–334.

——, and M. Still. 1999. "Why Monogamy?" *Social Forces* 78, no. 1: 25–50.

Kanter, E. 1972. *Commitment and Community: Communes and Utopias in Sociological Perspective*. Cambridge, Mass.: Harvard University Press.

Karandashev, V. 2019. *Romantic Love in Cultural Contexts*. New York: Springer.

Koch, H. L. 1960. "The Relation of Certain Formal Attributes of Siblings to Attitudes Held Toward Each Other and Toward Their Parents." *Monograph of the Society for Research in Child Development* 25:3–124.

Komarovsky, M. 1967. *The Blue-Collar Marriage*. New York: Vintage.

Kozeny, Geoph. 1995. "Intentional Communities: Lifestyles Based on Ideals." *Communities Magazine*, "Intentional Communities and Cults," no. 88 (Fall 1996): 18–20.

Legros, D. 2014. *Mainstream Polygamy: The Non-Marital Child Paradox in the West*. New York: Springer.

Lepore, J. 2018. *These Truths: A History of the United States*. New York: Norton.

Leslie, P. 1993. *The Imperial Harem*. Oxford: Oxford University Press.

Levine, N. 1988. *The Dynamics of Polyandry: Kinship, Domesticity, and Population on the Tibetan Border*. Chicago: Chicago University Press.

——, and J. Silk. 1997. "Why Polyandry Fails: Sources of Instability in Polyandrous Marriages." *Current Anthropology* 38, no. 3: 375–399.

Levine, R. A. 1962. "Witchcraft and Co-wife Proximity in Southwestern Kenya." *Ethnology* 1, no. 1: 39–45.

Lilla, M. 2008. *The Stillborn God: Religion, Politics, and the Modern West*. New York: Vintage.

Lindholm, C. 1988. "Lovers and Leaders: A Comparison of Social and Psychological Models of Romance and Charisma." *Social Science Information* 27, no. 1: 3–45.

——. 1998. "Love and Structure." *Theory, Culture, and Society* 15, nos. 3–4: 243–263.

——. 2000. *Culture and Identity: The History, Theory, and Practice of Psychological Anthropology*. New York: McGraw Hill.

——. 2002 [1996]. *The Islamic Middle East: Tradition and Change*. New York: Blackwell.

Luhrmann, T. M. 2012. *When God Talks Back: Understanding the American Evangelical Relationship with God*. New York: Vintage.

Madhavan, S. 2002. "Best of Friends and Worst of Enemies: Competition and Collaboration in Polygyny." *Ethnology* 41, no. 1:69–84.

Marquis, K. 1993. "Cut Diamond Cut." In W. Chmielewski, L. Kern, and M. Klee-Hartzell, eds., *Women in Spiritual and Communitarian Societies in the United States*, pp. 187–202. Syracuse: Syracuse University Press.

Marty, M., S. Appleby, H. Hardacre, and E. Mendelsohn. 1991. *Fundamentalisms and Society: Reclaiming the Sciences, the Family, and Education*. Chicago: University Chicago Press.

Mason, K. 1982. "Co-wife Relationships Can Be Amicable as Well as Conflictual: The Case of the Moose of Burkina Faso." *Canadian Journal of African Studies* 22:615–624.

Mauch, A. 2022. "Sister Wives: Kody Brown Doesn't 'Feel Safe in an Intimate Place' with Meri—'Never Will Again.'" *People Magazine*, January 27, 19.

McClure, S. 2020. "The Amish Keep to Themselves. And They're Hiding a Horrifying Secret: A Year of Reporting by *Cosmo* and Type Investigations Reveals a Culture of Incest, Rape, and Abuse." *Cosmopolitan*, January 14, 23–27.

McCombs, B. 2016. "Warren Jeffs' Brother Extradited in Food Stamp Fraud Scheme." *Associated Press*, June 16, A1.

McDermottt, R., K. Monroe, B. Wray, V. Hudson, and R. Jevis. 2018. *The Evils of Polygyny: Evidence of Its Harm to Women, Men, and Society.* Ithaca, N.Y.: Cornell University Press.

McMahon, K. 1995. Misers, Shrews, and Polygamists: Sexuality and Male-Female Relations in Eighteenth-Century Chinese Fiction. Raleigh, N.C.: Duke University Press.

Meekers, D., and N. Franklin. 1994. Conflict of Interest: Gender Relations Among the Kaguru of Tanzania. University Park: Population Research Institute, Pennsylvania State University.

Miles, C. 2011. "'What's Love Got to Do with It?': Earthly Experience of Celestial Marriage, Past, and Present." In C. Jacobson and L. Burton, eds., *Modern Polygamy in the United States,* pp. 185–208. New York: Oxford University Press.

"Monogamy in Animals." 2006. Wikipedia, November 16.

Moore-Emmett, A. 2004. *God's Brothel.* San Francisco: Pince-Nez.

Morgan, E. 1944. *Puritans.* New York: Harper.

Mulder, M., and W. Miller. 1985. "Factors Affecting Infant Care in the Kipsigis." *Journal of Anthropological Research* 41, no. 3: 231–260.

Musser, J. 1944. *Celestial or Plural Marriage.* Salt Lake City: Truth.

Musun-Miller, L. 1993. "Social Acceptance and Social Problem Solving in Preschool Children." *Journal of Applied Developmental Psychology* 14, no. 1: 59–70.

Nelson, A. 2021. "Sacrifice and the Agapic Love Gender Gap in South Korean Romantic Relationships." In C. Mayer and E. Vanderheiden, eds., *Handbook of Love in Cultural and Transcultural Contexts,* pp. 1013–1028. New York: Springer.

——, and W. Jankowiak. 2021. "Love's Ethnographic Record: Beyond the Love/Arranged Marriage Dichotomy and Other False Essentialisms." In C. Mayer and E. Vanderheiden, eds., *Handbook of Love in Cultural and Transcultural Contexts,* pp. 23–40. New York: Springer.

Nelson, A., and K. J. Yon. 2019. "Core and Peripheral Features of the Cross-Cultural Model of Romantic Love." *Cross-cultural Research* 53, no. 5: 447–482.

Nevo, V. S., A. Al-Kremni, and B. Yuval-Shani. 2008. "Polygynous Marriage in the Middle East: Stories of Success and Failures." *Ethnology* 47, no. 3: 195–208.

Niebuhr, G. 1998. "Southern Baptists Declare Wife Should 'Submit' to Her Husband." *New York Times*, June 10, A1.

Noonan, P. 2018. "Republicans Need Artists, Not Economists." *Wall Street Journal*, April 12, A13.

Norenzayan, A., and A. Shariff. 2008. "The Origins and Evolution of Religious Prosociality." *Science* 322:58–62.

Norman, J. 2015. *Edmund Burke: The First Conservative*. New York: Basic Books.

O'Dea, T. 1957. *The Mormons*. Phoenix: Phoenix.

Osburg, J. 2013. *Anxious Wealth: Money and Morality Among China's New Rich*. Stanford: Stanford University Press.

Paladino, T. 2013. *Presences: A Poem of Decantos*. Boston: Virgo.

Palmer, L. 1964. *Aaronic Priesthood: Through the Centuries*. Salt Lake City: Deseret.

Parish, S. 1994. *Moral Knowing in a Hindu Sacred City: An Exploration of Mind, Emotion, and Self*. New York: Columbia University Press.

Parker, S., J. Smith, and J. Ginat. 1973. "Father Absence and Cross-Sex Identity: The Puberty Rites Controversy Revisited." *American Ethnology* 2, no. 4: 687–706.

Peirce, C. S., and J. Buchler, eds. 2012. *Philosophical Writings of Peirce*. New York: Dover.

Peirce, L. P. 1993. *The Imperial Harem: Women and Sovereignty in the Ottoman Empire*, Princeton, N.J.: Princeton University Press.

Peristiany, J. G., and Pitt-Rivers, J. 1992. *Honor and Grace in Anthropology*. Cambridge: Cambridge University.

Peterson, A. 2005. *Seeds of the Kingdom: Utopian Communities in the Americas*. Oxford: Oxford University Press.

Pitzer, D. 1997. *American Communal Utopias*. Raleigh: North Carolina University Press.

Porter, D. 2008. "Polygamy Uncovered: What It's Really Like for the Women Who Have to Share a Husband." *Daily Mail*, September 18, A1.

Putnam, R. 2020. *The Upswing: How America Came Together a Century Ago and How We Can Do It Again*. New York: Simon and Schuster.

Qi, X. 2020. *Remarking Families in Contemporary China*. New York: Oxford University Press.

Quinn, M. 1991. "Plural Marriage and Mormon Fundamentalism." In M. Marty and S. Appleby, eds., *Fundamentalisms and Society*, pp. 181–224. Chicago: University of Chicago Press.

Reddy, W. 2001. *The Navigation of Feeling: A Framework for the History of Emotions*. Cambridge: University of Cambridge Press.

———. 2012. *The Making of Romantic Love: Longing and Sexuality in Europe, South Asia, and Japan, 900–1200 CE*. Chicago: University of Chicago Press.

Reiss, D., J. Neiderhiser, E. Hetherington, and R. Plomin. 2003. *The Relationship Code: Deciphering Genetic and Social Influences on Adolescent Development*. Cambridge, Mass.: Harvard University Press.

Reynolds, T., R. Baumeister, and J. Maner. 2018. "Competitive Reputation Manipulation: Women Strategically Transmit Social Information About Romantic Rivals." *Journal of Experimental Social Psychology* 78, no. 3: 195–209.

Robertson, A. F. 1991. *Beyond the Family: Social Organization of Reproduction*. Berkeley: University of California Press.

Ross, M. 2007. *Cultural Contestation in Ethnic Conflict*. Cambridge: Cambridge University Press.

Rossi, A. 1965. "Naming Children in Middle-Class Families." *American Sociological Review* 30:499–513.

Sa'ar, A. 2004. "Many Ways of Becoming a Woman: The Case of Unmarried Israeli-Palestinian Girls." *Ethnology* 43, no. 1: 1–18.

Sanderson, S. 2001. "Explaining Monogamy and Polygyny in Human Societies: Comment on Kanazawa and Still." *Social Forces* 80, no. 1: 329–335.

Saul, J. 2004. "The Collapse of Globalism." *Harper's*, March, 33–43.

Schachit, R., and K. Kramer. 2019. "Are We Monogamous? A Review of the Evolution of Pair-Bonding in Humans and Its Contemporary Variation Cross-culturally." *Frontiers in Ecology and Evolution* 7, no. 2: 1–8.

Schlegel, A. 1972. *Male Dominance and Female Autonomy*. New Haven: Human Relations Area File Press.

———. 2013. "Perspectives on Adolescent Identity." In Bonnie Hewlett, ed., *Adolescent Identity: Evolutionary, Cultural and Developmental Perspectives*, pp. 301–318. New York: Routledge.

———, and H. Barry. 1991. *Adolescent: An Anthropological Inquiry*. New York: Free Press.

Schmidt, S. 2006. *His Favorite Wife: A True Story of Violent Fanaticism*. Guilford, Conn.: Lyons.

Schwartz, G. 1987. *Beyond Conformity and Rebellion*. Chicago: University of Chicago Press.

Segal, N. L. 2012. *Born Together—Reared Apart: The Landmark Minnesota Twin Study*. Cambridge: Harvard University Press.

Seidman, S. 1991. *Romantic Longings*. London: Blackwell.

Sered, H. 1994. *The Mother Goddess*. New York: Oxford University Press.

Sered, S. 1994. *Priestess, Mother, Sacred Sister: Religion Dominated by Women*. New York: Oxford University Press.

Singular, S. 2008. *When Men Become Gods: Mormon Polygamist Warren Jeffs, His Cult of Fear, and the Women Who Fought Back*. New York: Norton.

Skeen, P., B. E. Robinson, and C. Flake-Hobson. 1984. "Blended Families: Overcoming the Cinderella Myth." *Young Children* 39:64–74.

Small, M. F. 1992. "The Evolution of Female Sexuality and Mate Selection in Humans." *Human Nature* 3:133–156.

Smuts, B., and D. Gubernick. 1992. "Male-Infant Relationships in Nonhuman Primates: Paternal Investment or Mating Effort?" In Barry Hewlett, ed., *Father-Child Relations*, pp. 1–30. New York: de Gruyter.

Solomon, D. 2004. *Daughter of the Saints: Growing Up in Polygamy*. New York: Norton.

Soloway, J. S. 1990. "Affines and Spouses, Friends and Lovers: The Passing of Polygyny in Botswana." *Journal of Anthropological Research* 46:41–66.

Sosis, R., and E. Bressler. 2003. "Cooperation and Commune Longevity: A Test of the Costly Signaling Theory and Religion." *Cross-cultural Research* 37, no. 2: 211–239.

Spencer, I. 2007. *Shattered Dreams: My Life as a Polygamist Wife*. New York: Center Street.

Spencer, M. 1979. "The Social Psychology of Max Weber." *Sociological Analysis* 40, no. 3: 240–255.

Spigelman, G., A. Spigelman, and I. L. Englesson. 1992. "Analysis of Family Drawings: A Comparison Between Children from Divorce and Nondivorce Families." *Journal of Divorce and Remarriage* 18:31–54.

Stacey, J. 2011. *Unhitched: Love, Marriage, and Family Values from West Hollywood to Western China.* New York: New York University Press.

Stegner, W. 1942. *Mormon County.* Lincoln: University of Nebraska Press.

Strassmann, B. 1997. "Polygyny as a Risk Factor for Child Mortality Among the Dogon." *Current Anthropology* 38:688–695.

——. 2000. "Polygyny, Family Structure, and Child Morality: A Prospective Study Among the Dogon of Mali." In L. Cronk, N. Chagnon, and W. Irons, eds., *Adaption and Human Behavior*, pp. 49–67. New York: Aldine de Gruyter.

Sulloway, F. 1996. *Born to Rebel: Birth Order, Family Dynamics, and Creative Lives.* New York: Pantheon.

Tiwari, G. 2008. "The Interplay Between Love and Sex and Marriage in a Polyandrous Society in the High Himalayas of India." In W. Jankowiak, ed., *Intimacies: Between Sex and Love*, pp. 122–147. New York: Columbia University Press.

Tomasello, M. 2009. *Why We Cooperate.* Boston: MIT Press.

Turley, J. 2004. "Polygamy Laws Expose Our Own Hypocrisy." *USA Today*, March 3, 13A.

Udall, B. 1998. "The Lonely Polygamists: Meet Bill. He Has Four Wives and Thirty-One Kids. And Something's Missing." *Esquire*, February, 129.

Ulrich, L. 1982. *Good Wives: Image and Reality in the Lives of Women in Northern New England, 1650–1750.* New York: Oxford University Press.

——. 2017. *A House Full of Females: Plural Marriage and Women's Rights in Early Mormonism, 1835–1870.* Cambridge, Mass.: Harvard University Press.

Vaillancourt, T., and A. Sharma. 2011. "Intolerance of Sexy Peers: Intrasexual Competition Among Women." *Aggression Behavior* 37, no. 6: 569–577.

Van Gulik, R. H. 1961. *Sexual Live in Ancient China.* Leiden: Brill.

Van Wagoner, R. 1986. *Mormon Polygamy: A History.* Salt Lake City: Signature.

Wall, E., with L. Pulitizer. 2008. *Stolen Innocence: My Story of Growing Up in a Polygamous Sect.* New York: William Morrow.

Watson, R. 1985. *Inequality Among Brothers: Class and Kinship in South China.* Cambridge: Cambridge University Press.

Weisner, T. 1982. "Sibling Interdependence and Child Caretaking: A Cross-cultural View." In M. E. Lamb and B. Sutton-Smith, eds., *Sibling Relationships: Their Nature and Significance Across the Life Span,* pp. 305–4327. Hillsdale, N.J.: Erlbaum.

Western, C. 2005. *Child Brides: Real Life Stories.* Waltham, Mass.: Infinity.

White, D., and M. Burton. 1988. "Causes of Polygyny: Ecology, Economy, Kinship, and Warfare." *American Anthropologist* 90:871–887.

Whitehouse, B. 2023. *Enduring Polygamy: Plural Marriage in a Twenty-first-Century African Metropolis.* Rutgers, N.J.: Rutgers University Press.

Wieseltier, L. 1993. "The True Fire." *New Republic,* May 17, 25–27.

Williams, R. 1991. "Movement Dynamics and Social Change." In M. Marty and S. Appleby, eds., *Accounting for Fundamentalisms*, pp. 181–224. Chicago: University of Chicago Press.

Wolf, M. 1972. *Women and the Family in Rural Taiwan.* Stanford: Stanford University Press.

Wuthnow, R., and M. Lawson. 1991. "Sources of Christian Fundamentalism in the United States." In M. Marty, S. Appleby, H. Hardacre, and E. Mendelsohn, eds., *Fundamentalisms and Society: Reclaiming the Sciences, the Family, and Education,* pp. 20–49. Chicago: University Chicago Press.

Young, K. 1954. *Isn't One Wife Enough?* New York: Henry Holt.

Zablocki, B. 1980. *Alienation and Charisma.* New York: Free Press.

Zoellner, T. 1998. "Polygamy on the Dole." *Salt Lake Tribune,* June 28, A1.

Zurndorfer, H, 2014. "Polygamy and Masculinity in China: Past and Present." *Nan/Nu* 18, no. 2: 224–256.

# INDEX

adolescence, 220; against male, 230; as distinct life stage, 227; successful, 236

Agar, Michael, 15

agency: women, 9, 105; as individualism, 215

alcohol: consumption of, 31; turn to, 231

allocare parenting, 172

Allred, families, 76, 80, 83, 110, 174, 180, 239, 250

Alman, Irwin and Joseph Ginat, 27, 174, 251

altruism, sense of, 8

American middle-class values, 24, 214

ancestor reverence, Chinese, 48

authoritarian orientation, 68–69; authoritarian approach, 70, 90

authority, displays of, 77

autobiographical accounts, 15; escape narratives, 158; ubiquity, 157

Barash, David, 2; and Judith Lipon, 6

Barash hypothesis, 2

Bennion, Janet, 27, 141, 176, 179–180, 222, 244, 255, 274

Big Love, 20

birth control, 82

birth order, 207; a person's, 222

blended families, 26

bountiful, 30, 97

Bradburd, Dan, 17

Brethren, 100, 136; because the, 132; church meetings, 134; disagreement with, 111; following the, 108; instructing her, 135; not being the Brethren, 105

Brown, Kody, 248

celestial ranking, 33, 101

chaperonage, 9

character, more virtuous, 241

child-rearing practices, 224

church leadership, 53
City of God, 40
close-corporate society, 96
commitment: ethical, 6; moral, 6
communitarian impulse, 33
community: closed, 36; social
    constructions, 14
communes: known, 39; Oneida,
    Kerista, and New Buffalo, 10
communitas, 92
comothers, 207
complex family, 13–18; marriage
    system, 14
concurrent love, 5
conflict: between cowives, 181;
    family, 228; female-to-female, 127
confluent love, 2, 10
consensus, family management, 70
consensus ethos, 130
conventional wisdom, economic, 88
cosmology, 17; community's, 150;
    inclusive, 213; inspired ideal,
    276; model, 196; official, 231
cowife: bond, 11; competition, 55;
    core values, 238; couples, open,
    3; exchanges, 176; friendship
    with, 270; hierachal, 4;
    indepedence, 71; instrumental,
    175; interfamilial, 239; new to
    lifestyle, 4; personal development,
    161, 169; responses, 171; rivalry,
    181; values of, 218
creed, official, 41
cross-cultural research, 7

Daoulah, Amin, 264
demographic realities, 236

Diderich, Monique, 200
dignity, 139
divorce, 138–139; comment on, 151;
    wives, 141
dyadic bond, 2, 125; as complete,
    143; descent system, 9;
    emotionally exclusive, 275;
    exclusiveness, 6; friendships,
    179; intimacy, 143, 183; love, 256,
    269; love bond, 260; mindset,
    178; nature of, 10; orientation,
    11; primacy of, 6

education, value on, 35
elopement, 105
emotions: angst, 4; avoidance of,
    256; belonging, 8; bond, 131;
    costs, 5; equity, 120; exclusivity,
    115; existential struggle, 3;
    experience, 12; detachment, 259;
    intimacy, 258–261; involved, 3;
    monogamous, 6; reorganization,
    8; richer 156; toll, 250; value of, 108
entrepreneurial strategy, 2
escapist literature, 15–18, 28
ethnographic record, 2; accounts,
    2, 15
Euro-American ideals, 7
existential doubts, 15

family: code word, 19; competitive
    nature, 224; complex system,
    278; cooperation, 202; cooperative
    spirit, 129; disagreement, 76;
    disunity, 249; dysfunctional, 177;
    elite, 233; extended, 2; founder
    generation, 188–190; harmony,

harmonious families, 122, 156, 177, 182; harsh reality, 72; Heavenly Father's ideal, 65; high functioning 74–75, 280; identification with, 210; interdependency of, 12; low-ranking, 274–275; management, a man's philosophy, 72; managing, 80, 85, 90; model, 9; nonelite, 76; organization style, 73, 78, 216; patriarchal, 70; prayers, 73; religious system, 74; system, 16–19, 267; unhealthy, 87, 157, 214, 223; Victorian image, 219; well-functioning, 254

father: accomplishment, 52; active involvement, 101; adjudicator, adjudication by, 44–45, 54; admired, 61; adoration of, 41, 193; advice by, 102, 219; attitudes toward, 64; behavior, 68; bifurcation of, 64; birth, 203; child interaction with, 62; commitment to, 195; competing images of, 62; core dilemma of, 121; dead, 59; disagreements, 26, 56; discourse centered on, 50, 71; emotional bond with, 61; exchanging daughters, 76, 96; glorification, 41, 67; harmony, 170; high-functioning father, 174, 176; idiom of, 49; leadership position, 42; love of, 47; name of the, 212; obligation, 138; pivotal axioms, 199; plural, 87; power of, 59; problems, 154; public images, 64; religious authority,

100; reversal of, 51; and son relationship, 43; support, 87; favorite wife, 8; husband of the, 8

female choice, 20, 272

filial affection, 49

Fisher, Helen, 7–8

FLDS, 25–28, 30, 86–90, 97, 98, 158, 239, 250

fumarate deficiency, 273

Fundamentalist Church of Latter-Day Saints. *See* FLDS

genetic complications, 273

Gospel, 57, 137; learning the, 149

government support, 88

group loyalty, promoting, 49

guilt, 3; conscious, 256; experience of, 261; feeling, 18, 130, 217; gender ideals, 19; internalized, 18; personal, 257

hagiographic accounts, 46

harem: Ottoman, 23, 83; polygamy, 9

health: emotional, 273; mental, 273

hierarchy, social, 17

household labor, organized division of, 74

husband: attention, 181; deceased, 182; detached, 251; diplomatic skills, 122; emotional well-being, 246; good, 120–121, 251; high status of, 140; ideal, 99; indifference, 72; relationship, 127; story, 156; and wife bond, 117, 183

Hutterites, 36

identity: autonomous, 195; individual, 60; political, 137; polygamous man's, 243, validating, 154
ideology, official, 75
Imperial China: concubines, 83; families, 153; polygamous family, 23
inclusive fitness, 209
individualism, self-actualization, 238
intentional community, 22, 87, 276
intergenerational antagonism, 231–232
Illouz, Eva, 3
Irons, William, 271

Jacobson, Cardell and Lara Burton, 17
jealousy: cowife, 171, 174; intensify only, 226
Jeffs, Brent, 153, 216, 222
Jeffs, Warren, 20; sect, 34, 263
Jessop, Carolyn, 85
journalistic accounts, 19

Kanazawa, Satoshi and Mary Still, 21
Kerista (commune), 10, 184

LeBaron, Alma Dyer, 95
LeBaron, Mexico, 27, 95, 158, 170, 180, 239, 250
life orientation, 74–75
limited good, 87, 171
love: around, 149; being in, 7; bond, 127, 185; bond, illicit, 275; comfort,

165; confluent, 2; crush, 108, 229; domain, 6; exclusivity, 4; expression of, 12; form of, 184; group arrangement, 10; harmonious, 12–18, 93, 147, 256; hierarchical, 91; ideal of, 147; letters, 12; middle-class configuration, 2; mutual, 4; noble, 65, 91; passionate, 4, 113, 166, 258–262; plural, 3–12, 235; power of, 260; presence or absence, 12; psychophysiological characteristics, 7–8; sex, 10; spiritual, 11; true, 103–104; types, 6
Luhrmann, Tanya, 13

male authority, 131
marital problems, 272
Marty, Martin and Scott Appleby, 39
maternal investment hypothesis, 187
mating frenzy, 94
matricentric focus, 195
matrifocal units, 55, 222
meaning, quest for, 22
media accounts, 28; image of, 237; mainstream, 133
Medicaid, 89
men: court, 109; effort, 135; household complex, 9; marital disagreements, 129; married, 110; motivational priorities, 4; wealthy, 2
Melchizedek priesthood, 43
monogamous, monogamy: blended, 200; bond, 1;

emotionally monogamous, 4;
family, 15, 208; love, 10;
marriage, 20, 267, 274;
marriage system, 2, 19; mate
selection, 246; pathogen stress,
20; society, 199
moral community, 57
moral framework, 110; conflict, 119;
dilemma, 215, 263; leader, 245;
struggle, 240
Morgan, Edmund, 92
mother: admiration for, 195; birth
different from, 210–211; birth
order, 196; crucial role, 55;
intrusive outsiders, 85;
mother-centric focus, 268;
mother-child bond, 223;
organized around, 54
Mother's Day, 212
millennial narrative, 34

naming: bond, 187; daughters
of, 194; decisions, 187; linkage,
196; maternal kin after, 193;
micropolitics of, 188; paternal,
191; pattern, 188, 197; politics
of, 186, 189, practices, 185;
preference, 196; process, 193;
studies, 186; variation, 196
natal: affection, 195; family, 204,
208; subunits, 211
network, female-centered, 86
Nevo, Vered Slonim, Alean
Al-Kremni, and Bar
Yuval-Shani, 246, 264
norms: dominant, 85; folk, 85;
in-group, 239

O'Dea, Thomas, 238
offspring behavior, 9
Oneida community, 9, 184
orthodox-liberal function, 37

pair bond: cultural construction,
12; enduring, 1; exclusive,
13; format, 128; forming, 1;
ideal, 12; preference, 8;
species, 1, 276
Palestinian polygamy, 21, 246–247
parental investment, 191, strategy,
197, studies, 280
passion, satisfying, 6
paternal certainty, 197
patriarchal ideology, 192; ideal,
193
patriarchy: committed to, 142;
different, 247; glorification of,
215; ideal, 68; male embodiment
of, 57; pawns of, 23; and separate
personae, 5
Pinesdale, 77, 98, 141, 164, 174, 176,
236, 239
Pioneer Day, 36
placement marriage: absolutism,
238; assumed, 112; becoming,
111, 125; benefits of, 108;
dissatisfying, 106; doctrine of,
94; ethos, 120; family, 124, 167;
orthodox, 168; societies, 139;
unpracticed, 95
plural love: celebrating, 164; family,
12, 141, 143, 183; living, 244;
marriage, 126; hierarchical, 2–3;
practitioners, 4; phenomenon
of, 275; united, 2, 181

polyamory: communities, 27, 146;
complexity in contemporary, 2;
deliberations, 102; ethical
commitment, 144; family
arrangement, 277; fascination
with, 22; forming, 98; ideal unit,
2; living, 255; marriage, 31;
participants, 95, 149; system,
13–15
polyandrous: arrangement, 201;
family system, 8; household, 65;
social organization, 53; societies,
142
prodigal daughters, 234
pro-polygamy.com, 24
Puritans, 57,92

Quinn, Michael, 245

*Raise the Red Lantern*, 122
Rapture, 34
Reddy, William, 92
righteousness, 58, 218, 240
redistributive practice, 79
religious community:
accommodating to, 40;
cooperation, degree of, 39;
ethos, 270; ideals, 58;
salvation, 271; sectarian, 35
reproduction glorified, 81
resource allocation, 21
rituals, 47
romantic love: establishment of
boundaries, 4; interests, 3;
intimacy, 55; marriages, 114;
posture toward, 107; power, 18;

presence of, 260; research
discovered, 257; specific set of
characteristics, 8; superiority,
93; warned against, 226
Rossi, Alice, 190
rotation systems: laissez-faire and
fixed system, 83; preferred, 84

sacrifice: often, 152, 258–260; a man
to, 251; need for, 217; self-sacrifice,
209; willing, 143, 148
Saint Augustine, 145
Schacht, Ryan and Karen L.
Kramer, 1
Schlegel, Alice, 9
Schmidt, Susan, 127
seclusion, of women, 9
self-identification, 57; sense of, 91
self-mastery, 215; identification,
269; reflection, 242; sufficiency,
89
sex: attraction, 9; casual, 2;
frequent, 9; passionate, 10;
sisterhood, 147
sexual: appetite, 23, 82; behavior,
32; monogamous species, 6;
premarital, 32; restraints, 81;
secrets, 126; social regulation, 9;
youth, 219
Shakers, 10
shame, sense of, 128, 262
Short Creek, 88, 146, 174, 188
siblings: competition, 212; feeling
closer to, 207; full, 206, 269
Singular, Stephen, 160–161
*Sister Wives* (TV), 173, 248

sister-wives: abuse from, 253; antagonistism between, 148, 162; argument of, 173; desire, 82; dominance over, 185, 207; experienced, 162; family, 172; giving assistance to, 164; new, 167; partners, 10; perceiving themselves, 178; quality of, 146, 180; relationship, 180; rivalry, 172
Smith, Joseph, 125
social order, 11; coerciveness of, 20–21
social organization, specific, 15
solidarity: bonds, 200–201; bonding with, 234; degree of, 204; family, 202–203; full-sibling, 201, 211; half-sibling, 204–205
Solomon, Dorothy, 127, 157
song duels, 50
Sosis, Richard and Eric Bressler, 39
soul mate, 106
Spencer, Irene, 150, 263
Spigelman, Gabriella, 202
spouse abuse, 252
status competition, 245
status-leveling, 50; community, within, 53; competition, 51; family's low, 52
Sternberg, Robert, 4
structural tensions, 15

Tapestry Against Polgamy.com, 24
theocratic political system, 37; governed system, 163; tenets, 268
theological axioms, 41, 78; books, four foundational, 30; community, 83; convictions,
225; cosmological commitment to, 195; framed within, 242
Tibetan polyandrous, 200; family, 201
triadic arrangements, 6
Truthbearer.com, 24
Turley, Jonathan, 25

Ulrich, Laurel, 131
universal: near, 7; not as cultural, 12
utopian ideal, 24, 142

visions and dreams, 56–57

Wall, Elizabeth, 221
wedding ceremony, 115
Whitehouse, Bruce, 277
wife: abandoned, 139; anniversary and birthday, 115; assertive, 78; assessing quality of, 87; emotional needs of, 130; as emotional facilitator, 177; favorite, 8, 114, 150, 155; ideal, 98–99; longtime, 165; low-profile, 84, 150–155, 188; persona, 152; postmenopausal, 82; power of, 150; swearing, 153; well-being, 135
women: official standing, 43; plight of, 18; regrets, 28; socializing, 14
Work, the, 148; dedication to, 152; living the, 234

Young, Brigham, 125
Young, Kimball, 141, 166
youth: acute anxiety, 236; American, 10, 220; fearing it, 226; freedom of, 107; men in high school, 257;

youth (*continued*)
Mormon fundamentalist, 228; retained, 232; secretly gathered, 228; socialized in, 250; romantic and involved, 230; unmarried male, 231

Zablocki, Benjamin, 10